The History of Siberia

The History of Siberia

From Russian conquest to
Revolution

Edited and introduced by
Alan Wood

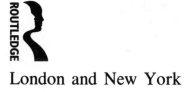

London and New York

First published 1991
by Routledge
11 New Fetter Lane, London EC4P 4EE

Simultaneously published in the USA and Canada
by Routledge
a division of Routledge, Chapman and Hall, Inc.
29 West 35th Street, New York, NY 10001

Phototypeset in 10pt Times by
Mews Photosetting, Beckenham, Kent

Printed and bound in Great Britain by
Biddles Ltd, Guildford and King's Lynn

British Library Cataloguing in Publication Data
The history of Siberia : from Russian conquest to
  revolution.
  1. Russia. Siberia
  I. Wood, Alan *1943–*
  957
  ISBN 0-415-05873-2

Library of Congress Cataloging in Publication Data
The History of Siberia: from Russian conquest to revolution / edited
  and introduced by Alan Wood.
       p. cm.
  ''Third volume of essays on Siberia to result from the activities
  of the British Universities Siberian Studies Seminar'' — Pref.
  Includes bibliographical references and index.
  ISBN 0-415-05873-2
  1. Siberia (R.S.F.S.R.) — History. I. Wood, Alan, 1943–
  II. British Universities Siberian Studies Seminar.
  DK761.H57   1991
  957-dc20   90-38468
                                                                    CIP

Contents

Contents

The contributors

J.L. Black is Professor of History, and Director of the Centre for Canadian-Soviet Studies, Carleton University, Ottawa. He has published twelve books and many articles on Russian and Soviet history, including, most recently, the second volume of *USSR Documents Annual*, of which he is editor, *Perestroika: the Second Stage, 1988* (1989); (with D.K. Buse) *G.-F. Müller in Siberia, 1733–1743* (1988); and (with Norman Hillmer) *Nearly Neighbours: Canada and the Soviet Union from Cold War to Détente and Beyond* (1989).

John Channon is Lecturer in Economic History at the School of Slavonic and East European Studies, University of London. He is the author of numerous articles on Russian and Soviet agrarian history, with special reference to regional studies of the peasantry and land reform. He is currently engaged in research for a study of *Gorbachev's Agricultural Reforms in Historical Perspective*.

David N. Collins is Lecturer in Russian History at the University of Leeds. He has published a number of articles on Russian and Siberian history and historiography, including 'Colonialism and Siberian Development: A Case-Study of the Orthodox Mission to the Altay, 1830–1913' (1989) and is editor (with J.D. Smele) of *Kolchak and Siberia* (1988). He is at present working on a bibliography of Siberia.

Basil Dmytryshyn is Professor Emeritus of History, Portland State University, Oregon. His major publications include *A History of Russia, USSR: A Concise History, Medieval Russia, Imperial Russia* and (with J.M. Letiche) *Russian Statecraft: the 'Politika' of Iurii Krizhanich* (1985). He has also edited (with E.A.P. Crownhart-Vaughan and Thomas Vaughan) *Russia's Conquest of Siberia* (1985), *Russian Penetration of the North Pacific Ocean* (1988) and *The Russian American Colonies* (1989).

James Forsyth is Head of the Department of Russian, University of Aberdeen. He has written extensively on Russian language and literature, but has concentrated for several years on the history and ethnography of the peoples of the Soviet Union, in particular Siberia. He has recently completed *Russia's Northern Empire: A History of the Peoples of Siberia* (forthcoming).

James R. Gibson is Professor of Geography at York University, Toronto, and an associate editor of the journal *Soviet Geography*. His major works include *Feeding the Russian Fur Trade, 1639–1856* (1969), *Imperial Russia in Frontier America, 1784–1867* (1976) and *Farming the Frontier: The Agricultural Opening of the Oregon Country* (1985). His latest book on the maritime fur trade of the north-west coast, *Otter Skins, Boston Ships and China Goods*, is now in press.

Leonid M. Goryushkin is Doctor of Historical Sciences and Professor and Head of History at the Institute of History, Philology and Philosophy, Siberian Branch of the USSR Academy of Sciences, Novosibirsk. He has written and edited a large number of works on the history of Siberia, especially on the peasantry and the exile system. Among his most recent books are (with N.A. Minenko) *Istoriografiya Sibiri Dooktyabrskogo Perioda* (*Historiography of Siberia before the October Revolution*) (1984), *Politicheskaya ssylka v Sibiri* (*Political Exile in Siberia*) (1987) and *Istochniki po istorii krestyanstva i selskogo khozyaistva vo vtoroi polovine XIX – nachale XX vv* (*Sources on Peasant and Agrarian History, late 19th– early 20th centuries*) (1988).

Alan Wood is Lecturer in Russian History at Lancaster University and Convenor of the British Universities Siberian Studies Seminar. He is also founder and contributing editor of the journal *SIBIRICA*. Among his recent publications on Russian and Soviet history are *Siberia: Problems and Prospects for Regional Development* (1987), (with R.A. French) *The Development of Siberia; People and Resources* (1989) and *Stalin and Stalinism* (1990). He is at present writing *A History of Modern Siberia*.

Editor's preface

This book is the third volume of essays on Siberia to result from the activities of the British Universities Siberian Studies Seminar, founded at Lancaster University in 1981. While the first two volumes have been multidisciplinary in character, containing chapters on the social and economic development of modern Siberia, foreign relations, transport, the oil and gas industry, and so on, the present collection is devoted entirely to aspects of the historical development of Siberia from the Russian conquest in the sixteenth century up to and including the Revolution of 1917 and the Civil War. The various topics and their significance are explained in the editor's Introduction.

All the authors, four from Britain, two from Canada and one each from the United States and the Soviet Union, have in one way or another been active participants in, or contributors to, a number of international conferences on Siberia which have been held over the past decade, and each has a well-established reputation in his own particular field of research. Especially welcome in the present volume is the contribution from Professor Leonid Goryushkin from the Siberian Branch of the Soviet Academy of Sciences in Novosibirsk. Soviet colleagues were initially slow to join in the enterprises of western 'Siberiologists', but the era of *glasnost* has led to more active and fruitful co-operation, of which Professor Goryushkin's essay is a gratifying example.

In quantitative terms, the historiography of Siberia has been on the whole poorly served by western scholars. There are a number of valuable monographs, written mainly by North American historians, on various aspects of Siberia's past, and references will be found to several of these in the following pages. However, no single-volume, comprehensive textbook on the history of Siberia so far exists in any western language. The editor knows of four which are at present in various stages of preparation – two in the USA and two in Britain – which in their quite different ways will help to fill that very large hole. But until they appear, it is hoped that the present collection will, if nothing more, act as a modest hors-d'oeuvre to whet the reader's appetite for the main courses to follow. It is also hoped that it may, by pinpointing a variety of controversial issues in the interpretation of Siberia's past, encourage further research and publication ventures.

For the purposes of this book, Siberia is defined as that part of the Russian Empire lying east of the Ural mountains and stretching to the Pacific Ocean, including the island of Sakhalin, the Aleutian and Kuril archipelagos, and, from the late eighteenth century to 1867, the territory of Russian America, now known as Alaska. Most of continental Siberia was incorporated into the empire by the end of the seventeenth century; the Gornyi Altai region was added in the eighteenth, and the Far Eastern maritime provinces of the Amur and Ussuri basin in the nineteenth century. The administrative subdivisions of the territory fluctuated considerably over the centuries of Russian rule, and are indicated at the appropriate place in the individual chapters.

Transliteration of Russian names, geographical terms, and technical expressions is based on the Library of Congress system, but without diacritical marks and with the initial vowels 'e', 'iu' and 'ia' rendered as *ye*, *yu* and *ya*. The 'soft sign' has been omitted throughout. No entirely satisfactory system of rendering the ethnonyms of the indigenous Siberian peoples into English has yet been devised. The practice adopted here has been to use the standard modern Russian terms with anglicized plurals. The solution is imperfect, but intelligible, and avoids some of the more bizarre forms which have been suggested.

I would like to express personal thanks to all who have helped either directly or indirectly in the preparation of this book: to Barbara Smith and Almina Geldart for retyping some of the chapters and notes and to Miss Smith in particular for compiling the index with her customary skill; to John Haywood for preparing the map on p. 138; to Peter Sowden for suggesting the book in the first place, and for his patience when unforeseeable circumstances delayed delivery of the typescript; to all those friends and colleagues in Britain, Europe, North America and the USSR who share my fascination with Siberia and have given me encouragement, support and advice in my efforts to enhance its study during the past ten years and, of course, especially to the present team of distinguished authors. The views they have each expressed and the judgements they have made are entirely their own, but, following normal convention, I take full editorial responsibility for any errors or inconsistencies which may still be detected in the final printed text.

Alan Wood
Halton-on-Lune

Glossary of specialized terms

Technical terms in Russian (and other, non-Russian, languages) which appear frequently in the text are translated into their English equivalent the first time they appear in each separate chapter. However, the following glossary has been included for easy reference purposes. Words indicating individual objects, institutions, and so on, are given in the singular; terms which are more usually used collectively are given in the plural form. Words which appear once or only rarely are not normally included.

amanat hostage (male or female), taken from the Siberian native peoples and held by the Russians to guarantee tribal loyalty and payment of fur tribute.

artel a co-operative or collective organization of people engaged in the same craft or other occupation.

ataman a cossack chieftain.

boyar member of the Muscovite hereditary landowning aristocracy.

boyarskaya duma the Council of Boyars, an advisory body to the tsar in Muscovite Russia.

brodyaga a vagrant or vagabond; used here usually of escaped exile criminals roaming Siberia.

brodyazhestvo vagrancy; vagabondage.

desyatina measurement of land equalling 1.09 hectares or 2.7 acres.

dyak a clerk or secretary in a government or administrative department in Muscovite Russia.

guberniya	liberally a 'governorship', that is, a major territorial-administrative unit of the Russian Empire, headed by a Governor or Governor-General.
GULag	Main Camp Administration; organ of the Stalinist security apparatus, responsible for running forced labour camps.
gulyashchie lyudi	literally, 'wandering folk'; term used to describe fugitive peasants, vagrants and other non-tax-paying itinerants in Siberia.
katorga	penal servitude with hard labour.
Litva	collective term used to denote prisoners-of-war and other foreigners sent to Siberia in the seventeenth century; they were often used for military or other duties.
maidan	underworld term for a prisoners' illicit grocery store-cum-gambling den.
oblast	region or district; a territorial-administrative unit on a lower level than a *guberniya*.
oblastniki	literally, 'regionalists'; used here of those who advocated some measure of regional autonomy, special treatment or even political independence for Siberia.
obshchina (or *mir*)	a commune; usually used of the Russian peasants' communal social organization.
ostrog	a fortified wooden stronghold or outpost.
poddyachii	an undersecretary or clerk, subordinate to a *dyak*.
pomeshchiki	literally, owners of a *pomeste* (an estate of land); generally, members of the landowning (and, before 1861, serf-owning) nobility.
pominki	gifts or bribes given to Russian officials by Siberian natives.
prikaz	an office, department or bureau of the Muscovite government administration.
pristanoderzhatelstvo	the illegal practice of harbouring an escaped criminal or exile.

promyshlenniki	literally, those engaged in some craft or trade (*promysel*); here denoting hunters, traders, artisans or individual entrepreneurs who flocked to Siberia during the Russian conquest and settlement.
pud	unit of weight equalling 16.38 kilogrammes or 36 pounds.
sazhen	measurement of length equalling 2.13 metres.
shaman	native Siberian 'holy man', witch-doctor, soothsayer and healer; an exponent of 'shamanism', the religion of most aboriginal Siberian peoples.
shert	in the seventeenth century, an oath of allegiance sworn to the tsar by Siberian natives.
Sibirskii prikaz	the 'Siberian Department'; central government office responsible for the administration of Siberia, 1637–1763.
sluzhilie lyudi	literally, 'service folk', that is, civilian or military servitors (the latter often called *voennosluzhilie lyudi*) working in various official capacities in the administration of seventeenth-century Siberia.
ssylka	exile; that is, punitive or administrative banishment to a specific location for temporary or permanent residence, with or without forced labour.
starozhily	'old inhabitants', that is, early Russian settlers in Siberia and their descendants.
streltsy	literally, 'shooters'; members of Muscovite regular military units. Many were used on service in Siberia.
taiga	the vast mixed coniferous and deciduous forests covering large areas of Siberia.
uezd	a district; territorial-administrative subdivision of a *guberniya* or *oblast*.
varnak	popular term used to describe dangerous criminals on the run from exile or imprisonment in Siberia.
versta	measurement of distance equalling 1.06 kilometres.

voennosluzhilie lyudi	military servitors (see *sluzhilie lyudi*).
voevoda	military commander; in seventeenth-century Siberia, the voevoda was the chief military, fiscal and judicial official appointed by Moscow to govern a specific area or town.
yasak	tribute (usually paid in fur) imposed by the Russian authorities on the Siberian native peoples. Both the term and the practice are Mongol in origin.
zakhvat	literally, 'seizure'; practice of establishing landownership by seizing and occupying an area of notionally 'unoccupied' land.
zemleprokhodtsy	pioneers in the discovery and opening-up of new territory; overland explorers; trailblazers.
zemstva	organs of rural local government established in Russia during the reforms of Alexander II; not introduced into Siberia until 1917.
zhigan	popular term used to describe an itinerant escaped exile (less denigratory than *varnak*).
zimove	a small winter outpost or shelter.

1 Introduction: Siberia's role in Russian History

Alan Wood

The breathtaking pace of political upheaval in Eastern Europe, the Baltic region and Transcaucasia in the last few weeks of the 1980s has naturally focused international attention on those parts of the Soviet empire lying to the west of the Ural mountains, including those countries which were allotted to Joseph Stalin's 'sphere of influence' at the end of the Second World War. The momentous events themselves and the amount of journalistic coverage and academic analysis they have received have understandably reinforced the tendency in most western historical literature specializing in Russia and the Soviet Union to devote the greater share of its attention to political, social and economic developments in the central, 'European' heartland of Russia and on its western and south-western rim. Uneven demographic distribution, diplomatic and military considerations, the location of major industries, commercial relations, cultural influences and the centralization of political and administrative power in either St Petersburg or Moscow (ancient and modern) have all helped to ensure that cis-Uralian Russia has enjoyed a near-monopoly of European and North American scholarship in this field. (A glance at the index of just about any reputable general text-book of modern Russian history will confirm this.) One of the direct results of this westwards orientation (or, more precisely, 'occidentation') has been the relative neglect by historians of the huge, seemingly limitless tracts of territory stretching eastwards beyond the Urals towards the Pacific coast, and encompassing on its north–south axis the frozen wastes of the Polar North and the deserts and mountains on the edges of Central Asia, Mongolia and China.

This enormous continent, covering no less than one-twelfth of the planet's entire land surface, and including the modern administrative region of the Soviet 'Far East', is traditionally known as *Siberia*.[1] It is, of course, both a name and a concept which readily stimulates knee-jerk responses, stereotyped visions and hackneyed images in most people's minds – images which will almost invariably feature great frozen wildernesses, blinding blizzards, steel-shattering frosts, and, of course, legions of fur-wrapped, fettered convicts and political prisoners – 'exiled to Siberia', in the chilling cliché – by the autocratic Russian state. In fact, such images do to a large extent reflect both the climatic and the historical reality of Siberia. The winters there *are* long, hard and cruel; two-thirds of the entire territory are grounded on 'permafrost' – permanently frozen earth, in many areas over one kilometre deep; eastern Siberia contains the northern hemisphere's 'pole of cold', at Oimyakon, several degrees *south* of the Arctic Circle where temperatures in this inhabited settlement sometimes sink to −70°C; major rivers, seas and ports are frozen solid for most of the year, and growing conditions are so disadvantageous as to create one of the most fragile ecological systems in the world. Countless similar facts and statistics could be adduced to substantiate Siberia's fearsome reputation for extremes of ice, cold and snow. But Siberia also encompasses the 'little Switzerland' of the Gornyi Altai, a region of spectacular alpinesque beauty; it contains the verdant grasslands around Lake Baikal where for centuries nomadic pasturalists have grazed their flocks and herds; Lake Baikal itself, the deepest in the world and 'the pearl of Siberia', is magnificent at any season and supports a micro-ecology with its own unique flora and fauna; from the Kamchatka peninsula towers Mount Klyuchevskii, the highest volcano in Eurasia, and there, too, is a hotbed of active, boiling springs and geysers; in the Vladivostok region on the Pacific coast grapevines are cultivated, and the jungles of the Amur and the Ussuri lowlands are still the stalking grounds of the great Siberian tiger. It is, in short, a land of astonishing geographical and climatic diversity, as befits its size, which to some extent belies the rigid, frigid snowscapes of the popular imagination.

As regards its notoriety as a 'land of damnation and chains', a domain of perpetual punishment and pain – this, too, is grimly rooted in the very real sufferings of generations of convicts, rebels, revolutionaries, common criminals and multitudes of often innnocent men, women and children, who for nearly four centuries have dragged themselves along the 'road of chains' (*kandalnaya doroga*) leading beyond the Urals. At first starting on an *ad hoc* and *ad hominen* basis before the birth of the Romanov dynasty, the system of transporting the unwanted criminal detritus and the antisocial, nonconformist and subversive members of the Russian social and political order – both tsarist and Soviet – steadily generated a huge sprawling diaspora comprising millions of wretched human beings who were banished to the living purgatory of Siberian exile. Amid the unspeakable sufferings, however, there are epic tales of courage and heroism; of those who voluntarily followed their banished loved ones into the unknown; of enlightened, cultivated exiles who chose to remain after their sentences were complete and devote themselves to the scientific, artistic and educational development of the region. At the same time it should be remembered that over the centuries, exiles and deportees have only accounted for a tiny fraction of the total population of Siberia, the vast majority of which was there as a result of voluntary emigration, fortune seeking or the process of natural procreation. As well as the horror stories of the tsarist penal system and the Stalinist *GULag*, there are also examples of those exiles who managed to lead a relatively comfortable, if spartan, existence, taking regular exercise, hunting for sport, reading, writing and corresponding fairly freely with fellow exiles, enjoying connubial pleasures and composing theoretical treatises – one thinks particularly of Vladimir Ilyich Ulyanov/Lenin who spent three reasonably fruitful and unexacting years, most of the time with his wife, Nadezhda Krupskaya, living as a political exile in the home of a rich peasant in the village of Shushenskoe in southern Siberia (1897–1900). But for the majority, conditions were so atrocious as to justify Dostoevskii's description of the Siberian penal system as 'The House of the Dead'.

There is, however, obviously a great deal more to the history of Siberia than a catalogue of criminality and cold. From the reign of Ivan the Terrible (1547–84) to the present day, Russia's northern empire east of the Urals has played an often crucial – sometimes direct, sometimes indirect – though frequently unacknowledged, role in the development of the Russian state and society. It was, after all, the conquest and settlement of Siberia in the late sixteenth and the seventeenth centuries which more than anything else – at least in terms of territorial aggrandizement – originally transformed the land-locked mediaeval Tsardom of Muscovy into the mighty Russian Empire, giving the government in Moscow and then St Petersburg virtually unchallenged, absolute sway over the whole of northern Eurasia and its polyglot peoples. During the period of Tatar domination from the thirteenth to the end of the fifteenth centuries, Russia under the Golden Horde had been the most westerly province of the great Mongol Empire founded by Genghis Khan; but from 1582 onwards the tide was turned and the European Slavs rapidly found themselves rulers of a vast colonial domain stretching across Asia to the northern Pacific. The Leningrad historian, R.G. Skrynnikov, has suggested, though not without challenge, that it was in 1582, rather than 1581, that the first foray or 'expedition' of cossack conquistadors under the leadership of *ataman* Yermak Timofeevich scored an unspectacular military victory over the tiny Tatar princedom of Sibir, then ruled by Khan Kuchum, thus laying the foundations for what was to be the irresistible Russian *Drang nach Osten*. Over the next hundred years a motley collection of military servicemen (*voennosluzhilie lyudi*), fur-hunters, merchants, government officials, Orthodox clergymen, fugitive serfs, entrepreneurs and tradesmen (*promyshlenniki*), convicts, religious dissidents, foreign prisoners-of-war (generically known as *Litva*, 'Lithuanians'), cossacks, artisans, adventurers and vagrants (*gulyashchie lyudi*) steadily overwhelmed the indigenous Siberian native population and established a strongly defended network of wooden fortresses, outposts and stockaded population points, several of which swiftly grew from small military and administrative settlements into substantial, bustling frontier towns, a process described in more detail by David Collins in Chapter 2 of this book.

The nature of Russia's 'conquest', 'subjugation', 'annexation' or 'assimilation' of Siberia has been the subject of a good deal of historical debate, and is indeed discussed briefly in some of the following chapters, particularly those by Basil Dmytryshyn, David Collins and James Forsyth – the last concentrating on the ambiguous impact of the incoming Slavs on the aboriginal Siberian peoples – but what is important to underline in this introductory essay is that Muscovy's expansion from the Urals to the Pacific in the seventeenth century was in a sense the territorial and colonial complement to the institutional consolidation of the political power of the Russian autocratic state. Although in the middle of the seventeenth century Muscovy was racked by a series of civil rebellions, peasant wars, religious turmoil and military mutiny, it was also during this period that the foundations for the political, social and economic structures of the tsarist imperial system were laid down. The salient features of this historical process were: the dynastic consolidation of regal authority in the Romanov family; the entrenchment of autocratic absolutism; the social ascendancy of the land-owning nobility (*dvoryanstvo*); the promulgation of a comprehensive Legal Code (the *Sobornoe Ulozhenie* of 1649); the burgeoning of a civil bureaucracy; the confirmation of the caesaro-papist principle (by crushing the popular *Raskol* (Schism) and curbing the authority of the patriarchate); the dependence on military prowess; and, above all, the final enserfment of the Russian peasantry. It was precisely at the same time as these processes, policies and institutions were being consolidated that the embryonic imperial regime found territorial expression for its increasing power in the colonial administration and economic exploitation of Siberia.

Indeed, one might even go so far as to say that, were it not for the 'discovery' of Siberia's seemingly inexhaustible resources of 'soft gold', that is, an abundance of fur-bearing mammals – in particular the highly-prized sable – the Muscovite government would have been without the economic foundation for the growth of its political power. Among western historians, Raymond Fisher has established the centrality of fur in the seventeenth-century Russian economy and, more recently, Janet Martin has demonstrated that control of the fur trade (the 'Treasure of the Land of Darkness') was an essential ingredient in the political domination of a succession of mediaeval states, culminating in that of the Muscovite Tsardom.[2] There is, of course, nothing novel in the idea that commercial and political power go hand in hand, but the sheer volume and importance of fur as the preponderating commodity on the mediaeval international market suggests that a monopoly in its procurement, sale and supply was, if not exactly a *sine qua non*, then at the least a decisive factor in the political hegemony of Muscovy. No doubt the proposition: 'Had there been no Siberian sable, there would have been no Muscovite empire', is somewhat fanciful, but there is no gainsaying metropolitan Russia's early economic dependence on the resources of her Siberian possessions.

There was, of course, as Basil Dmytryshyn points out in Chapter 1, no grand design or masterplan for the original Russian conquest of Siberia. It was the result of a complex intermixture of state enterprise, private initiative, 'geopolitical' imperatives, the urge to find 'natural' frontiers, serendipity and sheer adventurism. However, during the reign of Peter the Great (1682–1725), tremendous changes were introduced into every sphere of Russian life which, as far as Siberia was concerned, meant a greater element of state intervention, of *dirigisme*, particularly in the exploration and scientific investigation of Siberia's natural and economic resources. The motive force behind all of Peter's reforms was the greater glory of the Russian state, and to this end he sought to harness the entire human and material reserves of his extensive kingdom. How much more practically, efficiently and profitably those reserves could be utilized and exploited if the raw materials and the areas in which they were located or lay buried were systematically explored, charted, surveyed, investigated and catalogued.

Therefore, driven by a mixture of curiosity, practicality and *raisons d'état*, and encouraged by the councils of such western advisers as the Dutchman, Nicolaas Witsen, and the German philosopher, Gottfried Leibnitz, Peter ordered the kitting-out and dispatch at state expense of various expeditions for the scientific exploration and study of his Siberian treasure house. Of these, commencing its odyssey some time after Peter's death, and with the participation of the Academy of Sciences, the most famous was the Second Kamchatka, or 'Great Northern' expedition, led by the Danish seaman, Vitus Bering, who was to lend his name to the narrow straits separating Siberia from the American continent at the northern extremity of the Pacific Ocean. It is to this grandiose undertaking that J.L. Black's chapter in the present volume is devoted. Although this was the grandest, Bering's voyage of discovery was only one of many scientific expeditions in the eighteenth century, and through the efforts of government-sponsored explorers and private entrepreneurs – the latter seeking not so much scientific information as further killing grounds in the pursuit of the lucrative sea otter – Russia's political and commercial power began to reach out beyond the Siberian landmass across the northern Pacific, taking in the Aleutian and Kuril Islands, Russian America (the present Alaska), as well as establishing trading settlements down the western coast of America, and even making a short-lived foray into the Hawaiian archipelago. However, as James Gibson's chapter in the present collection makes clear, Russia's overseas colonial experience in the Americas was not a happy or successful one. The expense, the incompetence of the personnel, the distances involved, the lack of an agricultural base, the foreign competition, a reorientation of imperial policies in the Far East – these and a number of other factors analysed by Gibson eventually led to the sale of Russian America to the United States in 1867 'at two cents an acre'.[3]

Meanwhile, the colonization, settlement and economic exploitation of the Siberian mainland continued throughout the eighteenth and nineteenth centuries, binding the territory ever more closely to metropolitan Russia and reflecting, contributing to or suffering from every stage of the nation's overall historical development. One aspect of Peter the Great's reforming energy in the early eighteenth century, which had an indirect effect on the population dynamics of Siberia, was his massive use of convict and forced labour on his gigantic construction projects in European Russia, in particular the building of St Petersburg, the digging of canals and the fortification of new ports and harbours, like Rogervik, on the Baltic. As mentioned above, although the exiled inhabitants of Siberia never amounted to a large proportion of the total population, nevertheless they did make a significant quantitative and qualitative contribution during the seventeenth century to the region's manpower resources – accounting for around 11 per cent of the total, and engaged in a variety of administrative, military, clerical and agricultural occupations essential to the proper management of the newly-conquered territories. But Peter's preoccupations in the west, and his insatiable demand for recruits for both his military and civilian enterprises, meant that the flow of compulsory exiles into Siberia from European Russia was temporarily curtailed. On the other hand, Peter was responsible for the introduction of a punitive practice which was to remain at the centre of the tsarist criminal code and of the Siberian penal system until well into the twentieth century. This was the institution of *katorga*, or forced labour. One of the tsar-reformer's great achievements was the foundation of the Russian navy, much of it consisting of wooden galleys propelled by the collective muscle-power of conscript or convict oarsmen. The mediaeval

Greek word for galley is *katergon*, and it was in this nautical sense that the word first entered the Russian vocabulary. It soon lost its exclusively maritime connotation and, from denoting simply work as a galley slave, came to be applied to other forms of penal servitude with hard labour. As such, and particularly after Empress Elizabeth's *de facto* abolition of the death penalty for criminal offences in 1753, exile to katorga, followed by perpetual exile in Siberia (*ssylka na katorgu v Sibir*), was to be retained as the harshest form of punishment in the tsarist penal code until the revolutions of 1917 – though of course it survived far beyond that date under a different dispensation.

During the period of 'Palace Revolutions' following Peter's death, Siberia gained in notoriety as a place of exile and confinement as a result of the increasingly frequent banishment there of the victims of a sequence of palace conspiracies and coups. Between 1725 and 1762, scores of once-powerful imperial favourites, courtiers, viziers, royal lovers, politicians, patricians and plotters fell foul of this or that faction or clique in St Petersburg and found themselves temporarily or permanently imprisoned or exiled beyond the Urals, still alive but incapable of joining in the political intrigues of the capital.

Paradoxically, however, as well as becoming the classical place of banishment, Siberia was also fast developing into a haven and a land of freedom and opportunity for the steadily increasing numbers of refugees fleeing from the oppressive social, economic and political policies of St Petersburg. If the flow of compulsory exiles to Siberia decreased during the reign of Peter the Great, so did the rate of voluntary fugitives from central European Russia increase by leaps and bounds. And there seems little reason to doubt the conclusions of a number of pre-revolutionary and Soviet historians that the enhanced rate of peasant flight to Siberia in the late seventeenth and early eighteenth centuries was the direct result of the increasing burdens of the serf-owning economy and of Peter's oppressive fiscal policies, military recruitment, foreign wars and religious persecution. Between 1678 and 1710, for instance, the peasant population of Siberia, counted in number of households (*dvory*), increased by almost 50 per cent, while that of Moscow province alone declined by 27 per cent.[4] This trend continued in succeeding years so that during the three-quarters of a century between the first (1719) and the fifth (1795) official censuses, the Russian population of Siberia increased by almost two and a half times, from 169,000 adult males to 412,000, at a time when the population of the empire as a whole less than doubled.[5] The faster rate of population growth in Siberia than in the rest of the country demonstrates the rapid and determined process of

Siberia's colonization, settlement and russification, and is explained by a number of factors.

First was the continuing, and expanding, rate of peasant flight from European Russia, which peaked during years of harvest failure, and was a constant manifestation of discontent with the abuses of serfdom. Second, the discovery of mineral resources and the consequent development of metallurgical industries in Transbaikal and the Altai demanded more manpower than could be met from the local populations, and hence acted as a loadstone for the attraction of the necessary personnel to work them, in the form of both voluntary and forced labour. Third, the large number of commercial expeditions joining in the hunt for the maritime fur resources of the Far East and the North Pacific drew more and more merchants, *promyshlenniki* and ordinary peasants into those far-flung regions. Fourth, the regularization of commercial relations with China by the treaties of Nerchinsk (1689) and Kyakhta (1727), and also the building of fortified 'lines' (*linii*) in the relatively fertile southern borderlands, created stable conditions there for trade, agriculture and settlement, as did the annexation of the rich Gornyi Altai district to the empire in 1758. Fifth, after the comparative lull during the reign of Peter the Great, the St Petersburg authorities resorted with increasing frequency to the practice of exiling malefactors and malcontents to Siberia, with the twin aims of punishment and colonization. The reasons for this phenomenon are varied: the tightening bonds of serfdom and the greater degree of social regimentation introduced by Peter the Great meant that a number of previously innocent practices (tree-felling, salt-gathering, trespass, begging, vagrancy, and so on) were criminalized and punished with hard labour and exile; popular protest against the proliferating powers of the state in the form of minor revolts, mass insurgencies (for example, Bulavin, Pugachev), large-scale banditry and escalating rates of petty crime were similarly dealt with; the abolition of capital punishment for criminal offences in 1753 led to its replacement with 'civil execution' (public flogging and mutilation followed by perpetual katorga); and laws passed in 1766 and 1769 changed the usual place of penal servitude from Rogervik and other locations in European Russia to the silver mines and factories around Nerchinsk. But the steepest rise in the number of Siberian exiles was caused by the notorious legislation of 1760 which granted serf-owners the right to hand over disobedient, idle or refractory peasants to the state authorities for exile to Siberia, in return for a military recruit quittance. Incomplete figures reveal that between the third (1762) and fourth (1782) censuses, the number of exiled serfs almost quadrupled from around 2,500 to over 10,000 in the Tobolsk, Kolyvan and Irkutsk provinces alone, that is, not counting those condemned to hard labour in the mines at Nerchinsk.[6] All of these different circumstances, with the added natural factor of increased birth-rates in a non-serf-owning environment, resulted in Siberia being inhabited at the end of the eighteenth century by an overwhelmingly Russian peasant population.

The fact that central government was now beginning to regard Siberia as an integral part of Russia as a whole, rather than merely as a colonial appendage, was marked by the abolition in 1763 of the Siberian Department (*Sibirskii prikaz*), the central state bureau which had, with a brief interruption under Peter the Great, been directly responsible for the governance and administration of the territory since 1637. By the beginning of the nineteenth century Siberia was divided up into the three governorships (*gubernii*) of Tobolsk, Tomsk and Irkutsk, each of them further subdivided, like any other guberniya in the empire, into a number of regions (*oblasti*) and districts (*uezdy*). However, despite the formal integration of the territory into the regular administrative structure of the empire, a combination of human and material circumstances peculiar to Siberia served to preserve the particularity of the region in a number of ways, which led later 'regionalist' historians and thinkers to consider Siberia to be a quite distinct entity, in other senses than the merely geographical, from European Russia, with its own unique characteristics, needs and requirements.

One particular characteristic which had blighted the administration of Siberia throughout the period of Russian domination was the legendary rapaciousness, venality, corruption and brutality of many of even the region's most senior officials. Since the early seventeenth century, despite the central government's efforts to attenuate, curb or eliminate the worst abuses (to the extent of publicly hanging the first Governor of Siberia, M.P. Gagarin, in 1721), the tsar's 'Siberian satraps' enjoyed almost plenipotentiary powers in what they regarded as their own fiefdom, which they exercised with all the arbitrary and unbridled ruthlessness of a military dictatorship and the methods of a police state. Particularly notorious in the early nineteenth century, during the supposedly 'liberal' reign of Alexander I (1801–25), was the draconian regime of the Siberian Governor-General, I.B. Pestel (father of the executed Decembrist leader), and his assistant, the Civil Governor of Irkutsk, N.I. Treskin. Not only the Siberian natives, who had long suffered from the systematic cruelty and exploitation of the invading white men (see James Forsyth's account in Chapter 4), but also the 'old inhabitants' (*starozhily*), Russian peasants, citizens and merchants fell victim of their virtual reign of terror. Although, as Marc Raeff has pointed out, it was their methods rather than their aims which were at fault, it was nevertheless the inefficient, inhumane and corrupt administration of Siberia under Pestel and Treskin, last of a long line of government-appointed regional tyrants, that was to be tackled with such determination by Alexander's brilliant bureaucrat and disgraced official, Mikhail Speranskii (1722–1839).

Speranskii's own brief governorship of Siberia (from 1819 to 1821) was a minor turning point in the history of the territory. Indeed, one of Nicholas I's ministers, Count Uvarov, was later to remark that the history of Siberia could be divided into two periods – before and after Speranskii.[7] While Uvarov's periodization is obviously too clear cut, it is nevertheless true that Speranskii's reform of the territory's administration – including the operation of the exile system and the regularization of relations with the Siberian natives – created, in theory, if not always in practice, a more rational and equitable framework for the government and management of the Siberian lands which remained more or less *in situ* until the upheavals of 1917.

When the ostracized Speranskii learned of his appointment to the Governor-Generalship of Siberia, his own mental image of the place was similar to the popular stereotype described above – that of a vast, remote and inhospitable ice-bound prison. However, his on-the-spot tours of inspection, and his characteristically thorough investigations of the region's peoples, problems and resources, quickly convinced him of Siberia's enormous potential as a land of civilization and plenty, if only it could be provided with the necessary administrative, legal and political framework within which to develop its promise. Speranskii's consequent package of reforms is too complex to be analysed in detail at this point, and has in any case been thoroughly investigated by Marc Raeff.[8] Suffice it to say that, in the absence of a sufficiently 'mature', well-educated civil society in Siberia, Speranskii sought to design a structure of bureaucratic agencies and offices in which power was vested in institutions rather than personalities, which took full cognizance of individual regions' peculiar human and material needs and circumstances (both Russian and native), and which laid down proper codes of administrative procedures, legal practices and economic policies. In other words, he endeavoured to introduce into Siberia something which was after all only a rudimentary concept at that time in metropolitan Russia, that is, the 'rule of law'. Conscious of his pioneering role in this respect, and in thereby 'opening up' Siberia to the prospect of a more orderly and civically developed future, Speranskii compared himself, rather immodestly, with the traditional 'discoverer' of Siberia, Yermak.[9]

Despite his good intentions, and despite the more rational management principles and institutions introduced by Speranskii, the actual administration of Siberia, the manner of its economic exploitation, the low levels of popular enlightenment, the permanently suppurating sore of the exile system, the treatment of the native population – which still ranged from the paternalistic to the spasmodically genocidal – and the survival of traditional 'imperialist' attitudes in St Petersburg, meant that in practice the old core–periphery, metropolis–frontier relationships still remained in force, and Siberia continued to be treated and governed in a manner which reflected its original quasi-colonial status.

An attempt has been made by the present writer to convey something of the lawless nature and the rough, tough frontierland conditions of post-Speranskii Siberia in his later chapter comparing Siberia to the American 'Wild West' and analysing the relationship between exile, vagrancy and crime in the region. The reforming governor's efforts to place the hated exile system 'on a more orderly and business-like foundation' foundered on the twin reefs of underprovision of infrastructural resources, and the over-supply of vastly more compulsory settlers and convict labourers than the restructured system was designed or intended to cope with. From an average of 2,000–3,000 exiles a year during Alexander I's reign, by the middle of the century as many as 17, 18, or even 19,000 exiles were being annually transported to settle in Siberia – not even counting those sentenced to katorga. Apart from the thousands of common criminals who proved to be such a bane for Siberian society, the nineteenth century also witnessed a steady increase in the number of people who, either by judicial or administrative process, were banished to Siberia for political crimes – committed or suspected – against the state.

The first large contingent of political exiles in the modern period were over a hundred participants in the abortive military rebellion against autocracy in 1825 – the Decembrists. Even before their enforced sojourn in the tsar's eastern provinces, several of the Decembrist conspirators already had some experience of, or indirect connection with, Siberia. The leader of the Southern Society, Pavel Pestel – executed, not exiled – was the son of the notorious Governor-General mentioned earlier; G.S. Batenkov, himself of Siberian origin, acted as a close personal aide to Speranskii during the latter's governorship; Baron V.I. Shteingel was born in Perm on the western edge of Siberia, was raised in Kamchatka and served between 1802 and 1810 in Okhotsk and Irkutsk; D.I. Zavalishin was well travelled in both Siberia and Russian America; and, as James Gibson notes in his own chapter, several of the Decembrists (including the poet, Ryleev, who was hanged alongside Pestel) had connections of one sort or another with the Russian American Company. There is an enormous literature in Russian on the Decembrists' Siberian exile which accurately reflects the powerful impact which these 'first enlighteners of the Siberian people' had on the scientific investigation and cultural development of the region with which so many of them came to identify themselves, and where not a few chose to remain after they were eventually amnestied by Alexander II.[10] Just as their initial, ill-fated rebellion marked the beginning of the nineteenth-century Russian revolutionary movement, so did their exile beyond the Urals open a new phase in the history of political exile in Siberia and of the on-going battle between the radical intelligentsia and the autocratic Russian state.

The Decembrists were followed in 1849 by members of the Fourierist circle of M.V. Petrashevskii, including the young writer, Fedor Dostoevskii; by tens of thousands of Polish insurgents after the national uprisings of 1830 and 1863; by radical pamphleteers and adherents of the fledgling post-emancipation revolutionary groups; by the most famous of the exiled 'men of the sixties' and acknowledged figurehead of his intellectual generation, Nikolai Chernyshevskii, confined in soul-destroying conditions at the remote outpost of Vilyuisk in northern Yakutia; by propagandists and terrorists of the Populist revolutionary movement of the 1870s; and by the victims of the new catch-all legislation on police powers of surveillance introduced after the assassination of Alexander II in 1881. All these, as well as many of their innocent relatives and acquaintances, were to find themselves condemned to the mercies of a capricious and often brutal exile administration which many were neither physically nor spiritually able to withstand. The majority of these state criminals or politically 'untrustworthies' (*neblagonadezhnye*), sprang from Russia's educated classes and her critically-thinking elite, that is, the intelligentsia. They thus represented a specific stage in the history of the revolutionary movement as a whole – that of the largely non-gentry, *déclassé* radicals, or *raznochintsy*, of which Chernyshevskii was the archetypal figure.

Around the turn of the century, however, the social composition of Siberia's community of political exiles became more diversified, more 'plebeian', as thousands of striking workers, members of Marxist-inspired proletarian organizations, rebellious peasants, participants in national liberation movements in the non-Russian borderlands, anarchists, rank-and-file Mensheviks, Bolsheviks and Socialist Revolutionaries became involved in the empire-wide tidal wave of social and political protest during the dying years of the imperial regime. While the government was to some extent successful in thereby isolating its opponents from their comrades in European Russia and elsewhere, the 'democratrization' of the political exile operation only served to disseminate the seeds and agents of revolutionary change in greater numbers and into the remotest corners of the empire. Through the government's own policies, therefore, Siberia was well supplied with an experienced and committed cohort of exiled revolutionary activists when revolution itself, followed by civil war, swept across the country during and after 1917.

But before that stage was reached, the far-reaching social and economic changes brought about by the post-emancipation process of modernization, industrialization and the growth of capitalist relationships in Russia also found their idiosyncratic expression in Siberia, newly enlarged by the territory of the Amur and Ussuri regions which were incorporated into the empire at China's expense by the visionary efforts of the Governor-General of Eastern Siberia, N.N. Muravev-Amurskii (treaties of Aigun, 1858, and Pekin, 1860). Despite the obstacles to personal and geographical mobility posed by the communal organization of the liberated peasants, the abolition of serfdom in 1861 nevertheless created conditions in which an even greater number than ever before of voluntary emigrants and settlers from the land-hungry provinces of central European Russia flocked towards the fertile steppe and forest-steppe lands of west and south-west Siberia, thus massively augmenting the influx of peasant settlers already observed in the previous century.

In his contribution to the present volume, the distinguished Soviet historian, Leonid Goryushkin, has added fresh insights to the body of literature on nineteenth and early twentieth-century peasant migration patterns by demonstrating how these reflected the fluctuating social, economic and political policies of the late tsarist regime and by analysing their impact on the agrarian economy and village industries of Siberia in the decades before the First World War. Such factors as the government's initial anxiety to guarantee an adequate labour force to the ex-serf-owning nobility; the building of the Trans-Siberian Railway – centrepiece of Russia's late industrial revolution; the uncertainties caused by the 1905 revolutionary situation; Stolypin's political gamble on agrarian reform: all these circumstances influenced the rate of Siberian settlement in what was one of the largest population shifts in European history. Goryushkin's conclusion is that in the process of peasant immigration and colonization, not only did the incoming millions bring about innovations in agricultural methods, animal husbandry, cottage industry and the social customs of the Siberian peasantry, but they themselves were also deeply influenced by the traditional local practices of the old Siberians. The result was a two-way process which created a 'new amalgam of peasant traditions and cultures' and 'a close unity in the material and spiritual culture of European Russia and Siberia.'[11]

Be that as it may, there were still those in the late nineteenth and early twentieth centuries who still continued to look on Siberia as an exploited colony whose population and resources were recklessly plundered and despoiled by the central government, whose merchantry continued to suffer under the 'economic yoke of Moscow' and the commercial interests of the centre, whose native peoples were many of them doomed to extinction, where such civil and political rights and modern judicial institutions as existed in tsarist Russia were largely denied to the population of Siberia, where the cultural and educational infrastructure was inadequate for the region's needs, and which was still used as a distant dumping ground for the criminal sweepings of the rest of the empire. In the second half of the nineteenth century such sentiments had fostered the growth of a small but vigorous school of Siberian regionalist writers and political activists (*oblastniki*), some of whom had even gone so far as to envisage the complete political separation of Siberia from Russia and the establishment of a new, independent Siberian republic. The proponents of such outrageous plans were easily muzzled and isolated by the police and military authorities, but localized, 'patriotic' sympathies for some kind of regional autonomy continued to be cherished by a few individuals and groupings until the collapse of tsarist authority and the ensuing chaos of revolution and civil war created conditions in which the adherents of Siberian independence could now openly press their case and join in the bitter, fratricidal struggle of contending political and nationalist forces which raged across the country's huge expanses between 1917 and 1922.

The final chapter of this book, written by John Channon, comprises both a brief survey of the course of the Revolution and Civil War in Siberia, and, drawing on the work of a number of Soviet historians and also western experts such as Evan Mawdsley, Norman Pereira and Jon Smele, an analysis of the horrendously complex, bloody and confused antagonisms with which the entire territory was racked. During this agonizing period, Siberia was perhaps the most bitterly fought-over, and certainly the largest, theatre of military operations and political hostilities in the entire conflict. As it was the revolt of the Czech Legion on the Trans-Siberian Railway in May 1918 which in a sense signalled the start of the Civil War, so was it the taking of Vladivostok by the Red Army in 1922, the withdrawal of American and Japanese interventionist forces from the Siberian mainland, and the incorporation of the short-lived Far Eastern Republic into the Soviet Union which finally marked its end. In this way, as so often in the past, even in the throes of revolution and civil war Siberia once more demonstrated the intimate and inextricable connection between its own internal fortunes, the sufferings and achievements of its people and the historical development of Russia as a whole.

It is hoped that the following chapters, contributed by an international team of acknowledged experts in their own field of scholarship, will help to counter the peripheralization from which Siberian historiography has partly suffered in the west, will illuminate and underline both the importance and the fascination of Siberia's role in Russian history, and also act as a stimulus to further research and publication in this relatively neglected area.

NOTES AND REFERENCES

1 The study of Siberia's history in the west has, it must be said, been better served by North American than European scholars, those in the USA perhaps because of their Pacific perspective on Siberia and the Far East, and the Canadians because of certain similarities between Siberia's and their own country's geographical features, climate and colonial heritage. Without giving a full bibliography, the works of the following historians (in alphabetical order) are particularly worthy of note: USA – Basil Dmytryshyn, Raymond H. Fisher, Frank A. Golder, Robert J. Kerner, George V. Lantzeff, George A. Lensen, Marc Raeff, John J. Stephan, Donald Treadgold, and John A. White; Canada – J.L. Black, James R. Gibson, Norman G.O. Pereira and Richard A. Pierce; the geographer, Robert N. North, has also written a valuable monograph on the history of transportation in Siberia. Until very recent years the only two modern British scholars of any repute in the study of Siberia have been Terence Armstrong and Violet Conolly, neither of whom, despite the great historiographical value of their publications, would claim to be principally a historian.

2 Raymond H. Fisher, *The Russian Fur Trade, 1550–1700* (Berkeley and Los Angeles: University of California Press, 1943); Janet Martin, *Treasure of the Land of Darkness: The Fur Trade and its Significance for Medieval Russia* (Cambridge, London and New York: Cambridge University Press, 1986).

3 See Chapter 6, p. 112.

4 V.M. Kabuzan and S.M. Troitskii, 'Dvizhenie naseleniya Sibiri v XVIII v.', in *Sibir XVII–XVIII vv. Materialy po istorii Sibiri: Sibir perioda feodalizma* (Novosibirsk, 1962) p. 147.

5 Ibid., Table 3, p. 146; see also Chapter 5 of this volume, notes 5 and 6.

6 Ibid., Table 4, p. 150.

7 Quoted in Marc Raeff, *Michael Speransky: Statesman of Imperial Russia, 1772–1839* (The Hague: Martinus Nijhoff, 1957) p. 260.

8 Marc Raeff, *Siberia and the Reforms of 1822* (Seattle: University of Washington Press, 1956).

9 Letter from Speranskii to his daughter, 1 February 1820, quoted in Raeff, *Michael Speransky*, op. cit., p. 267.

10 See, for example, N.M. Chentsov (ed.), *Vosstanie dekabristov. Bibliografiya* (Moscow-Leningrad, 1919); *Dvizhenie dekabristov. Ukazatel literatury, 1928–1959* (Moscow, 1960). Both contain references, albeit incomplete, to the Decembrists' activities in Siberian exile. See also the more up-to-date series published under the auspices of Irkutsk University, *Sibir i dekabristy*, 4 issues (Irkutsk, 1975–85), and L.M. Goryushkin (ed.) *Ssylnye dekabristy v Sibiri* (Novosibirsk: Nauka, 1985). In English, see Glynn Barratt,

Voices in Exile: The Decembrist Memoirs (Montreal and London: McGill-Queen's University Press, 1974) which contains selected translations of the Decembrists' own writings in Siberia; and Kupova M. Birkett, 'The Decembrists in Siberia, 1826–1856' (unpublished M. Litt. dissertation, University of Glasgow, 1988).

11   See Chapter 8, p. 156.

2   The administrative apparatus of the Russian colony in Siberia and northern Asia, 1581–1700

Basil Dmytryshyn

Russia's armed conquest of Siberia and the rest of northern Asia between 1581 and 1700 was of momentous historic, economic, political, cultural and geopolitical consequence. It brought under Moscow's control an enormous, albeit inhospitable, territory, rich in natural resources and inhabited by many primitive tribes with diverse cultures (see Chapter 4). It also transformed the relatively poor and weak East European, Orthodox, Slavic, Muscovite state into the powerful, resourceful, multinational, multi-ethnic and multicultural Empire of Russia. And, thanks to the process of cultural and ethnic cross-fertilization, many Asians became russianized and many Russians became asianized.

Scholars have offered differing interpretations of the Russian colonial venture. Some have called it 'a civilizing and Christianizing effort'. Others have characterized it as 'the gathering of the Russian lands'. Still others have viewed it as 'the urge to the sea'. A good many have perceived it as pure Russian imperialism, similar to that practised by such contemporary colonial powers as Spain, Portugal, France, England, and Holland. Soviet scholars have interpreted it as either 'a rapprochement (*sblizhenie*) between Russian and non-Russian peoples of northern Asia', or as 'a complex process of annexation (*prisoedinenie*) and assimilation (*osvoenie*)'.

While each of these views has some merit, none is entirely satisfactory. Russian expansion across Siberia and the vast region of northern Asia cannot be reduced to a single formula or a simple slogan. To do so would be inaccurate and misleading. Russian conquest of the area was not a meticulously planned and carefully executed undertaking, nor did it operate in accordance with a grand design or specific timetable. In fact, like contemporary West European colonial adventures, the Russian drive across the Urals to the Pacific was a convulsive process propelled by many pressures and forces that varied in purpose, skill, intensity and duration, but which, between 1581 and 1700, brought some 10 million square kilometres of territory under Moscow's control.

In theory, the tsar of Russia was the ultimate lord and master of Russia's colony that stretched from the Urals to the Pacific. This was natural, since, as an absolute and autocratic monarch, he wielded unrestricted authority. As the head of state and a theocratic ruler, he appointed and dismissed all top government and church officials, issued all major decrees and interpreted all laws. He was also the wealthiest landowner of the country and its chief merchant, and he had the power to expropriate the property of any citizen without compensation or due process of law. So inclusive, indeed, was the tsar's authority that he truly exercised the power of life and death over every one of his Russian and non-Russian subjects.

With the exception of Yermak Timofeevich's initial foray, the entire conquest of Siberia and of northern Asia was undertaken in the tsar's name or on his orders. The conquered areas were administered by his appointees and were defended by his military forces. The indigenous natives were forced to take the oath of allegiance to the tsar, and officials collected tribute (*yasak*) from them and a tithe from Russian merchants and hunters, and it went directly to the tsar's treasury. Contemporary official documents refer to Russia's new colony as the tsar's patrimony (*votchina*), and to him as 'Tsar of Siberia' and 'Lord of all the Northern Territories'. Because of his all-inclusive powers, no major policy, event or action developed with respect to Siberia (or for that matter the rest of the country) without the tsar's approval or authorization. He rewarded those Russians or natives who obeyed and carried out his orders, and punished, often harshly, those who disobeyed his commands.

In actual practice, however, the situation was different. The conquest, control, defence, and exploitation of Russia's new colony was administered and supervised by two intertwined bureaucracies. One was centred in Moscow; the other was dispersed throughout the colony. Until about 1650, the top Moscow-based administrative agency was the *boyarskaya duma* (aristocratic advisory council). The duma members were the *crème de la crème* of Muscovite society. They included influential landed aristocrats, descendants of appanage princes, talented members of petty nobility, capable bureaucrats and high-ranking church officials. The tsar appointed all members of the duma, which advised him on new laws, on vital issues of foreign and domestic policy, and on appointment and dismissal of high government officials (including military commanders) in Moscow and throughout the country. The duma also exercised control over most administrative departments (*prikazy*) of the government, including, of course, the *Sibirskii prikaz* (Siberian Department). It appointed all key officials of that prikaz in Moscow and in Siberia; formulated defensive and offensive strategies for the region; received reports from officials in Siberia on the state of the new colony, as well as petitions from Russian and non-Russian inhabitants; and made all major decisions concerning the exploitation and administration of the region. In short, the boyarskaya duma served as the most important agency dealing with the conquest and control of Siberia. After 1650, most of those functions were centred in the *Raspravnaya palata* (Chamber of Adjudication), which was created by the *Sobornoe Ulozhenie* (Code of Law) of 1649 to act as a unifying administrative superstructure over all departments of government.

The second important tier of Moscow-based bureaucracy in charge of the new colony consisted of officials of various departments of the Muscovite government. Until 1594, the *Posolskii prikaz* (Ambassadorial Department) was in charge of Siberian affairs. This came about because that department had handled Moscow's relations in earlier times with the Siberian Khanate, and also because it had received the first shipment of tribute collected from the natives by Yermak's men. Between 1595 and 1599, the affairs of Siberia were managed by the *Novgorodskii prikaz*, also known as *Novgorodskaya chetvert* or *Chet*, which oversaw the financial matters of Novgorod, Pskov, Arkhangelsk, and other peripheries of Muscovy. From 1599 to 1637, Siberia was administered by the *Sibirskii stol* (Siberian Desk) within the *Kazanskii dvorets* (Kazan Court), also known as *Meshcherskii dvorets* (Meshcherskii Court), that had jurisdiction over the basins of the Volga and Kama rivers and in newly-conquered western Siberia. In 1637, with approval of the boyarskaya duma, the tsar elevated the Sibirskii stol to Sibirskii prikaz, and made it responsible for the day-to-day operations of the ever-expanding colony. The prikaz exercised that responsibility until 1711, when Peter I (1682–1725) transferred many of its functions to the newly-established *Kantselyariya sibirskoi gubernii* (Office of the Guberniya of Siberia). In 1730, Empress Anna (1730–40) re-established some of the powers of the Sibirskii prikaz. Its respite was brief, however, for in 1763 Catherine II (1762–96) abolished this prikaz for good.

This résumé of events leading to organization of the Sibirskii prikaz as the principal department responsible for Siberia makes it evident that the prikaz emerged slowly and even haphazardly. The reason was that the central government did not have a grand masterplan for the conquest, exploitation, and administration of the region. Moreover, Moscow was preoccupied with such pressing problems as the 'Time of Troubles', and prolonged wars with Sweden, the Ottoman Empire, and the Polish-Lithuanian Commonwealth. Only after they resolved those matters, albeit partially, were the Muscovite authorities able to turn their attention to their newly-acquired colony. The elevation in 1637 of the Sibirskii stol to the Sibirskii prikaz was the first major step in that direction.

Once in place, the Sibirskii prikaz played a critical role in making Siberia and the rest of northern Asia an integral part of Russia. Throughout its existence the prikaz was headed by a *boyar* and two (and after 1660, three) *dyaki* (clerks) (singular *dyak*), who served as his principal advisers and assistants. As a rule, the boyar was a member of an influential, landed, aristocratic family of Muscovy and was appointed to his post by the tsar, with the approval of the boyarskaya duma. The dyaki were subject to the same appointment procedure. They were usually recruited from among less distinguished aristocratic families of Moscow, and frequently from among the privileged upper-class merchants known as *gosti* (singular *gost*), who were experienced and knowledgeable in economic and administrative matters. Both the boyar and his assistants were accountable for their policies to the tsar and the boyarskaya duma, and received generous compensation for successes and punishment for failures. Since Siberia possessed enormous riches (furs, gold, ivory, and other luxury items), there was never a shortage of officials for these posts.

Administrative rules of all departments of Muscovite government stipulated that the boyar and his dyaki participate jointly in the decision-making process in matters affecting vital interests of their respective departments. The purpose was to control the activity of pompous or arrogant boyars. For that reason, the dyaki kept records of all deliberations and of collective decisions. The boyar and his dyaki were helped by numerous senior, intermediate, and junior assistants known as *poddyachie*, and by scribes known as *poddyachie s pripisyu*, who actually prepared the texts of important documents and affixed their signatures to them. This was so because often neither the boyar nor his dyaki were literate. Moreover, since the head of the prikaz (as well as his dyaki) often had other obligations, the burden of running the department rested squarely on the shoulders of these poorly paid and overworked underlings, who, in the process, often abused their authority.

In addition to the senior officials, the rapid conquest of Siberia and all northern Asia, and with it the appearance of many problems, brought into existence new personnel to handle myriad details within the Sibirskii prikaz. The new personnel was assigned to various *stoly* (singular *stol*) or desks. Ultimately, two types of stol emerged. The first was in charge of administrative-territorial units (e.g. Tobolskii stol, Yakutskii stol, Yeniseiskii stol, Mangazeiskii stol, and the like). The second type handled specific matters. The *Razryadnyi stol*, for example, was responsible for military servitors; the *Denezhnyi stol* was in charge of financial affairs; the *Gosudareva* (Tsar's) or *Sobolinaya kazna* (Sable Treasury) received, appraised and disposed of furs. Each stol was administered by a *golova* (head), who was assisted by numerous lesser officials. In the Sable Treasury, these officials were *tselovalniki* (singular *tselovalnik*) – 'sworn men' – to insure their honesty. The senior personnel of the Sibirskii prikaz supervised the activity of these stoly and paid small salaries to their staff. Occasionally the boyar in charge of the Sibirskii prikaz bestowed a bonus of some goods on an enterprising golova or tselovalnik. On the other hand, the latter were obliged to make up any deficit created by their negligence or dishonesty.

To sum up, these Moscow-based officials of the Sibirskii prikaz were collectively in charge of daily operations of Russian colonial possessions in Siberia. They informed the tsar and the boyarskaya duma of happenings in the colony, and it was through them that the tsar and the duma forwarded instructions to colonial personnel in Siberia. These Moscow-based officials supervised the appointments and activity of all top Russian officials in the new colony and formulated detailed rules concerning their personal behaviour, their conduct toward their Russian subordinates, and their treatment of the indigenous population. They devised plans for Russian permanent settlements in the region, and prescribed guidelines concerning the exploitation of the area's natural and human resources. They also worked out elaborate schemes to protect the colony against outside powers as well as uprisings against Russian rule by the indigenous natives. These Moscow-based officials established the quotas for the collection of yasak from numerous natives of the region and of the tithe from Russian *promyshlenniki* (singular *promyshlennik*), that is, entrepreneurs of all kinds, and appraised the quality of the collected wealth. Finally, the officials of the Sibirskii prikaz, jointly with the boyarskaya duma, formulated detailed guidelines on relations with such formidable opponents to Russian presence in Siberia and in northern Asia as the Kirghiz, Kalmyks, Mongols, Manchu, and Chinese.

It should be remembered that, in addition to the elaborate bureaucracy of the Sibirskii prikaz, the Moscow-based bureaucrats of other prikazy also administered, albeit indirectly, many of the affairs of the new colony. Of course, this was inevitable, given the nature of Muscovite government. The *Razryadnyi prikaz* (Department of Military Affairs), for instance, recommended qualified military officers to the Sibirskii prikaz to serve as *voevody* (singular *voevoda*), that is, top Russian military and administrative officials, and it also provided troops for service in the new colony. The *Posolskii prikaz* oversaw all diplomatic contacts with such powerful southern neighbours of the Russian colony as the Kirgiz, Kalmyks, Mongols, Manchu, and Chinese. The *Streletskii prikaz* (Musketeer, or 'Sharpshooter', Department) supervised the diverse mounted and foot units of the *streltsy* (singular *strelets*) who served in the region. The *Yamskii prikaz* (Postal, or Communications, Department) was in charge of the postal, transportation, and communication systems. And several religious departments dealt with crimes against the faith, the appointment of clergy, the moral behaviour of Russian personnel, and conversion of the indigenous population to

Orthodox Christianity. In short, because of its size, potential, and problems, the new colony involved almost every department of the Muscovite administration, and, since each department had its own set of long-term goals and priorities, many conflicts of interest developed. These had to be resolved ultimately either by the boyarskaya duma or by the tsar.

Although Moscow-based officials of the Sibirskii and other prikazy played a critical role in the formulation of various guidelines on how to conquer, control, defend and exploit the new colony, credit for successfully subduing and transforming Siberia and the rest of northern Asia into a Russian land rests squarely on the shoulders of the personnel who went there. This effort was the product of eight distinct groups. These were:

1 Russian promyshlenniki (that is, entrepreneurs), who hunted and trapped fur-bearing animals, and who also procured furs from the Siberian natives through trade, extortion, theft, tribute, and other means;
2 state employees (known in contemporary sources as *sluzhashchie* or *sluzhilie lyudi*, that is, servitors). These encompassed various administrative officials and military personnel, including streltsy and cossacks, who were sent there by the central authorities to protect Russia's vital interests;
3 prisoners-of-war (Poles, Lithuanians, Ukrainians, Belorussians, Swedes, Baltic Germans, and other Europeans, known in contemporary sources as *Litva*), who were dispatched to the region for 'safe-keeping' by the central authorities;
4 Muscovy's political and religious dissenters, who were exiled to the inhospitable region, and who were used by local authorities to perform various assignments, including defence;
5 state peasants, craftsmen, priests, monks and nuns, who were dispatched to various points in Siberia to assist colonial administrators;
6 Muscovy's merchants, who went to the conquered wilderness voluntarily to seek their fortune;
7 the *gulyashchie lyudi* (that is, runaway serfs and other social misfits, unfortunates, and outcasts), who sought refuge in the new colony and who were willing and ready to join anyone on any assignment;
8 individual natives, and often whole native tribes, who served voluntarily as guides and interpreters, or who joined the Russians in their conquest to secure individual or group protection or other basic advantages.

Regardless of background or purpose, once they came to this inhospitable, harsh, and remote area, many of the newcomers developed greed and a passion for adventure, with the result that some became heroes, some beasts, and some both.

From the midst of these diverse and numerically insignificant groups, emerged many leaders of the Russian conquest of Siberia and of northern Asia. The most prominent were: Yermak Timofeevich, who in 1581 or 1582 initiated Muscovy's march across the Urals toward the Pacific; Fedor Dyakov, who, in 1601, founded Mangazeya, from where the Muscovites later subdued the Samoeds, the Ostyaks, and the Tungus; Petr Beketov, who, in 1632, founded Yakutsk, from where the Muscovite conquerors later gained control of the vast and rich Lena basin, and sent expeditions to the Amur basin; Postnik Ivanov, who, in 1638, reached the Indigirka river and subdued the Yukagirs; Vasilii Poyarkov, the first Russian to navigate, in 1643, the length of the river Amur; Yerofei Khabarov, who, between 1649 and 1653, led two expeditions into the Amur basin and terrorized its natives; Semen Dezhnev, the first known individual to sail, between 1647 and 1649, from Kolyma in the Arctic, around the Chukotsk Peninsula, to the Pacific Ocean; and Vladimir Atlasov, who, between 1697 and 1699, brought Kamchatka under Russian rule.

These and countless other *zemleprokhodtsy* (that is, overland explorers and travellers), and their willing and reluctant followers, were simple, and for the most part illiterate, men. Some of them were even criminals. Yet they were also extraordinary men, who, by chance and ambition rather than political design, achieved many 'firsts'. They were the first Europeans to navigate the major rivers of North Asia and the first to sail along the shores of the Arctic ocean. They were likewise the first Europeans to encounter many new species of animals, fish and plants of the region, and the first to meet, observe, and provide rough descriptions of the appearance, customs and habits of the indigenous natives. They also were the first Europeans to slaughter many species of fur-bearing animals to near-extinction; the first to perpetrate genocide against those native tribes who refused to obey their orders; and the first to establish – by terror, enslavement, exploitation, and cunning – a European colonial empire over an enormous part of the Asian continent.

The colonial empire that these zemleprokhodtsy built centred around the region's great rivers. Between 1581 and 1605, the nucleus of the new empire was located along the central and lower systems of the Ob and Irtysh rivers; that is, present-day West Siberia. By 1628 the empire spread over most of the Yenisei, the Lower and Stony Tunguska and the Angara rivers. In the 1640s the conquest encompassed the Lena, the Amur, Indigirka, Kolyma and the Anadyr rivers. And between 1638 and 1650 the conquerors annexed the entire region around Lake Baikal. As they sailed along these rivers and their tributaries, the new masters built permanent settlements at strategic locations to serve as centres of control and conquest: Tyumen in 1586, Tobolsk in 1587, Mangazeya in 1601, Tomsk in 1604, Yeniseisk in 1620, Yakutsk in 1632, Okhotsk in 1649, and Irkutsk in 1652. Between 1585 and 1666 the Russians built some fifty permanent fortified settlements known as *ostrogi* (singular *ostrog*) and numerous other semi-permanent units known as *ostrozhki* (singular *ostrozhek* – little fortified outposts) and *zimovya* (singular *zimove* – small winter outposts).

The most impressive aspect of Russia's conquest of Siberia and of northern Asia, and subjugation of its native inhabitants, is the speed with which a handful of wilful men accomplished it. Their feats may be explained by:

1 the existence of large navigable rivers that allowed the conquerors to cover great distances in a relatively short time;
2 the absence of any significant or sustained native resistance;
3 the disunity among and the technological primitiveness of the native population;
4 the conquerors' skill and technological superiority;
5 their adroit use of native guides and interpreters who were familiar with local and regional geography, trails, peoples and languages;
6 their ambition, cruelty, and determination to survive and to succeed;
7 the generous government support they received from Moscow;
8 the absence of any European opponents or competitors to challenge the Russian monopoly.

Thanks to the presence of these factors, the Russians were able to establish their hegemony over northern Asia with relative ease and transformed their serendipitous colonial adventure into a permanent conquest.

When they marched across northern Asia – from the Urals to the Pacific – the Muscovites acquired not only an enormous and highly resourceful territory, but a great diversity of peoples. Between the Urals and the Yenisei river, the principal tribes were the Voguls, Ostyaks, Samoeds, Tatars, Kirgiz, Kalmyks, Chats and Teleuts. Between the Yenisei and the Pacific Ocean the major peoples were the Buryats, Chakagirs, Mongols, Tungus, Yukagirs, Duchers, Daurs, Gilyaks, Koryaks, Yakuts, Chukchis, Lamuts, Itelmens and Kamchadals. Linguistically, these peoples belonged to the Ugric, Finno-Ugric, Turkic, Mongol and Tungus-Manchu families of languages. Technologically, all were primitive and often they were extremely hostile to each other. Most were nomadic. Their principal tools were stone axes, adzes, and fish-hooks; their weapon, the bow and arrow. Most lived on game and fish, and roots and berries. They had no complex political, economic, or social institutions. Some groups were numerically so small that they were actually large family units or clans, rather than tribes. It goes without saying that these factors and the dissimilarities among the natives allowed the Muscovites to conquer, exploit and rule them with relative ease (for more detail, see Chapter 5).

The exploitation and control of this vast colony and its inhabitants was the prerogative of colonial officials who were stationed in various fortified outposts throughout the region. The highest-ranking official was the voevoda. The term is Old Slavic and originally meant a military commander and leader of warriors. In Muscovy (in the sixteenth and seventeenth centuries) it also referred to appointed officials of an administrative unit called *voevodstvo*, with military, police, civil, judicial, and, in border areas, limited diplomatic powers. In Siberia and in northern Asia, the posts of voevody were located in every *uezd* (that is, an administrative unit similar to those of Muscovy, into which the new colonial region was divided) and circumstances there made it possible for each voevoda to wield the power of life and death over those under his control. Generally speaking, members of distinguished Moscow nobility with good family connections enjoyed monopolies on voevody posts, provided they had some previous experience in military and civilian affairs. Two prikazy were involved in the appointment process: the Razryadnyi prikaz, which recommended the person for the tsar's approval; and the Sibirskii prikaz, which formally announced the selection and subsequently supervised his activity. Because great fortunes could be made in Siberia, there was never a shortage of applicants for assignments in that inhospitable land.

To prevent graft, corruption and sedition, Moscow officials exercised great caution in their selection of appointees. They carefully screened each candidate's background and qualifications, and before they dispatched him to Siberia they gave strict instructions about his responsibilities and warned of the consequences should he fail to live up to expectations. Moreover, in an effort to monitor his activity, Moscow officials insisted that the voevoda communicate with them frequently; limited the tenure of a voevoda to two years (in 1695 it was expanded to six years); in key outposts appointed two voevody so they could check on one another's activities; allowed Russian and non-Russian subjects, hurt or offended by the voevoda's action, to petition the tsar, the boyarskaya duma, and the head of the Sibirskii prikaz; and frequently instructed the voevody's immediate subordinates (that is, dyaki) to participate in every major decision affecting the region.

Although Moscow officialdom tried in numerous ways to check and control the power of these colonial voevody, their authority was quite extensive. In his uezd, the voevoda was responsible for both internal and external security. Accordingly, he was the commanding officer of all military units in his uezd, and was also the chief of police, the principal judge, and head of the civilian administration, although there was very little civilian activity since Siberia was essentially a huge military camp throughout the entire seventeenth century. The voevoda controlled the mobility of every Russian as well as the activity of the indigenous population in his uezd. He controlled supplies, dispatched reconnaissance units to bring new territories under Russian control, and debriefed the leaders of such expeditions. He heard all petitions and complaints from Russians and natives, monitored carefully any signs of discontent, and kept his Moscow superiors, as well as other voevody in the new colony, informed of rumours and developments. In short, each voevoda wielded absolute power in his jurisdiction.

For his service, the voevoda received generous remuneration – about 250 roubles per annum in cash, furs and provisions. This was essential, since normally he brought along his family and servants on his assignment. In Siberia he was also expected to receive from local inhabitants all essentials for his needs. Moreover, all native subjects under the voevoda's jurisdiction were required to give him gifts known as *pominki* on all possible holidays. Those who failed to deliver them on time were subject to punishment. Because all the voevoda's subordinates also expected to receive their share of the pominki, the indigenous population had an enormous burden and their anger frequently expressed itself in widespread discontent and even violence.

In performing his assigned responsibilities, the voevoda was assisted by a large number of officials and formal groups. Initially the most immediate confidants were the *pismennye golovy* (literally, writing heads), who were literate, who were able to keep records and correspondence, and who, in the voevoda's absence, assumed his responsibilities. Later, patterned after the structure of the Sibirskii prikaz, these officials were replaced by the dyaki or the poddyachie s pripisyu. These men often accompanied the voevoda to his assignment and returned to their old posts in Moscow when their term of office expired. While their chief function was to keep records and do other clerical work, they frequently kept watch on the activity of the voevoda, and thus served as the eyes and ears of the Sibirskii prikaz.

Regardless of their assignments, the voevoda and his immediate assistants formed the elite of Moscow's colonial uezd administration. They performed their official functions in a wooden structure within the ostrog called the *prikaznaya* or *sezzhaya izba*; that is, the prikaz assembly office. There they formulated policies affecting the uezd, issued instructions to the zemleprokhodtsy before their missions and interrogated them upon their return, and met embassies from the powerful Kirgiz, the White or Black

Kalmyk, and the Mongol nations. From here they carried out correspondence with their superiors in Moscow and with other voevody. The prikaznaya izba served also as a repository of records, including those affecting the yasak. The voevoda and his immediate associates were aided by lesser scribes and by the *prikaznye lyudi* or prikaz agents. The voevoda selected these persons from among literate clergy, prisoners-of-war and semi-literate military personnel from his own area. Their number and responsibilities varied from ostrog to ostrog. In general they performed routine work, and some men served as leaders of isolated tribute collection centres.

In every ostrog or ostrozhek, colonial officials relied also on several military and paramilitary units in carrying out orders, directions and instructions that came from Moscow, and in enforcing their own policies. The presence of the military units was not unusual, since from 1581 to 1700 Russia's new colony was dotted with military outposts, and most administrators were military men. The elite of the military were the *deti boyarskie* or *syny boyarskie*, that is, impoverished Russian nobles. As a rule they served as unit leaders, in which capacity they went on special assignments, explored and brought new regions under Moscow's control, collected tribute from the natives, put down anti-Russian upheavals, and performed other valuable services. They received a fairly good salary and other material rewards.

Under these colonial military officers were six distinct military and paramilitary units. Four of these were Russian; two were non-Russian. The streltsy, that is, musketeers, or sharpshooters, both foot and mounted, formed the top Russian unit. Armed with muskets, swords, pikes and battleaxes, and led by their own officers or by deti boyarskie, the streltsy reconnoitred new territories, suppressed native discontent, defended Russian interests against native attacks, and collected tribute and convoyed it, as well as important officials, across hostile territory. Next were the cossacks, a term that applied to a great variety of men – adventurers, outcasts, restless misfits, homeless men – all of whom served, either on horse or on foot, to supplement the streltsy. Elderly cossacks were also used as sentries in the ostrog and as guards to defend the Russian agricultural population. The third Russian group consisted of the *gulyashchie lyudi*, or persons not assigned to any tax category. They included runaway serfs, itinerant workers, criminals, and all manner of unfortunates who sought refuge in the new colony. Because there was a constant shortage of manpower, colonial officials assigned these men to accompany the streltsy or the cossacks and they also used them for other tasks. The final Russian group was the promyshlenniki, that is, hunters, trappers, and petty traders, either self-employed or in the hire of wealthy Russian merchants. These men were not part of the official establishment, but, because of the perennial manpower shortage, colonial officials often deputized them to reconnoitre new territories, to collect tribute and to put down native discontent. The non-Russian units were: the *Litva* and the *sluzhilie lyudi yurtovskie*. The Litva were prisoners-of-war and other detained Europeans, such as Lithuanians, Ukrainians, Belorussians, Poles, Germans, and Swedes, whom Moscow officials sent to various outposts in Siberia for security reasons. The dispatch was usually for life. Because many of these men were educated and had diverse skills, Russian colonial officials used them in many ways. Some even rose to intermediate positions of authority. There were a few cases of insubordination, but for the most part the Litva fought alongside the streltsy and the cossacks to establish and maintain Russian hegemony in northern Asia. The sluzhilie lyudi yurtovskie were native Tatars who lived in settlements known as *yurty*, and who volunteered for Russian service. These men had their own special units that assisted the streltsy and the cossacks. They also served as guides and interpreters. Evidence indicates that some of them became converts to Russian Orthodox Christianity, while some deserted Russian service. Generally speaking, these six military and paramilitary units functioned as independent entities; however, there is also ample evidence that men from all the groups participated in given missions or assignments.

In addition to the military-administrative personnel, Russian colonial officialdom included priests, monks and nuns. Their presence there was neither unique nor unusual, since throughout Muscovite history very close ties existed between church and state officials. Because the tsar was the nominal head of the church, every ostrog had either a chapel or a church. The government supplied these churches with necessities, including salaries, furnishings, religious books, food, and land and peasants to farm it. Monasteries and nunneries, usually located near an ostrog for security reasons, received similar consideration. In return for their generous support, the ecclesiastical personnel was expected to care for the old and the disabled zemleprokhodtsy; to offer spiritual guidance and provide for the religious needs of Russian colonial functionnaries; and sometimes to administer the oath of allegiance to natives and baptize those who wished to convert to Russian Orthodox Christianity. Records indicate that military-administrative and ecclesiastical officials co-operated when their interests coincided. There were, however, many disagreeents between the two because the govern- ment failed to delineate clearly the functions of each group. Finally, it should be noted that, like their colonial military-civilian counterparts, some church personnel was involved in corruption, was susceptible to bribery and extortion, and was prone to alcoholism and loose morals.

Although they were not an integral part of the colonial administrative apparatus, Russian peasants also played a vital role in subduing Siberia and northern Asia. Most of them were state peasants (men, women and children), whom the government settled near various ostrogi to grow food for the garrison and to form the nuclei of permanent Russian settlements in the colony. The government provided seeds, equipment, livestock and land for that purpose. Unarmed and unskilled, these unfortunates were constantly harassed by the hostile natives. Many were killed, their few possessions destroyed, and their livestock scattered or stolen by the attackers. To enable them to cultivate crops in relative safety, local authorities frequently assigned aged cossacks to guard them. Often such protective measures came too late as many peasants had already been killed or had fled and joined the gulyashchie lyudi, or drifted to portages where they hauled heavy loads overland from one river landing to another, or signed on to various expeditions that were short of labour. The available evidence indicates that, as a group, Russian peasants suffered the most and paid the heaviest human price in subduing the new colony for Russia.

The last group of individuals, who also were involved indirectly with Russian colonial administration in the new colony, was indigenous women and their offspring. Although their role is highly critical, they have not received the recognition they deserve. Almost every Russian official in Siberia and in northern Asia, including cossacks and even priests, had native mistresses. Actually, they were personal slaves and they were frequently bartered among masters. These women and their offspring performed valuable services to local officials. Because they were familiar with the region and achieved bilinguality, they served the colonial officials as guides and interpreters and as informers on native discontent. And, although they were not too numerous, they contributed enormously to the speed and ease with which the Russians subdued the vast territory. They were also the first Asians to be russianized.

Except for when they were on special assignment (that is, collecting or convoying yasak, subduing rebellious natives, or reconnoitring in new territories), all Russian administrative personnel in the new colony, in the period under discussion, lived in the permanent settlements known as ostrogi or ostrozhki, that is, large and small fortified outposts. For defensive purposes, these settlements were usually located on a bluff overlooking a river or at some similarly strategic location. Each settlement was surrounded by a high timbered stockade with sharpened tops, and entry was through a main gate overlooked by two or three log towers six or seven metres in height. Each settlement, too, had a secret escape tunnel, preferably toward a river, to enable the garrison to communicate with other outposts in a crisis. Small cannon were located above the gate and in the towers, while along the walls were embrasures for sharpshooters. Wherever possible, to afford greater security, each fortified settlement was additionally surrounded by a deep, wide, water-filled moat. To permit it to withstand a prolonged siege, each garrison also had its own water supply system.

Within the walls of each fortified citadel or *kreml* (which was patrolled around the clock) were the official residences of the voevoda and his top associates; a church or a chapel; a supply depot; barracks to house the garrison; structures for equipment, weapons and wood for fuel; stockades where local authorities kept their own prisoners; and special cells that housed native hostages. Regardless of rank or status, life in such an enclosed environment was harsh. Because of the region's northerly location, summers were brief and humid and brought clouds of insects; winters were long, cold and dark. These climatic extremes affected all supplies, especially food, since provisions had to be hauled the great distances from European Russia. It sometimes took months (or even years) to transport heavy equipment. Failure to stock adequate supplies of food, weaponry and fuel, meant certain death for the entire garrison from starvation, scurvy, freezing, epidemics, or the native attacks that grew in direct proportion to their mistreatment or exploitation by the Russians.

Life within each palisade was grim, dangerous, spartan and boring. To prevent boredom from reaching dangerous levels, the voevoda and his staff devised various means to keep the garrison busy. They assigned the aged and infirm to sentry duty. Others were occupied with preparing food and cutting wood for fuel for the long winter. Still others were sent out on routine reconnaissance patrols to investigate suspicious activities among the natives, or to collect yasak, or to bring yet another region under Russian control. The few specialists were commissioned to repair and make ready equipment and weapons. In addition to these officially-sponsored activities, most men of the garrison found time to drink, gamble, sing, gossip, reminisce and to plan new expeditions that would free them from boredom or that would bring more natives under Russian rule.

A few of these fortified permanent Russian colonial settlements attracted merchants (Russian and Bokharan), craftsmen, and other professional people. Individually and collectively, these people offered valuable information, supplied useful goods and services, and in due time transformed the isolated outposts into towns. These new towns, however, were not true towns by West European standards. They were small, crowded and dirty, with few streets or essential services, and little sanitation. Houses were small and built of logs, with the result that they suffered extensive damage from native attacks or from accidental or arson-caused fires. Moreover, almost all commercial activity of towns in the new colony (as well as in European

Russia) was centred in the *gostinnyi dvor*, a primitive market-place where local officials scrutinized all transactions.

It should be remembered that the principal function of these Russian colonial outposts was not commercial. They were established to perform three critical functions: to gain physical control of the region; to exploit the region's resources and inhabitants; and to make the conquered region an integral part of Russia. Russian authorities neither articulated nor spelled out these goals at any length. They simply evolved out of practical experience and existing conditions and opportunities.

In most instances the scenario was as follows. A small group of cossacks or streltsy or some other well-armed unit, on orders from Moscow, or from local colonial officials, or sometimes on their own initiative, would invade a given territory. If the natives offered no resistance, the invaders simply seized some tribal leaders or their relatives as hostages whom they kept in specially-built cells within each outpost. Fellow tribesmen were then required to ransom these hostages through the payment of yasak or by taking an oath of allegiance to become loyal yasak-paying subjects of the tsar forever. Because most indigenous inhabitants resisted the conquering invaders, the Russians, 'invoking the tsar's help and God's blessing', used their superior knowledge and technology to overwhelm the opposition. As the survivors rushed into the wilds, the victors killed most of the men, seized their women, appropriated their food supplies, and forced on the survivors an oath of eternal loyalty to the tsar and an annual assessment of yasak.

All native men of Siberia and of northern Asia between the ages of 18 and 50 except for the crippled, blind, and converts to Russian Orthodox Christianity, were required to pay to the tsar annual yasak and pominki in prime sable furs. The amount of the payment varied from one area to another, depending on availability. Early in the seventeenth century, when sables were abundant, the assessed quota was twenty-two sables per man per year. By the middle of the same century, with the depletion of the animal, the quota had dropped to five. Whenever and wherever sables were not available, the Russians accepted prime furs from foxes, martens, lynxes, otters, beavers, squirrels, and other fur-bearing animals, as well as ivory from walrus tusks. Colonial authorities collected the assessed yasak in three ways. The first was by their own agents, who went annually to native settlements or encampments. The second required the natives to bring their assessed yasak to a designated collection point (ostrog, ostrozhek or zimove). And the third empowered local tribal chieftains, identified by contemporary Russian sources as *knyazhets*, *toyon*, *murza*, *taisha*, *taidzhba*, or *khan*, to perform that task.

In addition to imposing the payment of yasak and various pominki, colonial officials also forced many natives to supply food to them, and to

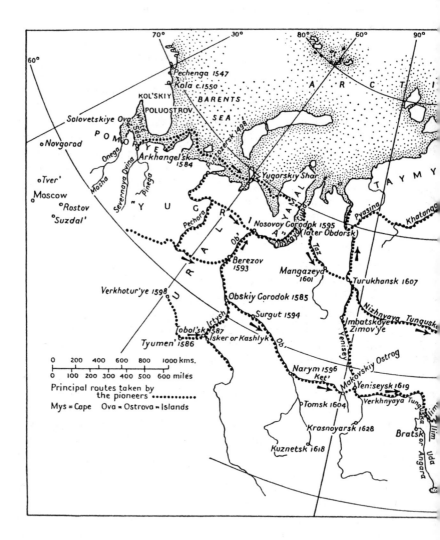

Map 2.1 The Russian advance across Siberia in the sixteenth and seventeenth centuries

Source: Terence Armstrong, *Russian Settlement in the North*, Cambridge University Press, Cambridge, 1965, p. 12. (with permission)

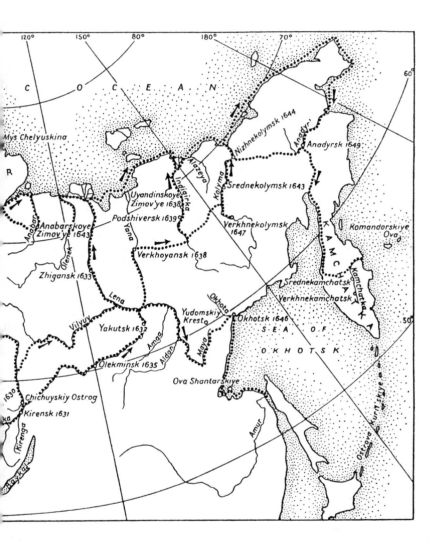

perform all kinds of work for them, including fishing, gathering berries, providing firewood, cutting logs for building, cultivating land, and to act as beasts of burden. Often the central authorities were unaware of many of these hardships imposed by local colonial officials on natives. Occasionally, when these excesses reached such dangerous proportions that they came to Moscow's attention, an official decree calling for a change in approach would be issued, or an official would be dispatched to investigate the abuse, especially when the abuse resulted in massive native defiance. In most cases, however, Moscow authorities simply sent additional military forces, not only to suppress native resistance, but also to insure that the region would be a permanent Russian colonial acquisition.

This brief survey of the Russian colonial administrative apparatus in Siberia and in northern Asia has brought forth the following salient features. The armed conquest of this vast region, rich in natural resources and sparsely populated by diverse and technologically primitive tribes, was of momentous historic and geopolitical consequence. It transformed the relatively poor and weak East European, Orthodox, Slavic, Muscovite state into the powerful, multinational Empire of Russia. In due time, thanks to the process of ethnic and cultural cross-fertilization, many Asians became russianized and many Russians became asianized. In due time, too, the Russians used the region to launch conquests against Central Asia, China, Korea, Japan, Alaska, and the islands of the North Pacific.

Scholars have offered differing interpretations of the Russian conquest of Siberia and of northern Asia. However, all evidence shows that it was a colonial and imperialist undertaking and that, like its contemporary West European counterpart, it originally had neither a clear blueprint nor a grand master-plan. It was propelled by many pressures and forces that varied in purpose, skill, intensity and duration. The conquest was a resounding success because the Russians possessed superior knowledge, skills, and technological superiority over the indigenous peoples; because the diverse bands of conquerors and pillagers received generous support and timely guidance from the government in Moscow; because they effectively exploited native animosities and adroitly utilized native guides and interpreters familiar with the local terrain and its inhabitants; and because they did not encounter sustained native resistance or competition, or challenge from European colonial powers.

These factors gave the Russians complete hegemony over all of northern Asia and enabled them to develop an effective administrative apparatus. This administration was carried out by two intertwined bureaucracies. One was centred in Moscow and included members of the boyarskaya duma and a host of officials of the Sibirskii and other prikazy, who formulated all defensive and offensive strategies for the region and made all major decisions concerning its administration and exploitation. The other bureaucracy, headed by scores of voevody, included a whole array of military and paramilitary groups (Russian and non-Russian), exiled prisoners and peasants, and church personnel. Stationed in strategically located fortified outposts, this personnel carried out orders from Moscow, exploited the region's resources and peoples, and brought still more new territories under Russian control. Of course, the tsar – the absolute and autocratic monarch – whose power was unrestricted, presided over both the Moscow- and colonial-based bureaucracies. Indeed, the entire conquest of the region was undertaken in his name, and the whole area was his patrimony, and the revenues went into his treasury. This arrangement met countless native challenges. None, however, succeeded in dislodging Russian hegemony over Siberia and northern Asia (see Map 2.1 which shows Siberia in the seventeenth century).

SELECTED BIBLIOGRAPHY

Aleksandrov, V.A. (1964) *Russkoe naselenie Sibiri XVII-nachala XVIII v.*, Moscow.

Alekseev, M.P. (ed.) (1936) *Sibir v izvestiyakh inostrannykh puteshestvennikov i pisatelei*, Irkutsk.

Andreev, A.I. (1960) *Ocherki po istochnikovedeniyu Sibiri. XVII vek.*, 2nd edn, Moscow.

Armstrong, T. (ed.) (1975) *Yermak's Campaign in Siberia. A Selection of Documents*, translated from the Russian by Tatiana Minorsky and David Wileman, London, Hakluyt Society.

Baddley, J.F. (1919) *Russia, Mongolia and China. Being Some Record of the Relations Between them from the Beginning of the 17th Century to the Death of the Tsar Aleksei Mikhailovich, A.D. 1602–1672*, 2 vols, London.

Bakhrushin, S.V. (1953) *Nauchnye trudy*, vol. 3., Moscow.

Butsinskii, P.N. (1889) *Zaselenie Sibiri i byt yeya pervykh naselnikov*, Kharkov.

Demidova, N.F. and Myasnikov, V.S. (eds) (1969–72) *Russko-Kitaiskie otnosheniya v XVII veke. Dokumenty i materialy (1609–1691)*, 2 vols, Moscow.

Dmytryshyn, B., Crownhart-Vaughan, E.A.P. and Vaughan, T. (eds) (1985) *Russia's Conquest of Siberia: A Documentary Record, 1558–1700*, Portland, Oregon Historical Society.

Dolgikh, B.D. (1960) *Rodovoi i plemennoi sostav narodov Sibiri v XVII veke*, Moscow.

Fischer, J.E. (1768) *Sibirische Geschichte von der Entdekkung Sibiriens bis auf die Eroberung dieses Lands durch die Russische Waffen*, 2 vols, St Petersburg.

Fisher, R.H. (1943) *The Russian Fur Trade, 1550–1700*, Berkeley and Los Angeles, University of California Press.

Gibson, J.R. (1969) *Feeding the Russian Fur Trade: Provisionment of the Okhotsk Seaboard and Kamchatka Peninsula, 1639–1856*, Madison.

Golitsyn, N.N. (1899) *Portfeli G.F. Millera*, Moscow.

Gurvich, I.S. (1963) *Russkie na severo-vostoke Sibiri v XVII veke*, Moscow.

Kuleshov, V.A. (ed.) (1888) *Nakazy sibirskim voevodam v XVII v. Istoricheskii ocherk*, Tashkent.

Kuznetsov-Kraskoyarskii, I.P. (ed.) (1890–97) *Istoricheskie akty XVII stoletiya, 1633–1699. Materialy dlya istorii Sibiri*, 2 vols, Tomsk.

Lantzeff, G.V. (1943) *Siberia in the Seventeenth Century: A Study of the Colonial Administration*, Berkeley.

Mirzoev, V.G. (1960) *Prisoedinenie i osvoenie Sibiri v istoricheskoi literature XVII veka*, Moscow.

Müller, G.F. (1937–41) *Istoriya Sibiri*, 2 vols, Moscow-Leningrad.

Nebolsin, P.I. (1849) *Pokorenie Sibiri*, St Petersburg.

Ogloblin, N.N. (1896–1900) *Obozrenie stolbtsov i knig Sibirskogo prikaza, 1592–1768*, 4 vols, Moscow.

Ogorodnikov, V.I. (1922) *Iz istorii pokoreniya Sibiri. Pokorenie yukagirskoi zemli*, Chita.

Orlova, N.S. (ed.) (1951) *Otkrytiya russkikh zemleprokhodtsev i polyarnykh morekhodov XVII veka na severo-vostoke Azii. Sbornik dokumentov*, Moscow.

Sadovnikov, D.N. (ed.) (1898) *Nashi zemleprokhodtsy (Rasskazy o zaselenii Sibiri) 1581–1712*, 2nd edn, Moscow.

Semyonov, Yuri N. (1963) *Siberia: Its Conquest and Development*, Baltimore.

Shunkov, V.I. (1956) *Ocherki po istorii zemlevladeniya v Sibiri, XVII v.*, Moscow.

Shvetsova, T.M. (ed.) (1970) *Materialy po istorii Yakutii XVII veka: Dokumenty yasachnogo sbora*, Moscow.

Slovtsov, P.A. (1838) *Istoricheskoe obozrenie Sibiri s 1585 do 1742*, Moscow.

Titov, A.A. (ed.) (1890) *Sibir v XVII veke. Sbornik starinnykh russkikh statei o Sibiri i prilezhashchikh k nei zemlyakh*, Moscow.

Veselovskii, S.B. (1912) *Prikaznyi stroi upravleniya Moskovskogo gosudarstva*, Kiev.

Yakor, Ya. P. and Grekov, B.D. (eds) (1936) *Kolonialnaya politika Moskovskogo gosudarstva v Yakutii v XVII veke*, Leningrad.

3 Subjugation and settlement in seventeenth and eighteenth-century Siberia

David N. Collins

First of all the native people had to be made to pay tribute, and this was achieved by the use of military expeditions . . . If the natives were 'disobedient', they were subjected to force of arms . . . The tents of the 'disobedient' were burnt down, their wives and daughters were taken into captivity, their fur stores were ransacked. Terrified by such an onslaught, the natives hastened to 'kow-tow' (*bit chelom*) by paying tribute in fur (*yasak*) . . .

The second stage was the construction of a fort (*ostrog*) in the centre of the newly discovered territory. This construction usually evoked great alarm among the surrounding natives and led to attempts to destroy the fort which had been built on their land. . . . There followed severe repression with the aim of terrifying the recalcitrant, and mutinous princelings usually paid for their revolt by death on a gibbet. . . .

[But] extermination of the natives was not in Moscow's interests. She needed not empty lands but fur, and the natives were the best suppliers of this fur. Therefore, having forced them to pay yasak, she strove to put an end to war. The native tribal organizations were even retained, since they could be used for yasak collection.

(S.V. Bakhrushin, 1929)[1]

Bakhrushin's rather harsh summary of Russian colonial policy in Siberia is characteristic of a certain strain of Soviet historiography. Even when the author credits the Muscovite government with moderate policies towards the Siberian natives, the motivation for its instructions that they be treated tenderly (*laskovo*) is held to be solely mercenary.[2] Other Soviet writers have reacted against the stress on the military nature of the colonial process evoked by terms such as *pokorenie* (subjugation) or *zavoevanie* (conquest), and instead have placed emphasis on the peaceful and progressive nature of the Russian presence, using more neutral vocabulary such as *prisoedinenie* (annexation) or *osvoenie* (assimilation) of the new territory.

The reasons for this have been discussed elsewhere.[3] The purpose of the present chapter is to investigate in more detail the nature of Muscovite colonial policies in the seventeenth and eighteenth centuries, drawing largely on the researches of a range of Soviet scholars, but particularly those of N.I. Nikitin and A.P. Umanskii, whose works form the basis of the following study.

During their progress across the Siberian landmass, the Russians came into contact with many indigenous peoples. Though it is impossible to estimate their numbers with accuracy, the generally accepted total for all the peoples together is only between 200,000 and 220,000 in the late sixteenth century.[4] Settlement was very sparse in the far north and north-east on the tundra, whose inhabitants relied on hunting migratory reindeer or sea mammals. Populations were slightly higher in the wooded taiga zone further south, where the abundance of game, fowl and fish supplied enough food for denser settlement. The largest indigenous groupings occurred further south still, in the wooded steppe and the immense grasslands, where it was possible to herd large numbers of domestic animals, as well as engaging in hunting and primitive forms of agriculture. All the peoples traded in the products of their particular region, exchanging goods by means of barter.

It has become clear that the process of Russian penetration into these far-flung regions was more complex than some writers have suggested. There were several intertwining strands which were mutually interactive and dependent upon one another. There was a close relationship between state and private initiative. Sometimes an expedition under orders from the *Sibirskii prikaz* (Siberian Department) in Moscow would be the first to penetrate into a region; at other times hunters and traders would investigate a new river system on their own, later reporting their success to the local military governor (*voevoda*), who would then penetrate the region asserting government control over the inhabitants. On occasion groups of private traders would collect fur tribute in the name of the tsar, though this was rather irregular. Subsequently a small fort would be constructed, a garrison would be placed there to collect *yasak* and to protect the private traders. Around the fort would grow a tiny settlement which gradually, if the fort were well situated on what was to become a primary trading route, evolved into a complex settlement including military servicemen and their families, traders, artisans and peasants. Once this base had been consolidated, forays would be made deeper into the wilderness, this time, perhaps, with a cossack military unit establishing a blockhouse (*zimove*) to contain the furs collected from the next tribe to be located. Some blockhouses were small and short-lived, but others proved to have been placed advantageously and after several years would be reconstructed on a larger scale to form a frontier town.[5]

Such was Irkutsk. Founded in 1652 as a cossack zimove to collect yasak from the Buryats and Tungus (Evenkis), in 1661 it was rebuilt into an ostrog. Originally this had four towers and a wooden palisade to protect the inhabitants. By 1684 it had developed into a key centre with its own voevoda, a full range of administrative buildings, warehouses, baths, a merchants' hall, cottages for the garrison and civilian inhabitants, a guard house and a church in the centre. Raised in status to a *gorod* (that is, a town, a higher administrative level than an ostrog) in 1686, it was substantially rebuilt in 1693 with stout fortifications. There was an inner bailey containing the buildings of greatest importance. Outside this was a citadel, fortified like the inner bailey, but containing a greater number of buildings. Beyond this was a third fortified settlement, irregular in shape in contrast to the other two. The outer settlement was for artisans, peasants and other civilian personnel. By 1699 there were 1,000 inhabitants. Situated at a crossroads for the colonization, trade and post routes, with good arable, pasture and fishing facilities, Irkutsk became a major centre in which the various strands of Russia's colonization came together. Apart from the military and administrative functions of the town, which included offices for collecting taxes from native and Russian alike, there was the beginning of a parish structure established by Orthodox clergy who had accompanied or soon followed the first government forces. There were craft workshops, shops and counting houses for the commercial and artisan community. There was a market for the sale of products of the forest (meat, fish, nuts and honey) and agricultural goods (grain, sheepskins and vegetables).[6]

The Russians could not hope to settle or control the whole Eurasian continent at this period. Instead they penetrated along river routes, fortifying strategic points such as confluences and portages from one river system to another. Muscovite settlements were, in fact, little islands in a vast ocean of forest, tundra and steppe, linked by fragile transport routes. All the participants in the process of control and settlement were mutually dependent.

Two other significant strands of Russia's colonial expansion into Siberia deserve mention. The first consisted of religious groups; the second comprised peasant colonists. There were two different types of religious groups. Approved by the government were members of the Orthodox clergy who began to establish a parish and diocesan network in Siberia early in the seventeenth century. As well as catering for the spiritual needs of the Russian settlers, monks, sometimes with lay assistants, participated in the colonial process by establishing small monastic communities which soon attracted peasants and became the focus of new communities.[7] Attempts by the Orthodox clergy to convert the indigenous peoples, mainly shamanists, to Christianity were in some cases approved of by the authorities, but generally in the period under study there was a reluctance to permit the baptism of natives, since they then ceased to pay yasak. Relations between church and state in Siberia were mixed. Whilst in general each supported the other, there were clashes from time to time, both sides accusing the other of reprehensible acts. There is still no satisfactory study of the church's role in Siberia, though in recent years some work on it has begun both in the Soviet Union and in the West.[8]

The other religious groups were Old Believers (that is, Schismatics) trying to escape from persecution in Russia. Their communities were generally established in remote locations far from possible government interference, so on the whole they were to one side of the main process of ingesting Siberia into the Russian state. Yet they added their own particular flavour to the developing Siberian community, retaining seventeenth-century ways even until 1917 and beyond.[9]

Peasants arrived in Siberia by various means. Some were forcibly settled there by government directives, imported to help provide food resources for the remote garrison settlements. On other occasions they came independently, fleeing from oppression to the fabled free lands beyond the Urals. Legends such as the tale of the Land of White Water (*belovodie*)[10] drove them onwards away from Europe into the dense forests where serfdom was but a memory until a voevoda's troops stumbled upon them, making them pay taxes by growing grain for the troops or by carting goods – one of the harshest occupations in this severe land. Some Soviet writers have overstressed the importance of free peasant settlers in the early years, regarding their spontaneous settlement among the native inhabitants as evidence of a happy intermingling of the peoples of the Russian Empire, a sort of prelude to Lenin's nationality policy. Such colonization occurred on a large scale mainly in western Siberia, in areas nearest to the peasants' departure point, and in regions largely pacified by the troops by the mid seventeenth century. Peasants tended to move onwards in short stages, so their progression across Siberia was not sudden. It was more a trickle than a flood, for peaceful homesteads could be successfully built only where there was relative security, and where there were known to be agriculturally suitable regions.[11] Peasants were dependent on the government for protection, and the garrisons could not survive without foodstuffs produced by the peasants.

Short of reliable military forces the government obtained its troops from many sources: some regular dragoon regiments were sent as garrisons, particularly during the eighteenth century. Prisoners-of-war, wandering free men, peasants and natives were mobilized from time to time into detachments of foreign servicemen (*Litva*) or cossacks, and there were service gentry from European Russia stationed in the region for periods of several years.

During emergencies, when indigenous tribes attacked, every available person, male or female, would be brought into the common fight for survival. It thus becomes clear that an intricate web of mutual dependency existed between the state and private individuals, between the military, the hunters, the peasants, the craftsmen and the merchants. Even hardy explorers needed strongpoints to which they could return after exhausting expeditions into unknown regions. Sometimes there was harmony between the different groups, sometimes clashes occurred. The state supported private activities for its own ends, and vice versa. One might almost speak of a complex symbiosis of different elements in society.[12] It is indeed difficult on occasion to know how to untangle the strands. For instance, as Nikitin points out, it is impossible to categorize those garrison troops who undertook private trading against their superiors' orders, or those private individuals who voluntarily joined armed detachments going out on campaign under orders from Moscow.[13]

One thing which it is difficult to deny is that military strength was vital for Muscovite survival in this massive frontier land. The first campaigns in Siberia against Kuchum and his khanate were quite blatantly military, as were many actions further east. Yet there is a strong emphasis among some historians on the voluntary submission of native peoples. There are indeed cases of leaders of aboriginal groups *offering* to pay yasak. Yet it would be anachronistic to assume that they had surrendered their rights in anticipation of Marxist theories about the superiority of the all-Russian market, or that they felt a particular brotherly love towards the Great Russian folk. It is quite clear from studies of aboriginal peoples elsewhere that they could be astute traders and politicians, using the European newcomers for their own ends as much as they were being used.[14] Quite often submission to the Russians was a calculated act based on one or more of several considerations. For instance, seeing how firearms had decimated their neighbours, they might decide to bow to the inevitable and offer tribute before it was demanded with menaces. They might well have had experience at second hand of Russian trade goods, and thus have resolved to pay tribute to obtain these benefits. And on occasion some groups would choose to submit themselves to the Russians as the lesser of two evils when called upon to supply tribute to a third party with whom they were not on good terms.[15]

In the shifting pattern of dominance and submission which characterized tribal life, with warfare being carried out now against one, now against another group, it was natural that on occasion peoples should ally themselves with the Russians. A Buryat tale relates how one of their groups decided to link itself with the Russians because their own khan chopped off heads for crimes which merited mere birching in Muscovite territory.[16] We hear of other cases where the decision was based on Russian tribute being lighter than that of other overlords.[17] Of course, this might have been no more than a diplomatic ruse by the Russians to initiate a dependence which would permit a later imposition of heavier tribute payments without negative results.

Russian concepts of suzerainty and subjection were not always the same as those of the peoples they were hoping to subdue. For the Russians the payment of the yasak made the natives permanent vassals. The very word for citizenship in Russian, *pod-danstvo*, implies being under tribute payment. When first a new people group was contacted, the leaders were asked to pay tribute, and then they were often persuaded to make a solemn pact or covenant (*shert* or *prisyaga*). The customs of the locals were investigated to elicit information about what sort of oath would be regarded as the most binding. Naturally these varied depending on the beliefs of the people in question. In general there was the invocation of one or more deities to bear witness that a binding contract was being undertaken. The subjects vowed eternal fealty to the 'White Tsar', to be loyal and to pay dues on time. In return the monarch undertook to protect those who had come under his 'high hand'. Ostyaks (Khantys) swore in front of a bearskin on which were laid an axe, a knife and some bread. If they broke the vow a curse would ensue according to which they would be savaged by a bear, split apart by an axe, knifed to death or even choked by food. Some Yakuts split a dog in half and walked between the pieces with a lump of earth in their mouths, saying that if they did not observe the vow they would be split in two and buried in the earth. Altaian tribes 'drank gold', drinking from a vessel into which a gold object had been placed.[18]

The voevody took the words of the vows literally, as 'an obligation made before the tsar to be eternally faithful and devoted to him and to give yasak to the Treasury'.[19] However, the natives, who had known yasak, or *alman*, before the Russians arrived on the scene, and regarded it as a payment by a vanquished people to its conqueror, in the time-honoured manner would pay only as long as it suited them. It appears that the blood-curdling nature of the vows made little impression on them. This part of the ceremony was regarded as nothing more than formal ritual.

Such misunderstandings between the colonizers and the colonized naturally led to problems. Russians would regard as treason any switch of alliance against them, whilst in the steppe lands, particularly, switches occurred regularly. Reneging on the terms of the agreement was not only done by the natives. The Russians undertook to protect their new vassals, but were often not disposed to or were too poorly endowed with manpower to help when asked to do so. This, of course, demonstrated to tribespeople that the Russians understood their ways, and that either side could break the agreement if it were expedient to do so. Other causes for disagreements between natives and Russians abounded. In order to secure the payment of tribute, servicemen would often resort to taking hostages (*amanaty*). Usually members of the more prominent families would be taken. They would be kept under house arrest within a fort until the yasak payment season came round. They would then be exposed before the kinsmen, complete with presents such as metal dishes, tools and beads given by their captors, to demonstrate that they were still in one piece, and even being treated well. After a couple of years they would be exchanged for someone else of sufficiently high position.[20] On occasion, not surprisingly, raids were mounted to regain hostages. This would lead to Russian reprisals, and sometimes to an escalation of conflict with which the sorely pressed garrisons in the wilderness were ill equipped to deal.

There was also trouble with *yasyri*, that is slaves seized, not for formal reasons like the amanaty, but for the personal use of men far from home and family. Peasant settlers were short of womenfolk,[21] as were the soldiers and hunters.[22] Young women would be seized from their home tents and taken to Russian fortresses where they would often be sold, to end up as common law wives or concubines. Cases of this traffic in women are legion in seventeenth- and early eighteenth-century Siberia.[23] On occasion girls were sold by their parents. Where such a transaction had taken place there were no problems, but naturally any forced seizures caused bitterness and could well lead to bloodshed. The progeny of mixed marriages contributed to a 'metisization' of the Russian population, the greater part of which occurred in the regions most remote from Europe.[24]

Clashes also occurred because of the rapacious actions of some Russians, because of the infringement of native hunting territories, and the settlement of peasants on pastures essential to the yearly migrations of pastoralists' herds. Russian peasants were bound to come into conflict with the indigenous inhabitants. Apart from extending agriculture into lands which were not free, as they seemed, but part of an ancient patrimony, they hunted fur-bearing animals as well as birds and fish and in other ways competed with the existing population for scarce resources.[25] When the natives had to pay yasak in furs and Russians were killing the dwindling stocks, or when, as in Chukotka, both sides were very short of provisions and the Russians, desperate for food, stole reindeer in large numbers, hostilities were more or less inevitable.[26]

It was all very well for the government in Moscow to lay down severe penalties for its servants who maltreated the natives.[27] The conditions of service, the harshness of the environment, the atrocious difficulties associated with travel and food supplies, the ravages of scurvy, and the sort of men who went out in search of new lands for the tsar, all contributed to the tense atmosphere which sometimes erupted into bloody conflict. Not that the natives were always hostile in intent or capability. Nor were the Russians always spoiling for a fight. They were used to rubbing shoulders with Tatars in regions west of the Urals, and seem to have had few traces of the sense of racial superiority which other European colonists took with them. In general they got along with their new neighbours.[28] Most of Siberia was conquered and held without the serious levels of bloodshed experienced in the American West. The exceptions were in four main areas: in the west during the first onslaughts when the khanate of Kuchum was being eliminated; in the far north-east against the Chukchis and Kamchatkan Itelmens (here Russian losses may not have been very severe, but the effects on the aboriginal population were catastrophic); in the south-east in the struggle with the Manchus for domination of the Amur, where the Russians were beaten; and finally in the south-west against the nomadic horsemen of the steppes who were a thorn in the Russians' flesh for over a century.[29] (For further discussion of the Russians' impact on the natives, see Chapter 4.)

The Russians, small in numbers, relied on their firearms for victory. Whenever powder became damp or ran out, whenever shot was lost in a river or was used up, fear stalked the camp. It was essential to prevent the enemy obtaining harquebuses or cannon. Government orders forbade anyone to show the natives how to use such weapons, yet inevitably they did on occasion obtain them and use them to deadly effect, though their culture might be basically Stone Age. Even without them, some groups were particularly effective fighters. Marksmen with the bow and arrow, slings or spears, they inflicted grave wounds and death upon many Russians. They often stormed and burned ostrogi, soon realizing that the 'thunder and lightning' weapons were slow. Indeed, the primitive matchlocks could only be discharged a maximum of sixteen times during a whole day of battle.[30] In the cavalry skirmishes against Kalmyk, Kirgiz or Mongol horsemen, who almost lived in the saddle and were 'a numerous, highly manoeuvrable and well armed foe, a serious and dangerous enemy', Russian firepower proved of very little advantage. It was most useful in defensive positions.[31]

> A specifically military form of life was characteristic for pratically all areas of southern Siberia. Inhabitants of the *uezdy* (districts) there had to be ready at any moment to leave their homes and fields to get under cover of the walls of the fortresses.

All field-workers took weapons with them, and would venture forth to collect firewood only in large parties. Blockhouses were built in the fields, and sometimes the cattle were kept in fortified compounds to protect them from raiders. In the seventeenth century none of the Russian peasants in any of the regions of mass settlement lived without fear.[32] In a sideswipe at some earlier Soviet historiography, Umanskii writes that 'history does not need embellishments', and goes on to state that

a great share of the blame for military clashes lies with the tsarist voevody who organized campaigns deep into [native] lands to set up strong points, to search out new 'lands' and to return 'traitors and unruly elements' to subjection.

He continues:

In our view, we ought not to shut our eyes to these facts, or mask the dark sides of tsarist activities, or look for a justification for them in the need to protect Russian settlements from nomad onslaughts, and in the voevody's disobedience to the tsar, etc.[33]

For, in essence, the Russians were simply invaders and had to face the consequences of that fact.

Probably the most costly problems facing the Russian government, which was always eager to run its fur empire on a shoestring, were posed by the nomadic tribes of south-west Siberia referred to above. Whereas in sparsely populated regions of the north and east individual ostrogi may have been sufficient to take and hold territory, tribes and transport lines, the situation in the south was far more complex.

As Russians penetrated southwards from the forested zone (taiga) to the wooded steppe, and then the open grasslands, they built new fortresses. For instance, Tomsk, founded in 1604 on the orders of Tsar Boris Godunov, around 60 kilometres from the confluence of the Ob and Tom rivers, 'served as a defensive post for protection against attacks by the local population and for subjecting them to the payment of yasak'.[34] In 1607 detachments were sent out towards the Kondoma and Mrass rivers to collect fur tribute. With time it became clear that the new region was too distant from Tomsk to be controlled with ease. Consequently, in 1618 a new ostrog was established where the Kondoma joined the Tom. It was called Kuznetsk ('Smithtown') because the local inhabitants practised iron-working.

The only reasons for the establishment of Kuznetsk were to collect and trade in furs and control the natives. Kuznetsk is interesting in that, unlike Irkutsk, it was not near any main communication arteries and did not develop a secure economic base before the October 1917 Revolution. By 1700 it had an outer polygonal timber palisade one *sazhen* high (a sazhen is 2.13

metres) and 1,500 sazhens in length, with five towers set into it. The inner bailey had a circumference of ninety-four sazhens and three towers. There was slow development in the seventeenth century, and by the early eighteenth century decay was evident, despite the designation of the town as a centre of an administrative district (uezd) of Tobolsk Province. There were still only two churches, three large warehouses and a cluster of cottages to house the 674 households, with a total of 5,000 inhabitants. All the buildings were wooden. By the third census in 1763 the number of households had reduced to 500, and the inhabitants to roughly 3,000. In military terms the settlement had declined, so that in 1744 there were only 160 men in the fort.[35]

Yet circumstances were changing. Kuznetsk itself may not have developed, but in the Altai mountains to the south-east of the town, metallic ores including copper, silver-lead and gold had been found. Initially worked by a private company owned by Akinfii Demidov, whose main interests were in the Ural mountains, at his death the Altai mines and smelting works passed into the personal possession of the imperial family. Eager to enrich the treasury the Crown began a rapid development of these resources, settling the area with peasants who worked as a serf proletariat and maintained farms to feed themselves. The rise to prominence of the Dzhungar state in what is now Chinese territory, and the submission to it of tribes in the Altai and further west in present day Kazakhstan, were causing problems (see below for more detail on the Teleuts). Raids were becoming so costly by the mid-eighteenth century that the imperial government began to undertake substantial fortification work along the southern marches which resulted in the erection of a series of connecting fortified lines (*linii*) which stretched from the southern Urals to Kuznetsk. In doing this the government was employing techniques perfected from the sixteenth century onwards in the expansion of the Muscovite state towards the Black Sea and the Volga basin.[36]

Peter the Great's expansion was not limited to the west and south. His government claimed that the whole course of all rivers flowing into the Arctic Ocean was by right Russian territory. This had been so 'from ancient times' (*izdrevle*), and the peoples living within this vast area were said to be undertaking their seasonal migrations with Russian permission.[37] Yet this did not mean that the natives were aware that Russia had 'owned' the region from ancient times, or that they would be prepared to agree to this state of affairs. The Dzhungar state, the last in a long line of typical steppe nomad conglomerates descended from Genghis Khan's empire, also claimed the more southerly zone where lay the headwaters of the Ob-Irtysh river system. The Kirgiz-Kaisaks (Kazakhs), roaming in areas claimed by both sides, were in an uncomfortable position and from time to time paid fealty to both, meantime raiding on their own behalf and fighting amongst themselves. Owing to the immense distances involved it was impossible to construct a continuous fortification like Hadrian's Wall in Roman Britain. Yet constant raids were causing great losses and hardship. In the 1730s settlements in the Tobol region to the south-east of the Urals were being attacked. Villages were raided and burned, cattle were driven off, growing crops were trampled, hay stocks were fired and people were taken captive. Three raids alone in 1736 led to the loss of 1,026 head of cattle. In the summer of 1741 nomads penetrated the strategically important gap between the Ishim and Irtysh rivers devastating the hamlets of Zudilovo and Chausskaya. A traveller passing through the area afterwards reported scenes of utter devastation. In 1743 an attack on Bezrukovo near the Ishim led to the deaths of two people, the imprisonment of twenty-six more and the loss of eighty horses.[38] Extra artillery and troops were drafted in, and an attempt was made to plug the gaps with extra forts, yet by the 1740s the defence lines were crooked and poorly organized. Every 100 kilometres had approximately two defensive positions, 200 soldiers and five or six cannon. The raids continued. In 1742 the head of the Orenburg Expedition, Neplyuev, was sent to investigate the situation. In 1743, in consultation with the governor, he decided that an attempt should be made not to fortify the watersheds of all rivers leading to the Arctic – a mammoth task indeed – but to defend all the lands necessary and useful for the Province of Siberia, provided that care was taken not to include territories so important to the natives that a pretext would be given for an uprising. After two or more years' investigation and the resolution of differences about which locations should or should not be included, a plan was submitted to the Governing Senate in St Petersburg in 1746. It was approved only in 1752, during which year construction work began. The latest military technology was to be used in the construction of forts (*kreposti*) which were to be surrounded by massive earthworks, and to be of stone construction, unlike the seventeenth century ostrogi.[39]

Omsk alone required the excavation of 130,000 cubic metres of earth. In 1769 1,375 people were at work on it, many of them prisoners at forced labour. The construction works led to the severe exploitation of exiles, soldiers, cossacks, peasants and horses. Periods on guard duty alternated with heavy navvying. Not surprisingly, the work was plagued by desertions. Owing to the insanitary conditions and malarial swamps in some parts there was also a heavy incidence of disease.[40] Kuznetsk recovered from its period in the doldrums; in fact it was the only one of the old Siberian forts apart from Tobolsk to be rebuilt in stone,[41] since it formed the terminus of the most easterly section of the fortifications. Its stone fort with impressive barracks, powder stores, administration buildings and walls was substantially completed by 1813. The garrison consisted of a company of 200 soldiers and a detachment of up to ninety invalids. Yet with the destruction of the Dzhungar state by the Chinese towards the end of the eighteenth century, the military significance of the town declined once more. Since the fur trade was also well past its zenith, the town snoozed in a rural backwater. The fort became a prison and was blown up by partisans during the Civil War following the Bolshevik Revolution.[42]

Apart from the fortresses, the lines consisted of smaller forts (*forposty*), redoubts (*reduty*) and signal towers or beacons (*mayaki*). The forposty were sixty versts apart (a *versta* equals roughly one kilometre) and were a smaller version of the ostrog of wooden construction. The reduty were also wooden. They interspersed the forposty at twenty-verst intervals. Their dimensions varied, some being ten sazhens square with half-bastions at the corners, whereas elsewhere they were double the size, with full bastions. They held small detachments of troops on guard. The signal towers were tall observation posts eleven sazhens square. On the top was a pole wrapped in straw which could be ignited by the cossack sentry in case of enemy incursion. They were situated in positions which made them visible from the posts on each side. The overall length of the Siberian lines was 2,100 versts, and mounted cossack patrols constantly made the rounds to ensure that all was peaceful.[43]

The most easterly section of the Siberian Line was the Kolyvano-Kuznetsk Fortified Line. When the Demidovs had first built mines and smelting works in the hills, they had been fortified and special permission was obtained from the government for the industrialists to hire a private army for protection.[44] It is doubtful whether they would have been able to afford the elaborate system which replaced this piecemeal amateur effort, and in any case they were spared the necessity of any expenditure since the Empress Elizabeth seized their assets in 1747, just as plans were in hand to construct the new line. The eastern terminus was Kuznetsk. In the centre was Biisk, an ostrog on the Biya river, built in 1718 and later enlarged into a fortress, while at the opposite end lay Ust-Kamenogorsk, established in 1720. The first section to be built was the southern half. By 1757 this included Biisk, fifteen forposty, two small forts on the Anui and Katun rivers and three fortified factories. In that year hostile natives attacked the village of Praporshchikovo on the Irtysh river between the last forpost, Ubinsk, and Ust-Kamenogorsk. This led to the line being extended thither, the total length then being 380 versts. It was extended in the 1760s as the Russians had advanced slightly, to become 457 versts long. The northern section was built from the late 1760s to 1795. Between Biisk, which was relocated and strengthened, and Kuznetsk were three forposty and eleven beacons.[45]

Difficulties were experienced in the provision of construction workers since labour was scarce in Siberia, and the mine administration was competing for it as well. Gradually a mixed bag of cossacks, exiles and peasants settled the area, and as the natives became pacified so the military flavour declined. In 1816 a Special Commission resolved that Biisk was obsolescent, and by 1825 it was no longer on the list of active fortresses. The northern section was abandoned in 1848, though the southern maintained a shadowy existence until the 1890s. The cossacks were given allotments of land and farmed there as the wooden fortifications gradually rotted away. Today tourist trails follow the route of the old cossack patrols, and schoolchildren participate in archaeological investigations to discover the location of remnants of lost signal towers.[46]

A case study of Russian colonial relations with one Siberian native group, the Teleuts (otherwise known as the Telenguty or Belye Kalmyki) has been undertaken by Umanskii. He has investigated the subject with tenacity and in great depth, enabling us to understand a good deal about Russian and Teleut attitudes and activities.[47] The Teleuts were herdsmen, hunters, fishers, gatherers of natural produce, and superlative horsemen living in the upper reaches of the Ob river system. They were illiterate, mainly shamanist in religion and dominant over a number of other tribes in southwest Siberia. Their numbers seem to have grown from around 5,000 in the early seventeenth century to about 20,000 a century later. Since their traditional migration routes lay in areas which came under Russian influence fairly early (Tomsk, Kuznetsk and Tara districts), they established economic, political and cultural contacts with them in the seventeenth century. The Dzhungar khanate, established in 1635, also influenced them a great deal. They seem to have been in some sort of vassal relationship with the Dzhungars until they broke away in the 1650s and 1660s. Early in the eighteenth century they became more firmly subjected to Dzhungaria. A group of Teleuts, in tsarist documents known as the *vyezzhye belye Kalmyki*, moved into Russian-held territory and settled there out of reach of the Teleut princes.

The Teleuts made an agreement (shert) with Muscovite voevody, but never consented to pay yasak during the whole seventeenth century, even when offered the inducement of paying a nominal tenth of the usual quantity. They did give presents (*pominki*), but these were voluntary. It seems that this was their means of asserting their continuing independence of Moscow. It was normal diplomatic protocol to exchange presents when delegations met, and Umanskii detects a distinct difference between these gifts and those which yasak-paying tribes gave originally voluntarily, but later on under coercion. Nor did the Teleuts hand over hostages to the Russians, despite pressure being placed on them to do so. In fact their leaders were regarded as slippery customers by the Russians. One of them, Machik, 'manifested great inventiveness, cunning and insidiousness in his struggle against the Russian authorities, and the voevody could not take him at his word'. Umanskii concludes that their subjection to the Russians was nominal. Yet on the other hand an agreement had been reached for mutual military aid as early as 1609. There might appear to be elements of a feudal vassal status for the Teleuts here. In feudal Russia the petty princes had sworn allegiance to the crown and had to engage in military service, whilst retaining autonomy in their internal affairs, as the Teleuts did. But Umanskii sees a significant difference: feudal subjects of the seigneur are usually from the same nation as him. The Teleuts, however, had been sovereign in their own domains for a long period before the Russians arrived on the scene. Rather than being a case of feudal vassaldom, this has more of the characteristics of a military alliance between two states, an unstable one, it is true, and between partners of very unequal power.

Relations between the Teleuts and the Russians were not smooth. Periods of peace alternated with conflicts, some of them minor border skirmishes, others quite major clashes. The peaceful periods demonstrated that both sides had common interests. First, they had enemies in the Dzhungars, the Khalkha Mongols and the Yenisei Kirgiz. A common front could be made here. Second, they had mutual economic interests. The Teleuts needed Russian trade and agricultural products and the Russians were in desperate need of leather goods, cattle, horses and women. The Teleuts began to become dependent on Russian metalware but the Russians were unable to use this as a bargaining tool, since the Teleuts knew that the troops could not exist without their trade goods. If anything a mutual dependence was growing.

There were also sources of friction between them. The leaders of both sides wished to take yasak from the smaller Altaian groups, whose position became anything but enviable. The Kumandintsy are a good example of this. They were a collection of kinship groups (*seoki*) living around the river Biya. They were hunters, metal-workers, cattle raisers and also engaged in primitive agriculture and the gathering of roots and nuts. Throughout the seventeenth century they paid tribute to the Teleuts. From the 1620s the Russians started demanding payment too. Some of them also gave tribute to the Yenisei Kirgiz from the Minusinsk Depression. As the Teleuts became subject to the Dzhungars in the early eighteenth century, tribute had to go to them as well. The end of the Dzhungar state lightened their load, but the Russian yoke was never removed from their necks. Not only did they have to pay yasak, but Russians came and settled on their best lands.[48] Russian-Teleut clashes also occurred over trapping rights as well as over yasak payment from subject peoples. As fur resources dwindled and as Russian settlers moved ever onward, the pressures on Teleut traditional hunting grounds grew. There were, too, political conflicts. All Russian attempts to penetrate the Teleuts' territories were opposed, since they regarded themselves as overlords in the northern Altai. The Tomsk voevody wanted firm control over the region and were not satisfied to have the Teleuts as allies; they wished them to become permanent subjects. Russian forays deep into Teleut territory were regarded as provocations, and as an abrogation of earlier agreements between the two sides. Strains developed over the migration of the 'vyezzhye belye Kalmyki' to Russian territory, since the prince of the Teleuts regarded them as traitorous subjects and demanded their return. Russian failure to comply was regarded as unwarranted intrusion into their internal affairs. Also the Russians failed to help their Teleut allies in time of need.

By the 1660s the alliance was breaking down. Years of sporadic warfare followed, with both sides at one time aggressors, at another the victims. Peace came about in the 1680s through Teleut exhaustion. Their economy and population were both suffering, but also they were becoming wary of the Dzhungars' increasing strength. Russia wished to use the Teleuts as a buffer against the Dzhungars, but in the end they were overwhelmed by a superior power and began raiding Russian lands again around 1700 at the behest of their new masters, as did the Kazakhs further west. A Russian–Dzhungar struggle ensued over the Ob-Irtysh area which was only ended when the Chinese Empire crushed the Dzhungars.[49] Pacification of the Teleuts, now really weakened, followed, and in the end many became completely russified.

Russian colonial policies in the seventeenth and eighteenth centuries were aimed at maximizing the income of the state by the subjection of aboriginal peoples to fur tribute. It was fashionable at one time to see this process crudely in terms of mere military subjugation. Then the pendulum swung too far in the other direction, towards an assertion that the Russians avoided the unpleasant aspects of colonialism as exemplified in Spanish, Portuguese or British experience. Neither position, however, contains more than part of the truth. Fortunately we are now able to see the complexity of the processes more clearly through the painstaking researches of Soviet scholars. Russian servicemen were sometimes, but not always, brutal exploiters; they often felt frightened, vulnerable and far from home. Native peoples were not simply savages unable to pit their wits against a superior enemy, nor were they the Russians' dupes. Weakened by warfare, imported diseases and the excessive demands of their overlords, they were obliged in the end to submit. Those who foresaw the inevitability of this could take one of three ways out: commit suicide like the Itelmens; resist and fight like the Chukchis; or learn to get along with the newcomers. Only those who chose the last option survived.

NOTES AND REFERENCES

1 S.V. Bakrushin, 'Sibirskie tuzemtsy pod russkoi vlastyu do revolyutsii 1917 goda', *Sovetskii sever: Sbornik* (1929): 70–71.
2 Ibid., pp. 79–82.
3 D.N. Collins, Russia's Conquest of Siberia: Evolving Russian and Soviet Historical Interpretations', *European Studies Review* 12 (1982): 17–44. See also L.M. Goryushkin and N.A. Minenko, *Istoriografiya Sibiri dooktyabrskogo perioda* (Novosibirsk: Nauka, 1984), pp. 14–31, 44–51. The debate about peasant predominance in Siberian colonization is evidently far from over. Goryushkin and Minenko decisively reject Nikitin's assertion that the theory 'at the present time no longer satisfies many researchers'.
4 N.I. Nikitin, *Sibirskaya epopeya XVII veka: nachalo osvoeniya Sibiri russkimi lyudmi* (Moscow: Nauka 1987). His work is based in part on a *kandidat*'s thesis, 'Voenno-sluzhilie lyudi Zapadnoi Sibiri XVII veka' (Moscow University, 1975), since published as *Sluzhilie lyudi v Zapadnoi Sibiri XVII veka* (Novosibirsk: Nauka, 1988).
5 Nikitin, *Sibirskaya epopeya*, op. cit., pp. 21–2. See also his 'Istoriya Sibiri v trudakh S.V. Bakhrushina', in *Problemy sotsialno-ekonomicheskoi istorii feodalnoi Rossii* (Moscow: Nauka, 1984), pp. 48–9.
6 F.A. Kudryavtsev and G.A. Vendrykh, *Irkutsk. Ocherki po istorii goroda* (Irkutskoe knizhnoe izdatelstvo Irkutsk: 1958), pp. 6–29; T.S. Proskuryakova, 'Planirovochnye kompozitsii gorodov-krepostei Sibiri', *Arkhitekturnoe nasledstvo* 25 (1976): 58–9.
7 R.J. Kerner, *The Urge to the Sea* (New York: Russell, 1971), M.M. Gromyko, 'Krestyanskie tserkovnye votchiny Zapadnoi Sibiri', *Ezhegodnik po agrarnoi istorii Vostochnoi Evropy za 1961* (1963): 262–70; L.P. Shorokhov, 'Vozniknovenie monastyrskikh votchin v Vostochnoi Sibiri', in *Russkoe naselenie Pomorya i Sibiri (period feodalizma)*, (Moscow: Nauka, 1973), pp. 148–63.
8 N.D. Zolnikova, *Soslovnye problemy vo vzaimootnosheniyakh tserkvi i gosudarstva v Sibiri (XVIII v.)* (Novosibirsk: Nauka, 1981). On Christian Orthodox missions there are several articles in recent issues of *Zhurnal moskovskoi patriarkhii*; see also David N. Collins, 'Colonialism and Siberian Development: A Case-Study of the Orthodox Mission to the Altay, 1830–1913', in Alan Wood and R.A. French (eds), *The Development of Siberia: People and Resources* (London: Macmillan, 1989), pp. 50–71; and Oleg Kobtzeff, 'Ruling Siberia: The Imperial Power, the Orthodox Church and the Native People', *SIBIRICA II* (1986): 6–15.
9 T.S. Mamsik, *Pobegi kak sotsialnoe yavlenie* (Novosibirsk: Nauka, 1978), and her 'Obshchina i byt begletsov-"kamenshchikov" ', in *Iz istorii semi i byta*

sibirskogo krestyanstva, (Novosibirsk: Nauka, 1975), pp. 30–70. See also N.N. Pokrovskii, 'Krestyanskie pobegi i traditsii pustynozhitelstva v Sibiri', in *Krestyanstvo Sibiri: klassovaya borba, obshchestvennoe soznanie i kultura* (Novosibirsk: Nauka, 1975), pp. 19–50; E.E. Blomkvist and N.P. Grinkova, 'Bukhtarminskie staroobryadtsy', *Materialy komissii ekspeditsionnykh issledovanii: seriya Kazakhstana* 17 (1930).

10 T.S. Mamsik, 'Belovodtsy i Belovody', in *Istochniki po kulture i klassovoi borbe feodalnogo perioda* (Novosibirsk: Nauka, 1982), pp. 135–64; 'Belovodskaya legenda i publitsistika 40–50 godov XIX veka', in *Istoriografiya agrarnoi istorii dorevolyutsionnoi Rossii: mezhvuzovskii tematicheskii sbornik nauchnykh trudov* (Kaliningrad: Kaliningradskii gos. ped. institut, 1982), pp. 138–48; and N.N. Pokrovskii, 'K postanovke voprosa o belovodskoi legende i bukhtarminskie "kamenshchiki" v literature poslednykh let', in *Obshchestvennoe soznanie i klassovye otnoshenii v Sibiri*, (Novosibirsk: Nauka, 1980), pp. 115–33.

11 Nikitin, *Sibirskaya epopeya*, op. cit., p. 23.

12 Ibid., pp. 21–3; P.N. Pavlov, *Promyslovaya kolonizatsiya Sibiri v XVII v.*, (Krasnoyarsk: Krasnoyarskii gos. ped. institut, 1974), pp. 3–5, 204–5; and his 'Vyvoz pushniny iz Sibiri v XVII veke', *Materialy po istorii Sibiri. Sibir perioda feodalizma*, (Novosibirsk: Nauka, 1962), pp. 137–8.

13 Nikitin, *Sibirskaya epopeya*, op. cit., p. 22.

14 To cite but a few referring to the similar situation in Canada: D. Wishart, 'Cultures in Cooperation and Conflict: Fur Trader Reactions to Aboriginal Americans', *Journal of Historical Geography* 2 (1976): 311–28; W.A. Sloan, 'The Native Response to the Extension of the European Traders into the Athabasca and Mackenzie Basin, 1770–1814', *Canadian Historical Review* 60 (1979): 281–9; and A.J. Ray, *Indians in the Fur Trade: Their Role as Trappers, Hunters and Middlemen in the Lands Southwest of Hudson Bay, 1660–1870* (Toronto: University of Toronto Press, 1974).

15 Nikitin, *Sibirskaya epopeya*, op. cit., pp. 14, 20.

16 Ibid., p. 148.

17 N.S. Modorov, 'K voprosu ob yasachnoi politike russkogo tsarizma v severo-vostochnom Altae v XVII veke', *Uchenye zapiski Gorno-Altaiskogo nauchno-issledovatelskogo instituta istorii, yazyka i literatury* 10 (1971) 47–8.

18 Bakhrushin, 'Sibirskie tuzemtsy', op. cit., p. 74; Modorov, 'K voprosu', op. cit., p. 49; A.P. Umanskii, *Teleuty i russkie v XVII–XVIII vekakh* (Novosibirsk: Nauka, 1980), pp. 12–23. An example of a *shert* conveniently given in English may be found in Basil Dmytryshyn, E.A.P. Crownhart-Vaughan and Thomas Vaughan (eds), *Russia's Conquest of Siberia, 1558–1700* (Portland, Oregon: Oregon Historical Society, 1985), pp. 198–9.

19 Modorov, 'K voprosu', op. cit., pp. 47, 49.

20 Bakhrushin, 'Sibirksie tuzemtsy', op. cit., p. 76; Modorov, 'K voprosu', op. cit., p. 49.

21 N.N. Ogloblin, 'Zhenskii vopros v Sibiri v XVII veke', *Istoricheskii vestnik* 41 (1890): 51; A.A. Ionin, 'Novye dannye k istorii vostochnoi Sibiri XVII veka', *Izvestiya vostochno-sibirskogo otdela IRGO* 26 (1–3, 1895, appendix): 153–4, 210–11; V.A. Aleksandrov, 'Cherty semeinogo stroya u russkogo naseleniya Yeniseiskogo kraya XVII – nachalo XVIII v.', *Sibirskii etnograficheskii sbornik* 3 (1961) 5–6; Z. Ya. Boyarshinova, 'Krestyanskaya semya

54   *The History of Siberia*

zapadnoi Sibiri feodalnogo perioda', *Trudy Tomskogo gos. universiteta: Seriya istoricheskaya* 190 (1967) *Voprosy istorii Sibiri* 3: 6–7; A.N. Kopylov, 'Gosudarstvennye pashennye krestyane Yeniseiskogo uezda v XVIII v.', *Materialy po istorii Sibiri. Sibir perioda feodalizma* (Novosibirsk: Nauka, 1962), pp. 37, 44–5.

22 Ogloblin, 'Zhenskii vopros', op. cit., p. 196; Aleksandrov, 'Cherty', op. cit., pp. 7–8; N.A. Minenko, 'Gorodskaya semya zapadnoi Sibiri na rubezhe XVII–XVIII v.' in *Istoriya gorodov Sibiri dosovetskogo perioda* (Novosibirsk: Nauka, 1977), pp. 183–4; A.D. Kolesnikov, 'Rost, soslovnyi sostav i zanyatnost naseleniya dorevolyutsionnogo Omska', in *Istoriya gorodov*, p. 233; N.G. Apollova, *Khozyaistvennoe osvoenie Priirtyshya* (Moscow: Nauka, 1976), pp. 146, 148, 151; N.M. Yadrintsev, 'Zhenshchina v Sibiri v XVII i XVIII stoletiyakh', *Zhenskii vestnik* 8 (1867): 109.

23 Aleksandrov, 'Cherty', op. cit., p.4; G.-F. Müller, *Istoriya Sibiri*, (Moscow: Izdatelstvo Adademii Nauk SSSR, 1941) 2: pp. 430–2, 472–5; *Dopolneniya k Aktam istoricheskim*, reprint edn (Ann Arbor, Michigan: University Microfilms International, 1976), 3: 22–3, 223–4, 359, 361–4; I.P. Alkor and V.D. Grekov, *Kolonialnaya politika Moskovskogo gosudarstva v Yakutii*, (Moscow: Akademiya Nauk SSSR, 1936), p. 54; N.N. Bakai, 'Zakhvat, kuplya i prodazha inorodok Yakutskoi oblasti sibirskimi sluzhilymi lyudmi v pervoi polovine XVIIv.', *Izvestiya obshchestva arkheologii, istorii i etnografii (Kazan)* 11 (2, 1893): 1–3; P.N. Butsinskii, 'Mangazeya i mangazeiskii uezd 1601g.–1645g.', *Zapiski imperatorskogo Kharkovskogo universiteta* 1, (1893, chast neoffitsialnaya): 64–6; A.P. Okladnikov, 'Kureiskie tungusy v XVIII v.', in *Materialy po istorii Sibiri. Sibir perioda feodalizma* 3, (Novosibirsk: Nauka, 1968), p. 113.

24 See David N. Collins, 'Sexual Imbalance in Frontier Communities: Siberia and New France to 1760', unpublished paper, inaugural Conference of the British Universities Siberian Studies Seminar, University of Lancaster, September 1981.

25 Yu. S. Bulygin, 'Promysly sibirskogo krestyanstva v XVIII – pervoi polovine XIX v', *Aktualnye voprosy istorii Altaya: mezhvuzovksii sbornik*, (Barnaul: Izdatelstvo Altaiskogo gos. universiteta, 1980), pp. 143–51; Nikitin, *Sibirskaya epopeya*, op. cit., pp. 137–8.

26 Alkor and Grekov, *Kolonialnaya politika*, op. cit., *passim*; *Istoriya i kultura Chukchei. Etnograficheskie ocherki* (Leningrad: Nauka, 1987); G.V. Lantzeff and R.A. Pierce, *Eastward to Empire: Exploration and Conquest on the Russian Open Frontier to 1750* (Montreal and London: McGill-Queen's University Press, 1973), ch. 12.

27 Bakhrushin, 'Sibirskie tuzemtsy', op. cit., pp. 79–82; S.P. Nefedova, 'Yasachnaya politika russkogo tsarizma na Chukotke', *Zapiski Chukotskogo kraevedcheskogo muzeya* 4 (1967): 27–33.

28 Nikitin, *Sibirskaya epopeya*, op. cit., pp. 45, 140–2.

29 Ibid., pp. 52–3; Ya P. Alkor and A.K. Drezen, *Kolonialnaya politika tsarizma na Kamchatke i Chukotke v XVIII veke*, (Leningrad: Izdatelstvo Instituta narodov severa, 1935), *passim*; A.S. Sgibnev, *Istoricheskii obzor glavneishikh sobytii v Kamchatke s 1650 po 1856* St Petersburg, 1865) first section; Lantzeff and Pierce, *Eastward*, op. cit., chs 9, 10.

30 Nikitin, *Sibirskaya epopeya*, op. cit., pp. 53–6.

31 Ibid., pp. 56–7 (see also the documentary appendix).

32 Ibid., pp. 153, 156–7.
33 Umanskii, *Teleuty i russkie*, op. cit., pp. 30–3; see also Nikitin, 'Istoriya Sibiri', op. cit., pp. 41–3.
34 A. Pribytkova, 'Kuznetskaya krepost', *Istoricheskoe kraevedenie* 1 (1975): 231.
35 Ibid., pp. 231–2; Müller, *Istoriya Sibiri*, op. cit., (documents 62, 76, 78, 86, 87, 90, 95–9).
36 See D.J.B. Shaw, 'Southern frontiers of Muscovy, 1550–1700', in J.H. Bater and R.A. French (eds), *Studies in Russian Historical Geography* (London: Academic Press, 1983) 1: 117–42.
37 *Pamyatniki Sibirskoi istorii XVIII veka*, Tipografiya Ministerstva vnutrennykh del (1882), 2 (document 22): A.D. Kolesnikov, 'Pamyatniki voenno-oboronitelnogo iskusstva Sibiri', in *Pamyatniki istorii i arkhitektury Sibiri* (Novosibirsk: Nauka, 1986), pp. 4–10.
38 Kolesnikov, 'Pamyatniki', op. cit., pp. 11–12; F. Laskovskii, *Materialy dlya istorii inzhinernogo iskusstva v Rossii* (St Petersburg, 1865) 3: 46–8, 133–4.
39 Kolesnikov, 'Pamyatniki', op. cit., pp. 12–15; Laskovskii, *Materialy*, op. cit., pp. 133–5, 720ff; N.V. Gorban, 'From the History of the Construction of Forts in the South of Western Siberia: the New Ishim Fortified Line', *Soviet Geography* 25 (1984): 177.
40 Kolesnikov, 'Pamyatniki', op. cit., pp. 15–17; Laskovskii, *Materialy*, op. cit., pp. 134–40, 146–7; Gorban, 'From the History', op. cit., pp. 180–1; Proskuryakova, 'Planirovochnye', op. cit., p. 65.
41 Pribytkova, 'Kuznetskaya krepost', op. cit., p. 232.
42 Ibid., pp. 235–40.
43 Laskovskii, *Materialy*, op. cit., pp. 46, 138–46; Proskuryakova, 'Planirovochnye', op. cit., pp. 64–7; *Voennaya entsiklopediya* (St Petersburg, 1913), 13: 48–9; Gorban, 'From the History', op. cit., p. 180; see also I. Stebelsky, 'The Frontier in Central Asia', in Bater and French, *Studies in Russian*, op. cit., pp. 144–56, which has very helpful maps of the fortified lines.
44 A. Sergeev, 'Oboronitelnye sooruzheniya Kolyvano-Kuznetskoi linii', in *Pamyatniki istorii i kultury Sibiri*, (Novosibirsk: Nauka, 1978), pp. 43–4, 47; see also his *Tainy altaiskikh krepostei*, (Barnaul: Altaiskoe knizhnoe izdatelstvo, 1975) pp. 4–5, 11–12, 14.
45 Laskovskii, *Materialy*, op. cit., pp. 152–7, 708–9; *Voennaya entsiklopediya* 13: 48–9; Sergeev, *Tainy*, op. cit., pp. 15, 45–6; Kolesnikov, 'Pamyatniki', op. cit., p. 83; Proskuryakova, 'Planirovochnye', op. cit., pp. 67–8.
46 Sergeev, *Tainy*, op. cit., pp. 20–4, 39; M. Strukov, *Kratkii ocherk Altaiskogo okruga*, (St Petersburg: Tipografiya glavnogo upravleniya udelov, 1896), p. 24; *Kratkii istoricheskii ocherk Altaiskogo okruga*, (St Petersburg: Tipografiya A.S. Suvorina: 1897), pp. 36, 111; *Turistskie raiony SSSR: Altaiskii krai* (Moscow: Profizdat, 1987), pp. 184–5 (map), 190–2.
47 Umanskii's book, *Teleuty i russkie*, is based on work done for his *kandidat's* thesis, 'Teleuty i ikh tyurkoyazychnye sosedy v XVIIv.' (Novosibirsk, 1970), and his doctoral dissertation, 'Teleuty i russkie v XVII–XVIIIvv', (Novosibirsk, 1983). Apart from the book, at least a dozen articles have been published in provincial journals.

48   F.A. Satlaev, *Kumandintsy*, (Gorno-altaisk: Gorno-altaiskoe knizhnoe izdatelstvo, 1974), pp. 5–9.

49   The history of the Dzhungar state is briefly related in R. Grousset, *The Empire of the Steppes*, translated from the French by Naomi Walford (New Brunswick, New Jersey: Rutgers University Press, 1970), pp. 519–39.

4 Opening up Siberia: Russia's 'window on the East'

J.L. Black

In the voluminous annals of European exploration and expansion between the fifteenth and eighteenth centuries, Russia's efforts in opening up Siberia have been given rather short shrift. Studies on the growth of the great modern empires, above all the Dutch, Spanish and British empires, are preoccupied with maritime expansion. The search for riches, rather than trade and settlement, is the catalyst most often highlighted in examinations of the various European probings of continents and charting of sea routes. For Muscovy, the same period saw the beginning of overland expansion, at first to the south and south-east towards the Black and Caspian Seas; and then eastward towards the Pacific, through the vast reaches of Siberia. The expansion of Muscovy eastward, where Russians gradually destroyed the remnants of Golden Horde khanates and began to compete with China for territory and allegiances, has drawn little attention as a world political, commercial and strategic phenomenon even though the area concerned stretches from the Ural mountain range to the Pacific and from the Arctic Ocean to the borders of China.

The purpose of this chapter, however, is not to redress an historiographical imbalance; rather it is to delineate the magnitude, the complexity, the ambitions and the chief characteristics of Russian-sponsored exploration, exploitation and settlement of the vast expanses of Siberia. The intent here also is to demonstrate the variety of ways in which the history and character of Siberia can be approached and appreciated.

In so far as historiography is concerned, however, it is worth noting at the outset that, in contrast to the literature on western exploration, there are still many issues open to debate in the published history of Russian expansion eastward. Written references to the lands which became known as Siberia can be tracked to Marco Polo in the fourteenth century. Various early chronicles and stories of Siberia were printed and quoted by eighteenth and early nineteenth-century historians of Russia, such as V.N. Tatishchev G.-F. Müller, A.-L. von Schlözer, M.M. Shcherbatov and N.M. Karamzin.

A chronicle composed in the Stroganov family, the map-making exploits in Tobolsk of Ulyan Remezov and his son Semen during the seventeenth and early eighteenth centuries, another chronicle and an atlas left by the younger Remezov, and a huge body of literature on exploration and travel in Siberia which emerged in the eighteenth and nineteenth centuries, are among the many Russian-language sources often cited in research on Siberia.[1] There are many German-language accounts as well, prepared by early explorers and by naturalists,[2] but the fact that the opening up of Siberia attracted only peripheral attention in the larger overview of European expansion is exemplified by the number of contentious issues which still remain unsolved.[3]

Siberia can be studied from the perspective of cartography,[4] the search for sea routes,[5] the fur trade,[6] Russian settlement,[7] ethnography,[8] the exile system,[9] or from the point of view of Russian military, religious and political administration.[10] For reasons of space, this chapter will be limited first, to an overview of exploration and its various purposes in general and, second to a specific expedition of the mid-eighteenth century which in itself dramatically encompassed and symbolized all the characteristics of earlier and later Russian expansion through Siberia, that is, the Second Kamchatka (or Great Northern) Expedition of 1733–43.

The expansion of Muscovite suzerainty over an area four times its original size was remarkable for its speed. Between the early 1580s, when Yermak Timofeevich led free cossacks against Kuchum, Khan of Sibir, to the first third of the seventeenth century, Russian advances took them as far east as the Lena river, where Petr Beketov, another cossack, founded Yakutsk in 1632. A fortress (*ostrog*) had been founded at Tyumen on the Tura river as early as 1586 and was followed in rapid succession by Tobolsk on the Irtysh in 1587, Pelym (Tavda river), Verkhoture (Tura river), Berezov (lower Ob), and Tomsk (Tom) in the 1590s. Mangazeya was located on the upper Yenisei in 1601, and Yeniseisk in the south in 1619. These and other fortresses were built for purposes of military and political control (Kuchum was not finally defeated until 1598) and for the management of the fur and other trades (see Chapters 1 and 2).

Kuchum had been Khan of Tatars, but with their defeat the Russians found themselves faced by Kalmyks, so the fortresses had to be maintained. Soldiers, artisans, agricultural settlers, adventurers, prisoners-of-war (especially Swedes and Balts after the turn of the century), and religious dissidents flocked to the east. The process of conquest and settlement was followed by the establishment of Orthodox churches and attempts to proselytize the Russian religion to the indigenous peoples. The main incentive for early exploration was the seemingly inexhaustible supply of valuable furs, which were Muscovy's main source of foreign trade in the seventeenth century. To manage and protect this wellspring of wealth, the huge area was divided by the central government into military districts, each of them under the jurisdiction of a military governor (*voevoda*) (see Chapter 2).

In the 1640s a fortress was built at the mouth of the Kolyma and in 1648 there took place the famous voyage of Semen Dezhnev from the mouth of the Kolyma around the Chukotsk Peninsula and through what is now known as the Bering Strait to the Anadyr river on the Pacific. Cossacks sailed down the Lena to the Arctic Ocean in 1631; in 1641, the Sea of Okhotsk was reached. Lake Baikal was discovered two years later. By 1697 a Russian outpost had been established in Kamchatka by V.V. Atlasov, commandant of the Anadyrsk fortress.[11]

Although the direct Russian control of these sweeping areas was tenuous at best, information about the resource potential of the region, strategic considerations and competition for territory and discovery for their own sake, served as catalysts for a series of major exploratory, map-making, scientific and commercial expeditions which spread out over Siberia. Some of these expeditions were carefully planned by the state, others were the product of entrepreneurial campaigns undertaken by private enterprise families, the most famous of which were the Stroganovs and Demidovs. Russian diplomatic missions to China, for example, those led by N.G. Spatharius in the 1670s and by the Dane, Ysbrandt Ides, in the 1690s, gathered information about boundaries and territories; gold-seeking expeditions like those led by Ivan D. Bucholtz from western Siberia up the Irtysh in 1715 and by Major General I.M. Likharev in 1719 failed to disclose expected wealth in ores, but gave rise to ideas about river routes to India.

Visions of trade with Japan and China caused Peter the Great to send out geodesists Ivan M. Yevreinov and Fedor F. Luzhin in 1719 to gain geographical information on routes through Russian territory to the Pacific. In 1706 Peter also moved to tighten the Russian state monopoly over the valuable fur trade with China and ordered Siberian officials to forbid anyone to travel to China without specific permission from central government agencies. The Siberian fur trade itself became a state monopoly and still contributed enormously to the state treasury during the first third of the eighteenth century. Foreign travellers like Nicolaas C. Witsen, burgomaster of Amsterdam, and John Bell, a Scottish doctor, and others also provided interested European and Russian readers with a wealth of descriptive information on Siberia between the 1690s and the middle of the eighteenth century.[12]

Military pressures were exerted on the central Russian government to expand into Siberia when Kalmyks began to push into Kazakh territory from the east in the first half of the seventeenth century. The Kalmyks gradually conquered the huge Kazakh steppe during the last quarter of the century and came to threaten Russia's fortified position in southern Siberia. The founding of Omsk fortress on the Irtysh by Bucholtz in 1716 helped Russia play a direct role in the conflict between Kalmyk and Kazakh. By 1730 Russia had agreed to assist the Kazakhs in return for an oath of allegiance from the Kazakh khan.[13]

Conflict, tribal and otherwise, remained endemic to the Central Asian area, however, and forced Russian authorities to sustain their military presence. Similar conflicts occurred throughout Siberia and Kamchatka, with traditional territorial struggles between indigenous peoples continuing on the one hand, and, on the other hand, battles with the cossack agents of the Russians whose aim it was to force tribute (mostly in furs) and labour from local peoples. Tribal warfare, Russian military governance, and the fact that Siberia had already become established as a place for political, religious and criminal exiles from Muscovy and imperial Russia in the early seventeenth century, kept the territory in a state of flux about which, constantly, more needed to be known.

Peter had reorganized the Russian empire in 1708, dividing it into eight provinces (*gubernii*) of which Siberia, with its capital at Tobolsk, was one. In 1720, however, Siberia was divided into regimental districts, with each military group responsible for a town and its surrounding region. As a corollary of his attempt to make the management of the empire more efficient, Peter recognized that further geographical data were necessary. The fact that Peter the Great was advised to explore Siberia by the famous German academician, G.W. Leibniz, and a number of his own officials, has been well documented. So too has the fact that he had too little time or free funds with which to sponsor projects not associated with the Great Northern War until Sweden's offensive was broken at Poltava in 1709.

But it took an accumulation of reports of disorder and rebellion on the part of both cossacks and native peoples in Eastern Siberia between 1710 and 1714 to persuade Peter to act. He appointed a Great Kamchatka Command in 1716 to stabilize Russian control over Kamchatka, to establish outposts in, and gather information about, an area stretching from the Arctic to the Amur, and to investigate the possibility of trade with Japan. For lack of resources, the expedition collapsed. Nevertheless, it set the stage for post-petrine multipurpose projects like one directed by A.F. Shestakov and D.I. Pavlutskii between 1727 and 1732, which included exploration, charting of rivers, pacification of rebellious native peoples, the conquest of new territory, advances to the Kuril Islands, and the first European sighting of north-western America.[14]

Inland Siberia was explored on Peter's orders as well. Daniel G. Messerschmidt was contracted in 1718 to explore western and central Siberia, with orders to list plants, human resources and its natural history. Messerschmidt spent seven years gathering such information from his headquarters in Tobolsk and by 1727 was able to send numerous representative samples to St Petersburg. One of Messerschmidt's associates, P.J.T. Strahlenberg, published the first historical and geographical accounting of Siberia in Stockholm in 1730.[15] The most famous of Peter's attempts to discover the extent of his realm, however, was the First Kamchatka Expedition which was commissioned in December 1724. Its leader, Vitus J. Bering, set out from St Petersburg in January 1725, with his lieutenants A. Chirikov and M. Spanberg, and a huge team of geodesists, navigators, seamen, shipbuilders and soldiers. Bering had been assigned several tasks: to find out whether there was a north-eastern route by land between Asia and America; to prepare detailed maps of the eastern Russian Empire; to enumerate all its resources; and, above all, to reconnoitre the coast of America.[16] During five years of monumental hardship, his team reached Okhotsk, built a ship, transported goods to the western side of Kamchatka, provoked a bloody rebellion on the part of the Kamchadals (1730–31), constructed another ship at Nizhne-Kamchatsk, and sailed as far north as Cape Chukotka.

Bering returned to St Petersburg in March 1730 and immediately began to lobby for a second and more ambitious undertaking. He finally succeeded in getting a royal commission for a vastly more complex project of exploration, reorganization and mapping of eastern Siberia and Kamchatka. Decrees issued by the Empress Anna also required him to chart the Arctic coast of Siberia and visit the coasts of American and Japan for the purpose of arranging trade. The Academy of Sciences was ordered to outfit a scientific team to accompany Bering.[17] Support for Bering's expedition had been difficult to obtain until Ivan K. Kirilov, senior secretary to the Senate, and himself an enthusiastic statistician and geographer,[18] persuaded the powerful Count Ostermann to favour Bering by stressing the potential the enterprise had for trade, missionary work, and profit from natural resources. To a certain extent, these arguments demonstrated that the urge to explore for its own sake, which had been part of Peter's incentive, had fallen by the wayside.

About 600 persons were assigned to the Second Kamchatka Expedition. They were divided into three detachments: Bering's own group was to proceed in two stages, the first to go overland, build ships in Siberia and prepare for a voyage to Japan; the second was to build ships in order to sail to Kamchatka. The Academy unit was to follow Bering to eastern Siberia, exploring it en route and then accompany Bering to Kamchatka; a third group was to proceed by the northern sea route.

The Academy component of the expedition, accompanied by two landscape artists, a physician, an interpreter, an instrument-maker, four surveyors, five students to assist the professors, fourteen military guards and nine wagonloads of instruments and scientific materials, was led by two young German members of the Academy, G.-F. Müller and J.G. Gmelin, and an older Frenchman, Louis de l'Isle de la Croyère.[19] The story of the Second Kamchatka Expedition has been told often, but the scale of the venture in the context of eighteenth century exploration has often been underrated.

Bering's own herculean accomplishments are worth repeating here in brief. He reached Yakutsk in the spring of 1734, after spending a year in Tobolsk supervising the construction of a vessel (the *Tobol*) large enough to carry the first task force north on the Irtysh to the Arctic Ocean. In Yakutsk, Bering found that no provision had been made for him, and his supplies did not arrive until the following spring. But he built two more ships anyway, which he sent to the Arctic via the Lena. One of these was to turn west and chart the coast to the Yenisei, the other was to turn east and survey the coast to the Kamchatka Peninsula. Bering himself stayed in Yakutsk to organize the construction of more ships, dwellings, iron foundries and an entire complex from which to supply the constituent parts of his expedition. His work suffered constantly from obstructionism and resentment from local authorities who were expected to supply him at the expense of their own meagre resources. Later, when Bering moved on to Okhotsk, even the Academy representatives, to whom Bering refused to cater, sent hostile reports about Bering back to St Petersburg.

Accounts from spiteful Siberian officials made such an impression on officials in St Petersburg that Martin Spanberg's successful voyage to Japan in 1738, which had depleted Bering's supplies so much that his own trip to Kamchatka had to be delayed, was discounted in the capital city. Spanberg was intercepted by government officials at Kirenskii ostrog, where he had stopped on his way to report personally his discoveries to the senate. He was accused of deception and ordered to repeat his voyage to Japan.[20] Costs of the expedition had soared far beyond the original expectations by the late 1730s and Bering appeared to have little to show for it. Some members of the Senate suggested that the entire project be recalled; others demanded that Bering be dismissed. In 1737 he was deprived of part of his salary, with the warning that it would not be renewed until his expedition to Kamchatka actually got under way.

Bering was finally ready to leave Okhotsk in the summer of 1740, but unforeseen incidents – the change in orders delivered by Spanberg at the last moment, an accident which cost him valuable supplies, and a revolt by harshly overworked native peoples – resulted in his not reaching Kamchatka until September. By then it was too late in the year to undertake the voyage to America. Only in June 1741 were Bering's last two ships, the *St Paul* and *St Peter*, able to set sail from Petropavlovsk. After suffering six months of storms, bitter cold and raging disease which killed half of his crew, the 60-year-old Bering died. The famous Danish explorer was buried on a desolate island which later bore his name. His captain, A.I. Chirikov, suffered from scurvy, but survived only to die in 1748, shortly after his return to St Petersburg. The Second Kamchatka Expedition was terminated officially in 1743 but actually limped on until 1749 under two of Bering's other captains.

In its turn, the Academy contingent accomplished everything it was ordered to do and much more. Gmelin and Müller were granted permission not to accompany Bering to Kamchatka (de la Croyère died with Bering's group) and, instead, spent a full decade exploring and carefully putting to paper every facet of Siberia – its history, its flora and fauna, its climate, the customs, the religions and languages of its native peoples, its geography, trade routes and mineral resources. Müller's collection of historical documents, abstracts from old records, maps, drawings and artifacts filled dozens of wagonloads; his ethnographical and historical records (including verification of Dezhnev's 1648 voyage), comprised forty-two books of documents.[21] Müller also filed ten volumes of descriptive writings, town plans and diplomatic archives.

Gmelin's research led to the publication of a controversial four-volume memoir in Germany, and the first parts of his famous botanical work *Florica Sibirica*, appeared in St Petersburg in 1747. Gmelin's memoir, which was published in spite of the Russian senate's strict instructions that no information about the expedition was to be made public without its express permission, portrayed the harshness and brutality of life in Russia generally and in Siberia especially. It was translated into French and was widely read in Europe.[22] Works by other participants also reached large audiences: detailed accounts of Kamchatka by S.P. Krasheninnikov, one of the students with the Academy group, were published in two volumes in 1755, after their author's death; and J.-E. Fischer, a historian who joined the Academy expedition in its later stages, published a history of Siberia in 1767;[23] J.-W. Steller, who accompanied Bering and survived his voyages only to die in Tyumen in 1746, left accounts which were published in Germany in the 1770s.[24] These accounts included valuable information on Bering's discoveries, but were equally important for their records of animal and plant life. Another member of Bering's expedition, Ivan Sindt, survived to undertake further exploration, for he was later (1760s) assigned to an expedition to map the Aleutian Islands.

As a consequence of Müller's subsequent publicity-making, in part as official defender of Russia's role in the exploration of that area and the Pacific against challenges and criticisms from Europe, and in part in his role as founding editor of – and main contributor to – the most popular Russian journal (1755–1765), the vision of Siberia as a natural part of the Russian mission and destiny was assured.[25] The first volume of Müller's *Opisanie Sibirskago tsarstva* appeared in 1750 in St Petersburg. German language readers in Russia and Europe were given even longer accounts of Siberian history and geography on the pages of Müller's sporadic publication, *Sammlung Russischer Geschichte*. His materials on Siberia could be found also on the pages of important periodicals edited in Europe by Müller's friends and colleagues, among them the famous geographer, A.-F. Büsching, and the equally well-known historian, A.L. von Schlözer, and journalist J.C. Gottsched. Publicists J.L. Stavenhagen and Ulrich Weiss reprinted more of Müller's *sibiriana*. Aside from bringing a new object of curiosity to the attention of Russian and European scientists, diplomats and explorers, these publications helped shape a new image of Russia as a great world empire.

The consequences of Bering's second expedition to Kamchatka and its myriad by-products in public controversy, publications, information-collecting and image-making, are almost beyond counting. The expedition may have been the largest of all time, for it involved directly over 3,000 men during the decade of its official existence. It set forces in motion which accelerated and made more efficient state and entrepreneurial investment in trade, mining, agriculture and administration. Stories about, and examples of, new and apparently unlimited sources of furs from the North Pacific area (fox and sea otter) set off a new wave of Russian hunters, traders and trappers to the Irkutsk, Yakutsk, Okhotsk and Kamchatka region. Over forty organized groups of private entrepreneurs sponsored voyages in search of fortunes in the 'soft gold' business during the last half of the eighteenth century.[26] Information gathered by Müller, Gmelin, Steller, Krasheninnikov and others provided guidelines for the research undertaken by later eighteenth-century explorers in Russian service, Johann Falk, J.E. Georgi, A. Güldenstädt, Samuel Gmelin, Nicholas Rychkov, and, above all, Peter Simon Pallas. Each of these men, in fact, corresponded with Müller, the longest living major participant in the Bering expedition, who acted as liaison between them and the Academy of Sciences from the early 1770s until his death in 1783.

Surveys of the Arctic coast, new maps of, and information about, Japan, the official discovery of the northern coast of America and final proof of the existence of a strait between Asia and America, all represented new knowledge of far-reaching significance.[27] The way towards Russia's claim on Alaska was opened, the importance of control of the Amur river against Chinese inroads was recognized,[28] further attempts to establish trade relations with Japan were sponsored,[29] questions of the value of Russian colonization of Siberia by free peasants were raised and new expeditions were organized – all on the basis of information and ideas provided by participants in Bering's *tour de force*.

NOTES AND REFERENCES

1 For a still valuable overview of early sources on Siberia, see V.S. Ikonnikov, *Opyt russkoi istoriografii* II (2), (Kiev, 1908), pp. 1297–1307. See also A.I. Andreev, *Ocherki po istochnikovendeniyu Sibiri*, 2 vols (Moscow-Leningrad, 1960–5); R.G. Skrynnikov, 'Rannye sibirskie letopisi', *Istoria SSSR* (1979): 82–99, and Terence Armstrong (ed.), *Yermak's Campaign in Siberia: A Selection of Documents* (London: The Hakluyt Society 1975).

2 Among the best known of these were Messerschmidt, Gmelin, Müller, Fries, Adelung, Steller, Fischer and Lehrberg. One might turn to works like Albrecht Wirth, *Geschichte Sibiriens und der Mandschurei* (Bonn, 1899), and Albert Beveridge, *The Russian Advance* (New York, 1904), to get a picture of how politicized the 'expansion of Russia' to the Far East had become by the turn of this century.

3 See, for example, the questions raised in Raymond H. Fisher, *Bering's Voyages, Whither and Why* (Seattle, 1977); E. Stuart Kirby, 'The Trail of the Sable: New Evidence on the Fur Hunters of Siberia in the Seventeenth Century, *Slavic Studies* 25 (1981): 105–18; and R.G. Skrynnikov, 'Ermak's Siberian Expedition', *Russian History/Histoire Russe* 13 (1) (1986): 1–40. See also Skrynnikov's *Sibirskaya ekspeditsiya Yermaka* (Novosirbirsk, 1982); David N. Collins,'Russia's Conquest of Siberia: Evolving Russian and Soviet Historical Interpretations', *European Studies Review* 12 (1982): 17–44; and V.G. Mirzoev, *Istoriografiya Sibiri* (Kemerovo, 1965).

4 See, for example, L. Bagrow, 'The First Russian Maps of Siberia and their Influence on West-European Cartography of N.-E. Asia', *Imago Mundi* 9 (1952) and 'Semyon Remezov – A Siberian Cartographer', ibid., 11 (1954); Raymond H. Fisher, 'The Early Cartography of the Bering Strait Region', *Arctic* 37(4) (1984); B.P. Polevoi, 'Commemorating the Three Hundredth Anniversary of the "Godunov Map" of Siberia', trans. from Russian by James R. Gibson, *The Canadian Cartographer*, 8(1) (1971): 19–26; L. Bagrow, in Henry W. Castner (ed.), *A History of Russian Cartography up to 1800* (Ontario: Wolfe Island, 1975).

5 See, for example, T. Armstrong, 'In Search of a Sea Route to Siberia, 1553–1619', *Arctic* 37(4) (1984); Raymond H. Fisher (ed.), *The Voyage of Semen Dezhnev in 1648* (London: The Hakluyt Society, 1981).

6 Raymond H. Fisher, *The Russian Fur Trade, 1550–1700* (Berkeley and Los Angeles: University of California Press, 1943); and Kirby, op. cit.

7 Soviet scholarship tends to dwell on the colonizing, urbanizing and russianizing

of Siberia far more than do western studies. Such themes predominate in the 5-volume, *Istoriya Sibiri s drevneishikh vremen do nashikh dnei*, edited by A.P. Okladnikov (Leningrad, 1968–9). See also the early work by V.I. Shunkov, *Ocherki po istorii kolonizatsii Sibiri v XVII – nachale XVIII vekov* (Moscow-Leningrad, 1946); M.M. Gromyko, *Zapadnaya Sibiri v XVIII v.: Russkoe naselenie i zemledelcheskoe osvoenie* (Novosirbirsk, 1965); A.N. Kopylov, *Kultura russkogo naseleniya Sibiri v XVI–XVII vv.* (Novosirbirsk, 1968); O.N. Vilkov (ed.), *Goroda Sibiri* (Novosibirsk, 1974), and *Sibirskie goroda XVII–nachala XX veka* (Novosibirsk, 1981).

8   The early work of A.N. Pypin, *Istoriya russkoi etnografii* 4 (St Petersburg, 1892), is still valuable. See also M.O. Kosven, 'Etnograficheskie rezultaty Velikoi Severnoi Ekspeditsii 1733–1743 gg.', *Sibirskii etnograficheskii sbornik* 3 (1961): 167–212.

9   On two of the most famous seventeenth century exiles, see Basil Dmytryshyn, 'Iurii Krizhanich: The First Sibirologist', *Sino-Soviet Affairs* x (4) (1986–7): 195–211, and Alan Wood, 'Avvakum's Siberian Exile: 1653–64', in Alan Wood and R.A. French (eds), *The Development of Siberia: People and Resources* (London: Macmillan, 1989), pp. 11–34. For later periods, see George Kennan's well-known description in the late nineteenth century, *Siberia and the Exile System*, 2 vols, (New York: The Century Co., 1891), and a number of recent articles by Alan Wood listed in Chapter 7 (note 4) of the present volume.

10 See, for example, S.V. Bakhrushin, *Ocherki po istorii krasnoyarskogo uezda v XVII v.* (Moscow, 1959), and other such studies in his *Nauchnye trudy*; George V. Lantzeff, *Siberia in the Seventeenth Century. A Study of the Colonial Administration* (Berkeley, 1943); A.S. Donnelly, *The Russian Conquest of Bashkiria, 1552–1740. A Case Study of Russian Imperialism* (New Haven,1968); N.D. Zalnikova, *Soslovnye problemy vo vzaimootnosheniyakh tserkvi i gosudarstva v Sibiri XVIII v.* (Novosibirsk, 1981).

11 See Isaac Schottenstein, 'The Russian Conquest of Kamchatka, 1697–1731', PhD dissertation (University of Wisconsin, 1969).

12 Witsen, who was in Muscovy with a Dutch legation, published *Nord en osst Tartarye* in Amsterdam in 1692; Bell travelled with an embassy mission from St Petersburg to Pekin in 1719–22. His *A Journey from St Petersburg to Pekin, 1719–22* was printed first in Edinburgh in 1763. See also John Massey Stewart, 'Early Travellers, Explorers and Naturalists in Siberia', *Asian Affairs* 15(1) (1984): 55–64.

13 See, for general background, M.B. Olcott, *The Kazakhs* (Stanford, 1987), and E.N. Evseev, 'Ekspeditsiya I.D. Bukholtsa i osnovanie Omskoi kreposti', in Vilkov (ed.), *Goroda Sibiri*, op. cit., pp. 47–59.

14 Fisher, *Bering's Voyages*, op. cit., pp. 163–9; Schottenstein, op. cit., pp. 63–88.

15 Strahlenberg's *Das nord und östliche Theil von Europa und Asia*, was translated into English (1738) and French (1757). Messerschmidt's work was not published until recently – see E. Winter and N.A. Figurovskii (eds), *Forschungsreise durch Sibirien, 1720–1727*, 4 vols (Berlin: 1962–8). On Messerschmidt and Strahlenberg, see E.P. Zinner, *Sibir v izvestiyakh zapadnoevropeiskikh puteshestvennikov i uchenykh XVIII veka* (Vostochnosibirskoe izdatelstvo, 1968).

16 On this expedition, see Fisher, *Bering's Voyages*, op. cit.; P. Lauridsen, *Vitus Bering: The Discoverer of Bering Straits* (New York; 1969); F.A. Golder, *Bering's Voyages*, I–II (New York, 1922–3); L.S. Berg, *Otkrytie Kamchatki*

i *ekspeditsii Beringa, 1725-1742* (Moscow-Leningrad, 1946).

17 *Polnoe sobranie zakonov Rossiiskoi Imperii*, VIII, no. 6023, 17 April 1732, 749; no. 6041, 2 May 1732, 770-4. On the Academy of Sciences' part of the expedition, see J.L. Black, 'G.-F. Müller and the Russian Academy of Sciences' Contingent in the Second Kamchatka Expedition, 1733-1743', *Canadian Slavonic Papers* 25(2) (1983): 235-52.

18 Kirilov (1695-1737) prepared the first comprehensive corpus of geographical, historical, economic and statistical information on the Russian Empire: his *Tsvetushchee sostoianie vserossiiskago gosudarstva*, appeared in 2 volumes in 1727; in 1734 he published the first atlas of the empire.

19 For Müller's accounts of the ten-year expedition, see Carol Urness (trans. and ed.), *Gerhard-Friedrich Müller. Bering's Voyages: The Reports from Russia* (Fairbanks, Alaska, 1987); J.L. Black and D.K. Buse (eds), *G.-F. Müller in Siberia, 1733-1743* (Kingston, Ontario, 1988).

20 Lauridsen, op. cit., pp. 117-26; Müller, *Yezhemesyachnye sochineniya*, August 1758, pp. 116-17.

21 For a partial list of the documentation compiled by Müller, see N.V. Golitsyn, 'Portfeli G.F. Müllera (Svedeneniya o postuplenii ikh Arkhiv i opisanie 3-x portfeli)', *Sbornik moskovskogo glavnogo arkhiva Ministerstva Inostrannykh Del* 6 (Moscow, 1899), pp. 401-535.

22 See Gmelin, *Reise durch Sibirien*, 4 vols (Göttingen, 1751-2); *Voyage en Sibérie*, 2 vols (Paris, 1767). Gmelin left Russia for Göttingen in 1747 and did not return to St Petersburg, thereby breaking his contract with the Russian Academy of Sciences.

23 Krasheninnikov, *Opisanie zemli Kamchatki*, 2 vols (St Petersburg, 1755); Fischer, *Sibirische Geschichte von der Entdekkung Sibiriens bis auf die Eroberung dieses Lands durch die Russische Waffen*, 2 vols (St Petersburg, 1768). Müller prepared the Krasheninnikov work for publication and wrote an introduction to it, and provided Fischer with most of his information.

24 Steller, *Beschreiburg von dem Lande Kamchatka* (Frankfurt and Leipzig, 1774). On Steller, see L.Stejneger, *Georg Wilhelm Steller, The Pioneer of Alaskan Natural History*, (Cambridge, Mass., 1936). Krasheninnikov's work was published in English as *Explorations of Kamchatka: North Pacific Scimitar*, edited and translated by E.A.P. Crownhart-Vaughan (Portland, Oregon, 1972); Steller's record appeared in Golder, op. cit., II, 1922, pp. 9-187. A short account of Steller's life, published anonymously in Frankfurt in 1748, served as the first official report on Bering's voyage published from Russian sources. It has been translated by Olga M. Griminger and edited for publication by O.W. Frost - see *Alaska Historical Commission Studies in History*, 223 (1986). Lt Sven Waxell, second in command in Bering's ship, also kept a journal, which was published in Russian in 1940, and in English as *The American Expedition* (London, 1952) (reprinted in 1962).

25 The *Yezhemesyachnye sochineniya* (Monthly Essays) was published in twenty volumes, in which many accounts of Russian northern explorations, Siberian towns, peoples, trade, resources, gold discoveries, cossacks, and Siberia's vast expanses generally, attracted readers. On this, see the introduction to Black and Buse, op. cit.

26 See Basil Dmytryshyn, 'Privately-Financed Russian Expeditions to the North Pacific in the Eighteenth Century', paper presented at the Third International

Congress for Soviet and East European Studies in Washington, DC, November 1985.

27 For documents relevant to these discoveries, see A.I. Alekseev, A.L. Narochnitskii, I.N. Solovev and T.S. Fedorova (eds), *Russkie ekspeditsii po izucheniyu severnoi chasti Tikhogo Okeana v pervoi polovine XVIII v. Sbornik documentov* (Moscow, 1984); and Basil Dmytryshyhn, E.A.P. Crownhart-Vaughan and Thomas Vaughan (eds), *Russian Penetration of the North Pacific, 1700–1799, A Documentary Record*, II (Portland, Oregon: Oregon Historical Society, 1986).

28 See L.A. Maier, 'Gerhard-Friedrich Müller's Memoranda on Russian Relations with China and the Reconquest of the Amur', *Slavonic and East European Review* 59(2) (1981): 219–40.

29 See George A. Lensen, *The Russian Push Toward Japan: Russo-Japanese Relations, 1697–1875* (Princeton, 1959).

5 The Siberian native peoples before and after the Russian conquest

James Forsyth

The recorded history of Siberia begins (apart from some references in early Chinese works[1]) with its invasion by the Russians in the late sixteenth century. By then the ethnic composition of its native population was multifarious and complex, being the result of a long period of prehistoric development. Attempts to reconstruct the ethnogenesis of the peoples of Siberia have preoccupied many Russian scholars.[2] In ethno-linguistic terms the 'oldest' peoples of Siberia are those speaking the 'Palaeoasiatic' languages, which cannot be related to any known families of languages outside Siberia. These are the Chukchis, Koryaks and Itelmens of the extreme north-east and the Kamchatka Peninsula, the Yukagirs who in the seventeenth century inhabited a very large territory between Chukotka and the lower Lena, the Ainu of southern Kamchatka and the Kuril Islands, the Nivkhs of the lower Amur and Sakhalin, and the Kets of the Yenisei. The Eskimos are also often included among the old Siberian peoples.[3]

Movements of peoples in the historical period originated in the southerly latitudes of Inner Asia. It was presumably from present-day Manchuria that the Tungus tribes gradually spread northwards to pervade the taiga as far as the Arctic zone, from the Sea of Okhotsk in the east to the Yenisei in the west. A much more compact intrusion from Inner Asia was achieved, between the twelfth and fourteenth centuries AD, by the Yakuts with their Turkic language, whose culturally isolated community, based upon cattle and horse-breeding, was established among the Tungus on the middle Lena. At about the same period the Mongol-speaking Buryats moved into the steppes and forests around the southern end of Lake Baikal, where they subjugated the previous inhabitants.

One of the most widespread language families in Siberia was that now known as Samoed, the speakers of which at one time occupied a large part of southern Siberia from the Irtysh to the Yenisei, including the Altai-Sayan mountain region. These tribes, along with the Yenisei peoples whose last surviving linguistic descendants are the Kets, were profoundly affected by the northward expansion of Turkic peoples from Inner Asia and of the Tungus from the east. As a result, they were either pushed farther north or absorbed by the incomers. In western Siberia, while Turkic tribes from the steppes moved into the southern fringe of the forest and pressed upon the Samoeds, the Ugrian (Khanty and Mansi) peoples moving eastward from the Ural mountains into the Ob-Irtysh basin also mixed with the Samoeds, who by then occupied the northern forest and tundra from the White Sea in the west almost to the Lena in the east.

Among the sometimes rather speculative theories about these movements of peoples one thing is certain: contrary to the facile generalizations of many historians whose interest is almost entirely focused on the Russian element in Siberia, this vast area of northern Asia was not an 'empty' land in the sixteenth century. From the mountainous south to the treeless tundra, human communities had established themselves over several millennia, with a way of life which was nomadic or semi-nomadic. Except in the case of the Yakuts and the Turks and Mongols of the southern steppes, their economy was largely based upon the use of reindeer – in the first place by hunting wild herds during their seasonal migrations, and later by domesticating them to a greater or lesser extent.

The Russian conquest of northern Eurasia, which developed from the north-eastward territorial expansion of Novgorod and then Moscow, reached beyond the Urals into Asia only some sixty years after the Spanish conquest of Mexico, and twenty years before the first French and English colonies were founded in North America. The land into which the Russians advanced was similar in many ways to Canada in terms of terrain, climate and natural vegetation. Culturally, the native population encountered by the Russians was more varied than that found by the first Europeans in northern North America, but the general linguistic situation in the two regions was similar. This fact is generally obscured by the appearance of simplicity and tidiness imposed by the classification of the existing languages of the USSR, since, out of its approximately 105 recognized native languages, only about twenty-nine, belonging to eleven families, are indigenous to Siberia.[4] This appears to offer a contrast with the 200 native languages (in fifty-seven families) in present-day North America, of which about sixty-eight occur north of the 45th parallel (the zone comparable with Siberia). In fact the situation in sixteenth-century Siberia was rather different from what it is today, since a considerable number of languages, such as Kott, Yug, Arin, Assan, Pumpokol, Kamas and Mator, have died out completely. Moreover, the modern status of officially recognized 'languages', as opposed to 'dialects' – always a controversial question – obscures the fact that, for instance, Khanty has as many as five 'dialects' which are by no means mutually comprehensible; the far-flung Evenki Tungus have at least three groups of dialects, and their cousins the Evens as many as thirteen; and the Nenets Samoeds of the forest have three rather different 'dialects', although those of the tundra have a single common language. It is believed that the Yukagir people had many languages and dialects at the time of the Russian conquest, although only a small remnant of this nationality survives today. Of the larger nationalities, the Buryat Mongols have four dialects, the recently 'consolidated' Altaians about six, the Khakass about five, and the Tuvans four, while even such a small community as the Enets Samoeds has two quite widely differing 'dialects'. If these facts are taken into account, it seems probable that the number of indigenous languages spoken in Siberia when the Russian occupation began was over 120. The precise situation will never be known, since the Russian invaders, being interested only in extracting tribute in the form of sable and other furs, paid little attention to the linguistic complexity of Siberia. Like any other European colonialists, they were content to rely upon the services of interpreters from among the local people as they advanced farther into unknown territory.

Table 5.1 The peoples of Siberia in the seventeenth century (numbers)

Tatars	14,265
Teleuts and other Altai-Sayan Turks	11,300
Khantys and Mansis	16,260
Samoeds, including Nenets, Tavgi and Selkups	15,285
Kets	5,630
Tungus: Evenkis and Evens	36,235
Yakuts	28,470
Mongols, including Buryats	37,175
Yukagirs	4,775
Eskimos	4,000
Chukchis	8,500
Koryaks	11,000
Itelmens	23,000
Ainu	3,540
Nanais and Ulchas	3,500
Nivkhs	4,300
	227,235

The linguistic complexity of Siberia reflected its ethnic variety. The accompanying map (5.1) of seventeenth-century Siberia shows about twenty nationalities, but this too is a simplification. The reality of the ethnic situation is suggested by the folding map accompanying B.O. Dolgikh's study, based upon official contemporary records of tribute-exaction, of the clan and tribal composition of the peoples of Siberia in the seventeenth century. This shows at least 520 territorial groups recognized as administrative districts (*volosti*),

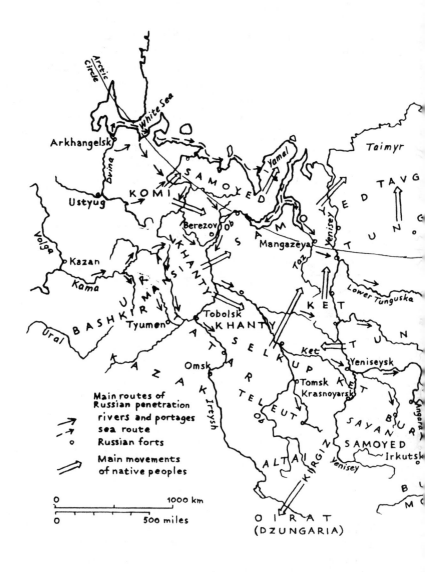

Map 5.1 The native peoples of Siberia in the seventeenth century
Drawn by James Forsyth.

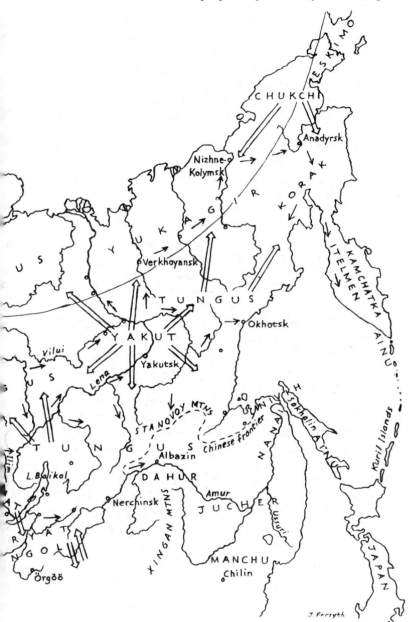

ESKIMO

CHUKCHI

Anadyrsk

Nizhne-
Kolymsk

YUKAGIR

KORAK

KAMCHATKA

ITELMEN

Verkhoyansk

TUNGUS

Okhotsk

AINO

Vilui

YAKUT

US

Lena

Yakutsk

STANOVOY MTNS

H

Sakhalin Ainu

Kuril Islands

TUNGUS

Albazin

Chinese Frontier

NANAI

L. Baikal

DAHUR

Nerchinsk

Amur

JUCHER

XINGAN MTNS

Ussuri

JAPAN

RYAT

NGOL

MANCHU

Chilin

Örgöö

J. Forsyth

which in some cases corresponded to true consanguineous clans, but in many other cases were merely 'clans' of convenience, rather arbitrarily designated by the Russian authorities. The population figures estimated by Dolgikh on the basis of this survey have become widely accepted in the Soviet Union. They show tribute 'constituencies' ranging from as few as fifteen persons to several hundreds or even thousands in the case of some of the bigger nationalities – in particular the Kangalas, Baturs, Borogon and Megin tribes of Yakutia, and the Bulagat and Tabunut tribes of Buryat Mongols. Aggregating Dolgikh's figures,[5] we can arrive at the approximate numbers for the peoples of Siberia in the seventeenth century (including some 69,000 people of the Altai-Sayan and the Far East who were not at this time Russian subjects) as shown in Table 5.1.

In view of the vast size of Siberia, the relatively small numbers of Russians operating there in the seventeenth century, and the difficulty of carrying out a census of a mobile population, it seems likely that these figures somewhat underestimate the number of indigenous Siberians before the Russian conquest.

In any case, by the beginning of the eighteenth century the native peoples were competing with a rapidly growing contingent of Russians in their midst: about 100,000 in 1701, increasing to some 700,000 in 1720. By that time the native peoples constituted a minority of only 30 per cent of the total population of Siberia, and they remained at that level until the end of the eighteenth century, although their own numbers increased from 288,000 in 1719 to 732,000 in 1795.[6]

Most Russian historians have presented the Russian occupation of Siberia as a culturally progressive phenomenon, and have shown the way of life of the native peoples in a negative light. For instance, much emphasis is placed upon fighting between tribes, which supposedly occurred with great frequency until such conflicts were stopped by the Russians.[7] This is a highly tendentious view. Of course native Siberians sometimes fought among themselves, just as the various national and religious communities of Europe were often at each other's throats. However, the scale of slaughter, cruelty and destruction involved in European wars of the seventeenth and subsequent centuries was immeasurably greater than that of the tribal conflicts of the 'savages'. The latter involved smaller numbers of people and were less indiscriminate and embittered, frequently being, like those of the North American Indians, somewhat ritualized and even limited to stand-up single combat between champions.[8] They can scarcely be taken as a serious reason for the 'backwardness' of the Siberian peoples, nor as a justification for their subjugation by the Russians.

So far as material culture is concerned, the Siberian peoples fell into two main categories. One consisted of the peoples of the forest and tundra, who chiefly relied upon reindeer skins for their clothing and shelter, and obtained their food by hunting game with spears, and bows and arrows, by fishing and by gathering nuts, berries and roots. Such were, for instance, the Khantys and Mansis, the Tungus (Evenki and Even), the Samoeds (Nenets, Enets and Nganasans), and the Yukagirs. The other group consisted of horse and cattle-herding peoples of the steppes and mountain pastures of the southern margin of Siberia who, while wearing animal-skin garments in winter, were also well acquainted with textiles. These included the Buryat Mongols, the Turkic peoples of the Altai-Sayan mountains, and the west Siberian Tatars. This division reflects one of several points of contrast between the Siberian natives and those of northern North America. Before the advent of the Europeans the latter lacked any contact with more 'advanced' cultures (except in so far as the influence of the Aztecs and other peoples of Central America may have percolated northward), whereas Siberia, as part of the 'Old World' cultural complex, was subject to many influences (however remote) from the great civilizations of Eurasia. Above all this meant China, but also included Persia, since the nomadic pastoralists of the steppes (who had their own, sophisticated equestrian culture) carried elements of these cultures to the northern forest peoples. As a result, metal-working (which was hardly developed at all in North American native cultures) was widespread in Siberia from the second millennium BC, and long before the seventeenth century AD all its indigenous peoples either worked iron themselves or used artefacts made of the precious metal when these could be obtained by trade.[9] Nevertheless, for many Siberian communities wood, stone and bone remained the principal materials for making tools and weapons.

There were few exceptions to the rule that the peoples of Siberia were illiterate before the Russians came. Only the west Siberian Tatars, as Muslims in touch with Bukhara and other Islamic centres of Central Asia, were familiar with Koranic Arabic, while the Buryat Mongols east of Lake Baikal used classical Mongolian, written since the thirteenth century in a vertical script, and later, as a result of conversion to Buddhism in the seventeenth and eighteenth centuries, received its scriptures in Tibetan. Lack of writing, however, did not mean the absence of creative composition in words: in every native community recitation was prized, and oral traditions, often partly historical, were highly developed, as, for example, in the Yakut epics known as *olonkho*.

So far as observation and knowledge of the world is concerned, the beliefs of the northern peoples have been dismissed equally by the Russian Orthodox Church and by the Communists as benighted superstition which imprisoned them mentally in a fear of evil spirits. Nevertheless, even if their cosmology, like that of all religions, was expressed in fantastic terms,[10] the Siberian natives, like the 'primitive' peoples of any land, had a rational enough view of the world which surrounded them, in addition to a wealth of practical knowledge about the forest and its fauna, and about crafts and hunting techniques. Nor did they lack ethical principles – contrary to much biased misunderstanding on the part of Russians with their Christian European prejudices, especially in the field of sexual mores. One of the most striking social norms of all the hunting peoples was sharing of the spoils of the hunt among all members of the community, even if they had played no part in the hunt – a practice to which the Evenki term *nimat* is often applied. Even Russian Communists, who dismiss most of the traditional aspects of mutual assistance within the clan as concealed exploitation of the poor by the rich, can find little to condemn in this indubitable manifestation of 'primitive communism'.[11]

It is generally accepted that most of the Siberian peoples were organized in clans, each of which traced descent from a common ancestor, and that marriage within this kinship group was forbidden. Thus the system of exogamy prevailed, according to which a bride had to be obtained from another clan, 'bride-price' and dowry being given according to an agreement between the parents. Awareness of belonging to one's clan – involving such obligations as mutual assistance and blood vengeance – was an important fact of life for all Siberian native peoples, except those of the extreme north-east – the Koryaks, Chukchis and Eskimos. The Chukchis in particular had no social unit greater than the extended family, and social coherence was achieved by neighbour association and (as also among the Nivkhs of the Amur) by 'group marriage', in which friends shared each other's wives.[12] In the far north-east and Kamchatka a common marriage practice was the residence of the husband in the family of his bride for a certain period of time, in order to pay for her by performing work for the family.[13]

Throughout Siberia (and indeed the European north as well), with the partial exception of the Muslim Tatar fringe in the west, the religion of shamanism was universal. Much has been written about the ritual practices, accoutrements, and spiritual calling of the *shaman*, who functioned as priest, soothsayer and healer.[14] The most conspicuous aspect of the shaman's ministry was his performance or dance (known in Russian as *kamlanie*, from the Turkic word *kam* 'shaman' – the word *shaman* itself being the Tungus term). During this, the shaman wore a special coat, often elaborately embellished with symbolic designs, trailing thongs, bells and iron pendants in the form of birds or chain 'snakes'. On his head was a special headdress of deerskin and feathers, and sometimes a metal crown bearing antlers or a bird effigy. Beating a similarly ornamented one-sided drum with a fur-covered stick, the shaman chanted and danced with increasing frenzy until he fell down in a trance. In this state his spirit was said to fly to the other world of spirits and there discover the cause of and cure for a person's illness, the identity of a malefactor, or the nature of events destined to occur. Shamans also used kamlanie to invoke the good will of spirits for such communal activities as hunting or warfare.

For long the shaman was treated in Marxist-Leninist writings as a mere charlatan who exploited the ignorance of his fellows in order to extort high fees for his services. In recent years, however, a less simplified and more generous interpretation has emerged, as noted, for instance, by Syroechkovskii: 'It is now clear beyond doubt that shamans were usually quite poor individuals, who stood out by reason of their intelligence or personality, and their authority was normally based upon this'.[15]

The shaman's journey to the land of the spirits is one manifestation of the animist religion of the Siberian native peoples. Their general reverence for nature spirits as the 'masters' of forest, rivers, mountains, and so on, took a very characteristic form in the cult of the supreme animal – for most Siberian peoples the brown bear. Although respect for the bear did not preclude killing it, due apology had to be made, and strict rules governed the disposal of its carcass. Consequently the bear-feast – ubiquitous in Siberia – was on the one hand a communal enjoyment of the cooked flesh of the animal, but on the other hand a sacred ritual intended to placate the bear-spirit and ensure that, while the dead animal would live again, its spirit would not seek vengeance on those who had killed it. In general, blood sacrifice was the principal religious rite of all Siberian peoples, the animal sacrificed being that which played the most important part in daily life. Thus most forest and tundra peoples sacrificed reindeer, but it was a dog which was killed (and eaten) by those peoples (Nanai, Ulcha, Nivkh and Koryak) who used dog-teams for transport, while the sacrificial animal of the Buryats, Yakuts and other Turkic peoples was the horse.

While idealization of, or sentimentality about, the way of life of primitive peoples must be avoided, there seems to be no doubt that among the Siberian peoples in their original state a certain harmony with nature existed, if only as a reflection of the unavoidable conditions in which they lived. These conditions embraced the realities of survival in an often hostile environment, and the mysteries of birth and death. Living meant constant activity to obtain food, shelter and clothing, and the way of life was an integrated one in which work was not distinguished from leisure, and every activity contributed towards the survival of the individual and the community. On this basis the Siberian peoples achieved a certain balance with nature. While they were at the mercy of erratic weather or changes in the migration routes of reindeer, so that they might suffer famine from time to time, they were generally well fed, more or less comfortably adapted to their environment, and enjoyed a surplus of resources sufficient to allow expenditure of time on the decoration of clothing and utensils, on story-telling and dancing. Their weapons were simple but not crude, and their clothing was meticulously formed and finished. As C.S. Coon has pointed out in regard to the world's hunting peoples in general, compared with urbanized people:

> Hunters live and work mostly out of doors. Their senses are acute and, like their bodies, well exercised. Their schedules and routines are seldom monotonous, but often adventurous. Their craftsmanship has to be accurate, for their success is at stake.

In contrast with 'overspecialized, overmechanized urban society' where the world of adults is sharply divided from that of children, those in hunting communities share in all adult activities and learn skills by example. Even if their way of life was uncomfortable by modern standards of luxury, the peoples of northern Asia in their original state, like other hunting peoples, 'had the energy, hardihood, and ingenuity to live and live well'. Their lives, in short, were not spent in misery before the Russians came among them.

This basic fact should be borne in mind when reading ideologically biased accounts of the benefits following upon Russian occupation, for, in the words of the same writer on the hunting peoples, 'In every well-documented instance, cases of hardship may be traced to the intervention of modern intruders.'[16]

The Russians came among the Siberian peoples in the late sixteenth century from two directions, which subsequently became established as the main regular routes. The northern (and earlier) approach was by passes across the Ural mountains to the lower reaches of the river Ob, and thence down the Ob Gulf by boat to the mouth of the Taz, which was ascended as far as a portage to the lower Yenisei; from there they followed an eastward course up the Lower Tunguska river, crossing a portage to the Vilyui and so to the Lena. The more southerly route lay across a gap in the Urals to the Irtysh and thence, after the Tatar khanate had been defeated, up the middle Ob and its tributaries, such as the Ket, to where a portage led to the middle reaches of the Yenisei; from here they ascended the Upper (or 'Stony') Tunguska as far as the Ilim, and so either by portage to the Lena or up the Angara towards Lake Baikal.

In many ways a parallel can be drawn between this river-borne Russian penetration and conquest of Siberia, with its combination of raiding and trading, and the invasion of the original land of the Slavs by the Varangians eight centuries before. Unlike the Scandinavian seafarers, however, the sixteenth-century Russians enjoyed an enormous military advantage over the indigenous people they encountered by having guns, and in addition they had behind them the organized power of the centralized state of Muscovy. In terms of military conquest, a considerable difference existed between the conditions encountered in the north and the south of Siberia. In the latter – the steppe and woodlands inhabited by Tatars, Altaians, Kirgiz, Buryats and Mongols – the Russians had to wage war against formidable enemies who were not only capable of putting up resistance to incursions into their territories, but also able to obtain support from the larger communities of Turkic-Mongol peoples to whom they were related. The steppe frontier from the Urals to the Altai was thus by no means 'open' to the Russians. The west Siberian Tatars of the Khanate of Sibir were subjugated or dispersed among the steppe nomads, but the presence of the latter (particularly the Kazakhs and Oirats) obliged the Russians to maintain fortified 'lines' in the south for over two hundred years (see Chapter 3). Farther east, Russian campaigns against the Buryats around the southern end of Lake Baikal went on from the 1630s to the 1680s, causing great turmoil as some Buryat and Mongol tribes withdrew to Mongolia, or were buffeted back and forward between the two aggressive empires of Russia and China.[17] At the farthest end of Russia's Inner Asian frontier, the Chinese, under the Ching (Manchu) dynasty, confronted the Russians on the Amur and put an end to their episodic marauding and colonizing activities around the fort of Albazin. The Russians were pushed back northwards to the Stanovoi mountains, where the frontier fixed in 1689 by the Treaty of Nerchinsk was recognized until the nineteenth century.

The smaller peoples of Siberia, living as they did in more or less dispersed clan communities or nomadic bands, also resisted the Russian conquerors wherever they could. Nevertheless, they were forced into submission, in the first place by a demonstration of the killing power of firearms. Thereafter they were obliged to register as payers of fur-tribute (for which the Russians used the Tatar term *yasak*). One of the means used to enforce this was the imposition of an oath (*shert*) by which the shamanist natives invoked the wrath of the spirits upon themselves if they broke their undertaking to the Russians. The other, more effective means, was the taking of hostages: chiefs or other tribesmen and their wives or children were seized and imprisoned in Russian forts as a guarantee of submission and tribute-payment on the part of their compatriots.

The most ruthless campaigns against northern peoples who refused to submit appear to have taken place in the east – perhaps because there the proximity of the Okhotsk coast, and the mountainous terrain, left fewer possibilities open for escape from the Russian soldiers. The 'Lamuts' (Even Tungus) of the Okhotsk region fought hard to preserve their freedom, while in Kamchatka the Itelmens, whose conquest did not begin until the early eighteenth century, were subjected to genocidal slaughter by troops using the up-to-date weapons of Peter the Great's military machine: muskets and hand grenades. The most determined resistance of all was put up by the Koryaks and Chukchis of the north-east, who faced a fierce and explicitly genocidal Russian campaign up to the 1750s.[18] Eventually this policy was abandoned because it was unprofitable for the Russian state treasury, and from then until the early twentieth century the Chukchis had the distinction of being recognized as 'not completely subdued', and were left largely to their own devices.

While the main west-to-east movement in the occupation of Siberia was accomplished by the first half of the eighteenth century, the frontiers of the Russian Empire continued to be pushed forward in various directions, thus bringing more peoples under its control. One important direction of expansion was southward into the Altai-Sayan mountain region on the border of Mongolia, where the Russian town of Kuznetsk was for long an outpost threatened from west, south and east by the 'White Kalmyks' (Teleuts and other Altaian tribes), the Oirats or western Mongols, and the Chinese. Intermittent warfare from the 1620s to the 1750s ended with the incorporation into the Russian Empire of many tribes speaking Turkic languages.[19] These included the Kacha, Kyzyl, Sagai, Koibal, Beltir and Shor tribes of the upper Yenisei basin (the 'Minusinsk Tatars') and the Altai Kizhi, Telengit, Teleut, Tölös, Kumanda, Tuba, and Chelkan, living between the Irtysh and the Yenisei, who are nowadays grouped together under the common name 'Altaians'.

Russian expansion in the Far East during the nineteenth century also involved the annexation of territory belonging to China, which lay in the Amur basin and the 'Maritime' region between the Ussuri river and the Sea of Japan. In addition to nomadic Tungus clans and the semi-nomadic Nanai, Ulcha, Udeghe, Nivkh and other small ethnic communities, this brought under the Russian flag considerable numbers of Han Chinese and Koreans who had migrated into these regions as seasonal labourers and agricultural settlers.

During the nineteenth century the absolute number of indigenous Siberians remained approximately the same as at the end of the eighteenth century, but their proportion in the total population of some five million fell to about 14 per cent. While the native people were fairly evenly distributed across Siberia from west to east (but with a greater concentration in the south than in the north), the distribution of the incomer population from west of the Urals was always very uneven. In the nineteenth century about 70 per cent of all Siberia's 'Russians' lived in the three most westerly provinces (Tobolsk, Tomsk and Yeniseisk), while only 30 per cent lived in the eastern half of Siberia.[20] There was an even greater variation in the various regions between the number of natives and of incomers. By the beginning of the twentieth century the latter made up about 90 per cent of the population of the three western provinces, and between 60 and 85 per cent of Irkutsk, Transbaikal and Amur provinces, but in the enormous Yakutsk province and the far north-east it was still the non-Russian indigenous population which predominated, in a proportion of 13:1.[21]

One of the major preoccupations of Soviet Russian ethnic historians, obliged to work within the framework of Marxist-Leninist dogma, is to define the level of social-political evolution which the peoples of Siberia had reached by the sixteenth century in terms of Marx's five universal stages. Not surprisingly, it was among the southern, pastoral peoples that social stratification had developed by that time, so that the label 'feudal' is attached, for instance, to the Buryat Mongols and the Tatars. The precise stage reached by the Yakuts remains more controversial, but Soviet historians generally agree that their tribal society was already decaying, so that the Russians found a community with marked class differences. Among the smaller northern peoples there was no tribal aristocracy, chiefs only being chosen temporarily for specific purposes such as war. They are considered to have been 'primitive-communal' societies based on the clan (*rod*). In some cases, however, such as the Khanty and Mansi, the accepted view is that even before their subjection to the Russians their clan system was in decline and 'feudal' relations were developing, with the emergence of princes and social inequality.[22]

Whatever stage of development any of the peoples of Siberia had reached, the occupation of their land by the Russians had a profound effect, either setting off entirely new social developments or accelerating trends which were already present. One of the principal ways in which the Russian state undermined native culture was by purchasing the collaboration of chiefs, where they existed, or could be arbitrarily designated. This led to the development of personal privilege and wealth as these native collaborators colluded in the exploitation of their compatriots. The indigenous way of life was greatly undermined by the burden of yasak, which diverted men from the essential hunting pursuits that provided food, clothing and other necessities, to the trivial occupation of hunting and trapping sable, arctic fox, squirrels and other fur-bearing animals. These were demanded relentlessly by the Russian government and by traders because of their commercial value, but they contributed nothing to the natural economy of the natives. Eventually this perversion of the natives' way of life led to their dependence upon Russian provisions – grain, bread, sugar, tea, and tobacco. Another key element in Russian culture was alcohol, the unscrupulous introduction of which to the unsophisticated natives by traders led in many cases to addiction, loss of the means of livelihood and eventual pauperization.

Colonies have always given scope to adventurers from the metropolis who have enjoyed irresponsible power over the natives, whether as administrators, police officials, soldiers, traders, or settlers (even if these were of the peasant class). Along with this power went a contemptuous attitude towards the natives as a 'lower race'. Such attitudes were familiar, for instance, in British imperial possessions in Africa, India and America, and there is no evidence that the Russian colonialists differed to any degree. In fact, the supposed readiness of Russians to 'accept' baptized or otherwise assimilated natives as Russians is in itself a manifestation of the national arrogance of the Russians, which eventually engendered a sense of inferiority among many of the indigenous peoples. Meanwhile the latter were looked upon by most Russian settlers as fair game to be preyed upon in a variety of ways.

Before the Russians came there was no landownership in Siberia, although rights to the use of hunting-grounds, fishing-grounds and pastures were respected by tradition or asserted by force. Under Russian rule many native communities were deprived of such rights by sheer seizure of land (*zakhvat*) or by forfeiting territory as a result of pernicious debtor-contracts into which they had been duped by unscrupulous settlers. Another direct result of conquest by force of arms was the development of slavery, which was widespread up to the beginning of the nineteenth century. The native slaves owned by Russians of all social classes were in the first place either prisoners-of-war or women and children captured after the men of a native community had been killed. Inevitably soldiers, officials and traders operating far from their home base needed women, so that the taking of native 'wives', either voluntarily or by force, was common, and prostitution, which had been unknown in traditional culture, also appeared. The general effect of widespread miscegenation was, as in North America, the creation of large number of *métis*, many of whom became assimilated into the 'Russian' population of Siberia.[23]

An involuntary, but major, effect of Russian intrusion among the Siberian peoples was the introduction of diseases which were endemic in European Russia but, apparently, were unknown in northern Asia. The most virulent of these were smallpox and measles, epidemics of which are noted in Russian colonial records from the 1630s onwards. Up to the middle of the seventeenth century they overran only western Siberia where, for instance, the number of Kets is said to have been reduced by half. Similar outbreaks spread east of the Yenisei in the 1650s, carrying away up to 80 per cent of the northern Tungus and Yakuts, while a widespread epidemic in the

1690s reduced the Yukagirs by 44 per cent. The Buryats are known to have suffered several epidemics in the middle of the eighteenth century, and later it was the Itelmens of Kamchatka who were reduced by almost two-thirds. In the nineteenth century these diseases ravaged the most remote populations: the Nganasans and Dolgans of Taimyr from the 1830s, the Chukchis and Koryaks of the far north-east in the 1880s. A more problematic infection which has been attributed to the Russians was the spread of syphilis, especially among the Nenets Samoeds.[24] These drastic reductions in population through disease must have been restored quickly; otherwise they are difficult to reconcile with the overall growth in numbers of indigenous people mentioned above.

Through the ideological prism of Marxist historicism some Soviet Russian historians see ample justification for the Russians' intrusion into the lives of the Siberian natives in the benefits of civilization which the latter are deemed to have received. These include their being brought out of geographical and cultural isolation into the sphere of a 'higher' (that is, Russian-European) culture. No doubt the material culture of the Russians was more highly developed than that of most Siberian peoples, in so far as they built log houses with wooden floors, windows and stoves; wore clothing made of textiles woven from linen, hemp or wool; used steam-baths; were able to shoot game (and people) more efficiently with bullets than with arrows; used vessels made of ceramics or metal; provided themselves with grain and vegetables where natural conditions permitted, and so on. On the spiritual side it was at one time also considered self-evident that the Russians' adherence to the Christian religion put them automatically on a higher plane than the heathen, raw-flesh-eating 'savages'. In reality, however, the Russians' 'higher' culture was represented in the seventeenth and eighteenth century by soldiers (men of service) and colonial administrators out for personal gain, and by peasants, whose building-tools were of the simplest – the axe, gouge and spokeshave (although they could do wonders with these).[25] The settlers' attempts at agriculture were frustrated, except on the southern steppe frontier, by frozen subsoil and the sub-arctic climate, and as they were carried out by the primitive 'slash-and-burn' method, were highly destructive of the forest environment. Even with regard to the Russians' superiority in weaponry, the high cost of firearms, powder and lead, not to mention the unreliability of early firearms, restricted their use. Even in the European North many peasants used old flintlocks right up to the first decades of the twentieth century,[26] and in Siberia the use of bows and spears by Russians was not unknown at least as late as the 1830s.[27] The high cost of transporting goods from European Russia made the Russians of Siberia, like the Mongolian and Turkic peoples of its southern regions, largely dependent upon textiles imported from that other centre of high culture – China.[28]

If the economic and social backwardness of the Russian metropolis itself is often invoked to justify the reforms of Peter the Great or the 1917 Revolution, the state of affairs in its vast eastern colony was inevitably much worse in many respects. So far as ethical standards are concerned, the history of armed conquest, yasak extortion, and unscrupulous exploitation by the Russians, speaks for itself, while the conversion of the natives to Orthodox Christianity was mainly a superficial phenomenon induced by threats or material bribes. In any case the ignorance and superstition of the Russians themselves was notorious. Even in regions much closer to the centre of Orthodoxy in Moscow, belief in the powers of wizards was still strong in the early twentieth century, let alone the seventeenth. In the remoteness of Siberia the doctrines of Christianity became very attenuated and distorted, and Russian settlers quite often resorted to the services of shamans – or indeed 'went native' altogether. Thus, if on the one hand the 'civilizing' role of the Russians in Siberia should not be belittled, neither should too much credence be given to nationalistic claims put forward in Russian accounts of the subject, whether before or after the 1917 Revolution.[29]

The many types of indigenous culture which existed in Siberia fall into approximately nine groups.[30] The classic type of pastoral nomadism was practised by the peoples of the south-central region between the river Irtysh and the Xingan mountains of Manchuria, namely, the Turkic tribes of the Altai, Minusinsk and Sayan steppe-lands, including some Kazakhs, and the Buryats and other Mongols south of Lake Baikal. Migrating from pasture to pasture with their herds of horses, cattle and other animals, they lived in a type of portable home (*ger*) consisting of a circular framework covered with felt (which the Russians incorrectly called *yurta*). Their costume reflected Mongolian and Chinese affinities, with coats always wrapped over to the right, having a band of decoration down the right edge, and soft leather, thick-soled boots.

West of the Irtysh in the woodlands along the northern edge of the Kazakh steppe lived the west Siberian Tatars and their neighbours in the Ural foothills, the Bashkirs.[31] These had originally also been nomadic pastoralists, but even by the time of the Russian conquest were partly settled and engaged in agriculture around the Tatar towns such as Tara and Tyumen. Here they abandoned the ger in favour of fixed houses ranging from wattle-and-daub huts in the Baraba steppe to log cabins heated by their own type of open stove, the *chuval*.

At the other extremity of southern Siberia, a number of peoples on the lower reaches of the Amur river, such as the Nanais, Ulchas, Udeghes and Nivkhs, as well as the Itelmens and the Ainu of Kamchatka, lived in the forest, moving between winter and summer villages, making much use of dugout or plank-built boats, and feeding themselves largely by catching fish. Their homes ranged from the large subterranean winter lodges of the Nivkhs to light summer huts of branches, reeds and bark which in some cases were raised on stilts. From the seventeenth century onwards a version of the Manchurian house with hypocausts became widespread among the peoples of the Amur. Here too Chinese influence was apparent in the left-to-right wrap-over outer garment, the shallow conical hat and cotton trousers, and the scroll patterns used for the decoration of clothing and utensils. All of these Far Eastern peoples used dog-teams to draw their sledges.

Dog transport was also the norm among the settled coastal Koryaks, Chukchis and Eskimos of the arctic regions of the extreme north-east, whose main source of food was walrus, seals and whales, to hunt which they ventured out on the cold arctic waters in boats made of walrus hide. A quite different (but economically interdependent) way of life supported the Chukchis and Koryaks of the interior, who roamed the tundra with reindeer herds. Their homes were large tents (*yarangas*) with partitioned-off sleeping quarters heated by means of seal-oil lamps. Originally the coastal Eskimos, Chukchis and Koryaks lived in subterranean lodges like those of the Nivkhs. All the peoples of the far north-east wore two-layer deerskin clothing, the men having a jerkin pulled over the head, while women wore a combination garment.

Among the peoples of the north the Yakuts were unique in having a way of life based upon cattle and horses which, like their Turkic language, betrayed their origins in the steppes of Mongolia. Milk products typical of nomadic pastoralists formed the mainstay of their diet. Their summer homes were large conical structures consisting of poles and bark, and in winter they moved into turf-covered timber lodges heated by open stoves. Craftsmanship in wood, leather, iron and silver was quite highly developed among the Yakuts in the seventeenth century, and they were almost the only north Siberian people to make pottery.

The immediate neighbours of the Yakuts were the Tungus (now known as Evenkis and Evens). They were the classic forest hunters of Siberia, whose family bands moved from place to place, camping in conical, deerskin-covered tents, the most common type of nomadic dwelling in the north, to which the Russians applied the Komi term *chum*. Like most peoples of the forest and tundra, the Tungus depended for their livelihood upon herds of domesticated reindeer, their use of which had several specific features. They did not harness the deer to sledges but transported goods on their backs and rode on them, and they milked the does. A similar way of life was followed by the Turkic-speaking peoples of the Sayan mountains known by two variants of the same clan name as Tuva and Tubalar (or Tofalar). The forest Tungus wore deerskin clothing consisting of long, supple leggings, a loin-cloth, and an edge-to-edge coat with a separate bodice to fill in its open front. On the other hand, the 'Horse Tungus' of the Mongolian borderland, like the related Oroch and Negidal peoples of the lower Amur, adopted the Mongolian wrap-over coat of deerskin or quilted material.

West of the Yenisei, the fishing and hunting economy of the Mansi, Khanty, Selkup and Ket peoples was largely based upon the use of dugout or plank boats, in which they navigated the numerous rivers, lakes and marshes of the Ob basin. Their winter homes were log cabins, either free-standing or half sunk in the earth and covered with turf. In summer they lived in conical tents or huts roofed with birch-bark, and sometimes on houseboats similar in appearance to the Chinese sampan. The transport animal in the middle Ob and Yenisei regions was originally the dog, but its use to pull sledges was on a primitive level, and only the Khantys and Mansis sometimes harnessed dogs in teams. Much of the clothing of the forest peoples of western Siberia was made of cloth woven from nettle or linen fibre, but garments were also made from the skins of deer, fish or birds.

The way of life of the northern Samoeds of western Siberia, now known as Nenets and Enets, was, like that of the Tungus, centred upon reindeer herding. The design of their various types of sledge, and their use of deer teams was highly sophisticated, but their reindeer were never ridden, nor were the does milked. In the arctic conditions of the forest margin and tundra, pullover parkas of deerskin, along with deerskin boots and fur caps, were worn by Nenets men, while women wore long wrap-over fur coats.

A different, and more primitive, form of reindeer culture existed among the Samoed people of the Taimyr Peninsula who were known to the Russians in the seventeenth century as Tavgi (today's Nganasan), and the Yukagirs who at that time occupied a very large area of arctic Siberia east of the river Lena. While each family possessed a few reindeer for harnessing to sledges, they had no herds, and depended entirely upon hunting wild deer, which they followed or waylaid on their seasonal migrations. Food, clothing, and covers for their conical pole-tents were all obtained from the kill, and fish and birds were also caught for food. Because of the roughness of the ground in Taimyr the Tavgi were the only Siberian people who did not use skis.

Neither the locations of the native peoples outlined above, nor their ethnic and cultural features, remained static during the period from the late sixteenth to the nineteenth century. Considerable physical migration took place –

mostly, but not entirely, caused by the activities of the Russians – and some peoples were reduced in numbers almost to vanishing point, while on the other hand at least one new ethno-cultural group was formed.[32] The principal directions of movement discussed below are indicated on map 5.1.

The Russians themselves, along with other people from west of the Urals, settled most densely in a zone approximately 400 to 700 kilometres wide, following the main land route across southern Siberia, with particularly large wedges near the Urals and between Omsk and Krasnoyarsk, where by the late nineteenth century practically no native people remained except for widely scattered villages of Tatars.

It was as a result of the Russian advance across the Urals that many Mansis and Khantys moved away from their homes, the latter crossing the Ob into the middle part of its basin, while some of the Selkups who had lived on the Ob, as well as Kets on the Yenisei, moved off to the north. In their northward migration toward the tundra these peoples encountered the Nenets Samoeds and adopted many features of their reindeer-herding way of life, so that a northern type of Khanty, Selkup and Ket culture developed. The Samoeds themselves, put into turmoil by the Russian invasion, moved partly to the north-east, where beyond the estuary of the Yenisei the separate Enets people became established.

Meanwhile the southern groups of Samoeds and Kets in the upper Yenisei and Sayan regions disappeared, having been assimilated by the Russian, Tungus, Buryat or Turkic peoples. The most important change in this region from the Russian point of view was the withdrawal of the Yenisei Kirgiz to Dzhungaria, which enabled the Russians to complete the subjugation of the Minusinsk 'Tatars' and the Altaians. Farther east on the southern frontier, the wars against the Buryats caused great turmoil up to the end of the seventeenth century, when the back-and-forth migrations of Buryat and Mongol clans was brought to an end by the closing of the frontier between the Russian Empire and Chinese 'Outer Mongolia'. East of Lake Baikal several clans of Evenki Tungus who had formerly herded reindeer went over to horseriding and were partly assimilated to the Buryats, especially in the context of native cossack units.

To the north-west of Lake Baikal it was the Evenkis who absorbed Ket people as they advanced westward to the Yenisei and beyond. Other Evenki clans sought to avoid subjection to the Russians by moving north of the Angara, and some of these also crossed the Yenisei into Nenets territory.[33] Farther to the north-east, in Taimyr, it was the influx of Evenkis and Yakuts into land inhabited by Tavgi Samoeds that led to complex ethnic mixing and the emergence of the new nationality known as Dolgans. This name comes from one of the Tungus clans, but their language is a dialect of Yakut. As a result of this intrusion the Nganasans were pushed farther north into the tundra, and a lasting enmity between them and the Dolgans was created. This was only one of the many directions in which the Yakut people spread from their homeland on the Lena.[34] Even before the advent of the Russians some Yakuts had established themselves far to the north on the river Yana, where the Russian fort of Verkhoyansk was founded. As they adapted themselves to reindeer-herding and continued to expand towards the north-east, the Yakuts absorbed the original Yukagir inhabitants of the tundra as far east as the Kolyma river. Far from being crushed as a nation by the Russian conquest, the Yakuts succeeded in adapting to the ways of their conquerors and extended their own influence over their Tungus and Yukagir neighbours, not to mention the Russians themselves. As a result, in the nineteenth century a national region which could fairly be called Yakutia extended over 1,6000 kilometres from the Vilyui river to the Kolyma and nearly as far from the middle Lena to the shores of the Arctic Ocean.

The other self-assertive people of eastern Siberia were the Chukchis who, despite the Russian campaigns of the eighteenth century, advanced far beyond their original homeland in the farthest corner of the north-east into the territory of the Yukagirs, whom they absorbed. Thus the Yukagirs almost disappeared as a people, partly through assimilation to their stronger neighbours, and partly because of the disruption of the whole Yukagir community by the recruitment of their menfolk as native auxiliaries in the Russian campaigns against other native peoples, such as the Lamuts or Even Tungus of the Okhotsk seaboard.

Other peoples which virtually disappeared from the map as a result of Russian colonialism were the Itelmens of Kamchatka[35] and, eventually, their southern neighbours the Ainu. The latter, a uniquely interesting people distinct from all their neighbours both physically and culturally,[36] were driven out of the Kuril Islands and Sakhalin by the Russo-Japanese territorial conflicts which began in the nineteenth century. Lastly, the sad record of colonialism in the far north-east includes the name of the Aleuts, who were largely annihilated by the Russians during the latters' trans-Pacific adventure in pursuit of sea-otter furs.

It is not surprising that the general trends for the indigenous population of the Russian colony of Siberia from the seventeenth to the nineteenth century were that some individuals, mainly 'chiefs' or traders, adapted to the ways of their conquerors and became successful according to the standards of Russian society, while the mass of their compatriots, exploited by the Russian system and lacking any means of redress, fell increasingly into poverty and degradation. It was because of this, along with the commonplaces of fashionable racial theory, that most educated Russians at the beginning of the twentieth century were convinced that practically all the smaller peoples of Siberia were irrevocably doomed to extinction.

NOTES AND REFERENCES

1 See N. Ya. Bichurin (Iakinf), *Sobranie svedenii o narodakh, obitavshikh v Srednei Azii v drevnie vremena* (St Petersburg, 1951), Pt I reprinted (Moscow, 1950).

2 See I.S. Gurvich (ed.), *Etnogenez narodov Severa* (Moscow, 1980); A.P. Okladnikov, 'Drevnee naselenie Sibiri i ego kultura', in M.G. Levin and L.P. Potapov (eds), *Narody Sibiri* (Moscow, 1956); A.P. Okladnikov, (ed.), *Istoriya Sibiri s drevneishikh vremen do nashikh dnei* 1 (Leningrad, 1968–9).

3 V.V. Vinogradov (ed.), *Yazyki narodov SSSR* (Moscow, 1966–8) vol. V, *Mongolskie, tunguso-manchzhurskie i paleoaziatskie yazyki.*

4 Vinogradov, *Yazyki narodov*, op. cit., vols II, III and V.

5 B.O. Dolgikh, *Rodovoi i plemennoi sostav narodov Sibiri v XVII v.* (Moscow, 1960); see also estimates in Okladnikov (ed.), *Istoriya Sibiri*, op. cit., 1: 412, 416, etc. The figures in the table given here are totals for these nationalities living at that time approximately within the borders of the present-day USSR. In the territory actually held by Russia during most of the seventeenth century, the total number of these nationalities was probably only about 160,000 (Dolgikh, p. 615).

6 Okladnikov (ed.) *Istoriya Sibiri*, op. cit., 2: 55–6, 183, 363; V.M. Kabuzan, *Dalnevostochyi krai v XVII-nachale XX vv.* (Moscow, 1985), p. 159. Up to the nineteenth century, population figures in the Russian Empire took account only of tax-paying adult males (*revizionnye dushi*). In order to arrive at an estimate of the total population including women and children, multiplication of such figures by four (sometimes more) has been widely used, as in the figures given here (cf. Levin and Potapov (eds), *Narody Sibiri*, op. cit., pp. 123–4; Dolgikh, *Rodovoi i plemennoi sostav*, op. cit., pp. 12–13).

7 For example, Dolgikh, *Rodovoi i plemennoi sostav*, op. cit., p. 617; Okladnikov (ed.), *Istoriya Sibiri*, op. cit., 2: 60, 98–9, 105, 294, 299 etc., and many other Soviet works.

8 L.V. Khomich, *Nentsy: istoriko-etnograficheskie ocherki* (Moscow, 1966), pp. 144–6; Okladnikov (ed.), *Istoriya Sibiri*, op. cit., 1: pp. 391, 398.

9 Levin and Potapov (eds), *Narody Sibiri*, op. cit., pp. 97, 101, 378, 935 etc.

10 I.S. Vdovin (ed.), *Priroda i chelovek v religioznykh predstavleniyakh narodov Sibiri i Severa* (Leningrad, 1976); A.F. Anisimov, *Religiya evenkov v istoriko-geneticheskom izuchenii i problemy proiskhozhdeniya pervobytnykh verovanii* (Moscow, 1958).

11 M.A. Sergeev, *Nekapitalisticheskii put razvitiya malykh narodov Severa* (Moscow, 1955), pp. 150–90, discusses *nimat* and other aspects of mutual aid.

12 V.G. Bogoraz, *The Chukchee (Memoirs of the American Museum of Natural History)* XI pp. 537–51, 598–607 (Leiden, 1904–9). L. Ya. Shternberg, *Gilyaki, orochi, goldy, negidaltsy, ayny. Stati i materialy* (Khabarovsk, 1933), pp. 30–45, 246–50.

13 Levin and Potapov (eds), *Narody Sibiri*, op. cit., pp. 870–2, 916–17, 966 and 981.

14 V. Diószegi (ed.), *Popular Beliefs and Folklore Tradition in Siberia* (Bloomington, 1968); V. Diószegi and M. Hoppál, *Shamanism in Siberia* (Budapest, 1978); U. Holmberg (Harva), *Finno-Ugric, Siberian (The Mythology of all Races)* IV (Boston, 1927); a recent work on a specific nationality is M. Kenin-Lopsan, *Obryadovaya praktika i folklor tuvinskogo shamanstva* (Novosibirsk, 1987).

15 Ye. Ye. Syroechkovskii, in V.A. Tugolukov, *Sledopyty verkhom na olenyakh* (Moscow, 1969), p. 9.
16 C.S. Coon, *The Hunting Peoples* (London, 1972), pp. 388–92.
17 M.N. Bogdanov, *Ocherki istorii Buryat-mongolskogo naroda* (Verkhneudinsk, 1926), pp. 44–76. The contorted process of diverting historians from the idea that the Buryats were conquered to the view that they submitted to the Russians voluntarily, and that their society was in the early stages of feudalism at the time, is traced in Ye. M. Zalkind, *Prisoedinenie Buryatii k Rossii* (Ulan-Ude, 1958). As a result of this ideological, pro-Russian, rewriting of history, the first volume of *Istoriya Buryat-mongolskoi ASSR* (1951) was deemed by the Communist Party to be incorrect, and replaced in 1954 by a new 'corrected' vol. I; cf. P.T. Khaptaev *et al.* (eds), *Istoriya Buryatskoi ASSR* II: 590 (Ulan-Ude, 1959).
18 Ya. P. Alkor and B.D. Grekov (eds), *Kolonialnaya politika moskovskogo gosudarstva v Yakutii XVIIv.* (Leningrad, 1936); Ya. P. Alkor and A.K. Drezen (eds), *Kolonialnaya politika tsarizma na Kamchatke i Chukotke v XVIII veke* (Leningrad, 1935).
19 B.P. Gurevich, *Mezhdunarodnye otnosheniya v Tsentralnoi Azii v XVII – pervoi polovine XIXv.* (Moscow, 1979).
20 *Entsiklopedicheskii slovar* XXIX: 759 (St Petersburg, 1890–1907), and articles on specific *gubernii* in other volumes.
21 G.V. Glinka (ed.), *Aziatskaya Rossiya* I: 82–5 (St Petersburg, 1914).
22 S.V. Bakhrushin, *Ostyatskie i vogulskie knyazhestva v XVI–XVII vekakh* (Leningrad, 1935).
23 The most informative accounts are: S.S. Shashkov, *Istoricheskie etyudy* II (St Petersburg, 1872); N.M. Yadrintsev, *Sibir kak koloniya* (St Petersburg, 1882); P.A. Slovtsov, *Istoricheskoe obozrenie Sibiri* (St Petersburg, 1886). The Soviet *Istoriya Sibiri* tones down the negative effects of Russian occupation.
24 I.S. Gurvich (ed.), *Etnicheskaya istoriya narodov Severa* (Moscow, 1982), pp. 58, 71, 95, 101, 103, 156, 164–5, 171, 176, 184, 216, 219.
25 V.A. Aleksandrov *et al.* (eds), *Russkie: istoriko-etnograficheskii atlas. Zemledelie. Krestyanskoe zhilishche. Krestyanskaya odezhda* (Moscow, 1967), pp. 168–70.
26 V.A. Aleksandrov *et al.* (eds), *Narody evropeyskoi chasti SSSR* I: p. 280 (Moscow, 1964).
27 Bogoraz, *The Chukchee*, op. cit., p. 698.
28 Levin and Potapov (eds), *Narody Sibiri*, op. cit., pp. 176–7.
29 See for example, Glinka, *Aziatskaya Rossiya*, op. cit., I: 200–25; Levin and Potapov (eds) *Narody Sibiri*, pp. 201–11.
30 In addition to *Narody Sibiri*, general accounts include S.A. Tokarev, *Etnografiya narodov SSSR* (Moscow, 1958), pp. 409–557; M.A. Czaplicka, *Aboriginal Siberia, a Study in Social Anthropology* (Oxford, 1914); V.I. Iokhelson, *Peoples of Asiatic Russia* (New York, 1928).
31 V.N. Belitser *et al.* (eds), *Narody evropeiskoi chasti SSSR* II: 682, 688–91 (Moscow, 1964).
32 Gurvich, *Etnicheskaya istoriya narodov Severa*, op. cit.; I.S. Gurvich (ed.), *Narody Dalnego Vostoka SSSR v XVII-XXvv.: Istoriko-etnograficheskie ocherki* (Moscow, 1985); Okladnikov (ed.), *Istoriya Sibiri*, op. cit., 2: 55–60, 285–99.
33 The widespread migrations of the Tungus are traced in V.A. Tugolukov, *Tungusy (evenki i eveny) Srednei i Zapadnoi Sibiri* (Moscow, 1985).

34 *Istoriya Yakutskoi ASSR* II: 145-6, 177-8 (Moscow, 1955-63).
35 A.S. Sgibnev, *Istoricheskii ocherk glavneishikh sobytii v Kamchatke s 1650 po 1856* (St Petersburg, 1869).
36 J.J. Stephan, *The Kuril Islands: Russo-Japanese Frontier in the Pacific* (Oxford, 1974), pp. 22-31, 46-55, 104-111.

6   Tsarist Russia in colonial America: critical constraints

James R. Gibson

Today the Soviet Union, notwithstanding anti-Soviet propaganda, encompasses less territory than the Russian Empire at its maximum. The USSR did gain considerable territory as a result of the Second World War, especially along its western frontier, but tsarist Russia had at one time or another possessed all of these lands (except the northern part of East Prussia and the Subcarpathian Ukraine) plus much more, including all of Finland and Poland, as well as Alaska. The last was one of the few acquisitions that she relinquished willingly. It was sold to the United States in 1867, the same year that saw the close of the colonial era in North America with the creation of the Dominion of Canada. Why Russian America did not last is the question this chapter seeks to answer (see Map 6.1).

Muscovy expanded slowly but steadily into the Russian Empire mainly from a need for more security. The location of the Eastern Slavs amid the Baltic Sea–Black Sea isthmus and alongside the Eurasian steppe corridor exposed them to frequent invasions by powerful and aggressive neighbours, be they Swedish armies, Germanic knights, or Tatar nomads. They had to be defeated and either repulsed behind defensible frontiers, such as the coasts of the Baltic and Black Seas, or annexed, like the cossack hosts and the Crimean Tatars. This precarious situation made for a garrison mentality and put a premium on security.

To the east, however, there was no major menace to Moscow. The khanates of Kazan and Sibir, likewise remnants of the Golden Horde but lacking a powerful ally like Ottoman Turkey, and a natural stronghold like the Crimean Peninsula, did not pose a serious threat. Here the motive for expansion was economic – 'soft gold'. Luxury fur-bearers, long a mainstay of the Russian economy, had by the seventeenth century been depleted in the 'land of darkness', that is, northern European Russia.[1] But the taiga habitat extended across the lowly Urals, so *promyshlenniki* (hunters) simply pushed eastwards on the 'river roads' to tap virgin stocks.[2] And once the Eastern Ocean was reached, Siberia's sables and squirrels were supplanted by the North Pacific's sea otters and fur seals. North China paid even more for sea-otter skins than Western Europe did for sable pelts. Sea-otter fur was so valuable that the Russians in Alaska did little else except pursue what they called the 'sea beaver', and they pursued the haplesss creature to the brink of extinction. So preoccupied were they with the fur trade that when it declined, thanks to the depletion of the fur source and the collapse of the fur market, so, too, did Russian America. As a government inspector concluded in 1862, 'the [Russian-American] Company', which ran the colony, 'has been preoccupied by profits to be realized from the fur trade and has consequently focused its attention exclusively on that subject'.[3] Economic diversification was attempted but it was late and lame, with only Alaskan ice being able to compete in distant markets.[4] Indeed, the most profitable of the company's new ventures, the Shanghai tea trade, did not even take place in Russian America, and was only partly based upon Russian American furs.

More importantly, Russian America really had no agricultural foundation. The mother country's serfs were immobilized until the emancipation manifesto of 1861, too late for the Alaskan colony (and even then their mobility was not full-fledged). Serfs did flee their oppressive landlords – state, church, or gentry – anyway, of course, but Russia's Ukrainian and western Siberian frontiers were much closer than Alaska's. And population pressure on the farmland of European Russia did not become uncontainable until well into the nineteenth century, again too late for Russian America.[5] Moreover, the intervening opportunities of southern European Russia and southern Siberia deprived Russian America of the benefits of 'pull' as well as 'push' factors. The southern steppe had what Alaska did not: plenty of fertile soil. So the Alaskan colony lacked an agricultural basis for both substantiating Russia's claim and sustaining its colonists.

The obsession with the fur trade was the fault of the Russian-American Company. It was a joint-stock concern which had been formed in 1799 by the merger of several private Siberian companies that had been competing intensely and sometimes violently for the peltry of the Gulf of Alaska. It was granted a twenty-year charter and a monopoly on the exploitation of Alaska. Founded under the patronage of the tsar, the company came under more and more state control as its profit margin increased and its foreign contacts multiplied. The firm's commercial affairs were managed by a board of four directors, who were elected by the stockholders. They constituted the Head Office, which was moved from Irkutsk to St Petersburg in 1800. In 1811 the Head Office was placed under the control of the Ministry of Internal Affairs, and in 1819 it was transferred to the jurisdiction of the Ministry of Finance.[6] The company's political affairs were directed by an imperial correspondent from 1799 and by a state council from 1804.

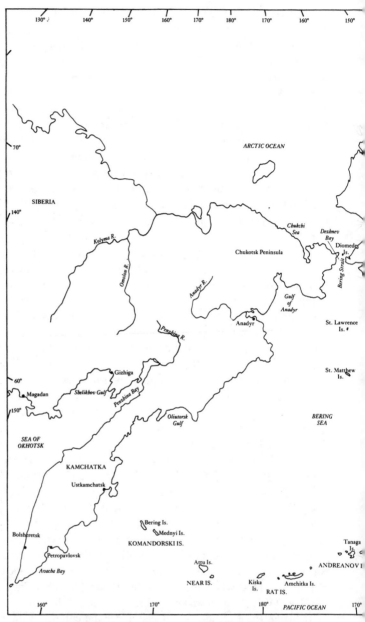

Map 6.1 Nineteenth-century Siberia and Russian America
Source: Dmytryshyn, B. Crownhart-Vaughan, E.A.P. and Vaughan, T. (eds) *Russia's Conquest of Siberia, a documentary record 1558–1700*: pp. xcii–xciii.

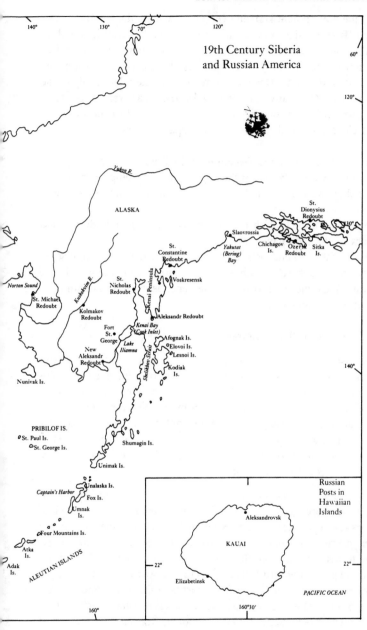

19th Century Siberia
and Russian America

Presumably the government kept an even closer eye on the company after the so-called 'first Russian revolution', the abortive Decembrist revolt at the end of 1825 on the part of young, idealistic radicals, many of them guards officers. The word 'presumably' is deliberately chosen because, despite the voluminous literature on the Decembrist movement, the relationship of the Russian-American Company and the *Dekabristy* has yet to be fully explored.[7] The tribunal of enquiry revealed that several of the insurrectionists had close links with the company, apparently owing to:

1. The keen interest of some Decembrists in Russian America, partly because they were in favour of the expansion of the empire and partly because they were interested in the Americas as sources of liberal political ideas.
2. The desire of the Decembrists to strengthen ties with disaffected members of the merchant class.
3. The liking of the Decembrists for the 'freedom and equality' of discussion within the company, with a variety of topics, including politics, being raised and the right to vote being dependent upon shareholding, not rank and station.[8]

In the words of one of the conspirators:

It [the Russian-American Company] was the sole institution whose general meetings offered some sort of model form of freedom and equality – freedom in the discussion of affairs outside the local and one-sided sphere of some narrow speciality and involving the management of an entire territory and, consequently and unavoidably, of political matters to some extent; and equality because here not rank and position in society, but the number of shares conferred the right to vote, and the petty bourgeois was equal to the noble personage.[9]

After the December fiasco on Senate Square the merchant element in the company was more quiescent, for several prominent members, including the directors Ivan Prokofev and Nikolai Kusov and the prominent stockholder Admiral Nikolai Mordvinov, were on friendly and even sympathetic terms with some of the would-be revolutionaries. One of the ringleaders, the poet Kondratii Ryleev, was the company's office manager at 72 Moika Street, where he had a free apartment that sometimes served as a meeting place for his fellow conspirators.[10] Several other Decembrists, including Wilhelm Küchelbecker, V.P. Romanov, Konstantin Torson, and Dmitrii Zavalishin, travelled to Russian America. In addition, it was intended that Zavalishin become commandant of Russian California and Gavril Batenkov, yet another Decembrist, governor of Russian America. Upon hearing that still another rebel, Orest Somov, was employed by the company, Nicholas I is reported to have said: 'You've collected some fine company there'.[11]

Not only was the company transformed from a business firm into a government department: at the same time it became less of a civilian and more of a military organization. From the very beginning naval officers were assigned to the company's ships, and from 1818 all governors of Russian America were officers in the imperial navy. In 1844, in accordance with the company's third (and last) twenty-year charter, the Board of Directors regained control of political affairs and was enlarged to five members, comprising one merchant and four military officers. From 1857 none of the directors was a member of the merchant class.[12]

These changes seriously impaired the efficiency of the company as a commercial enterprise. First, it was increasingly bureaucratized, which meant longer delays in decision-making, less attention to commercial and more to administrative matters, more reluctance to take risks, and a superfluity of personnel. For example, with the renewal of the company's charter in 1821, employees were placed on salaries instead of shares. Their incomes were thus stabilized but at the same time their incentive to produce was weakened. The second charter also saw the company provide more services – medical, educational, and ecclesiastical – in its colony, and in doing so the company acted more and more as an administrating body and less and less as a trading firm. Again, a golden opportunity to expand the company's exclave in California inland – and thereby render it agriculturally viable – was missed when the reactionary Nicholas I refused to have any relations with revolutionary and republican Mexico.[13] The company's overstaffing was remarked by officials of its British counterpart and competitor, the venerable Hudson's Bay Company. Chief Factor James Douglas, the future first governor of British Columbia, visited New Archangel (now Sitka), Russian America's capital, and the outpost of St Dionysius Redoubt, in 1840, and found that the company's business 'does not appear to be conducted with system or that degree of well judged economy, so necessary in extensive concerns'. He added that both establishments were 'crowded with men and Officers, living in idleness or in employments equally unnecessary and Profitless to the business'.[14] Douglas's boss, George Simpson, governor of the Honourable Company's territories in North America, and admittedly a stickler for economy, was similarly deprecatory. At New Archangel in 1842 he noted that the conduct of business

differs very much from that which we pursue, being characterized by a formal display and routine, in humble imitation of a Government establishment, admitting in my opinion of many improvements, and of curtailments or reductions, which of themselves would produce a very considerable gain in the shape of savings.[15]

In his published travel account Simpson stated that 'for the amount of business done, the men, as well as the officers, appear to be unnecessarily numerous'.[16] Four years earlier Simpson had visited St Petersburg to negotiate with the Russian-American Company's directors. There he met Baron Stenglozh, a leading banker and merchant and a major shareholder in the company, who told Simpson that its affairs were 'badly conducted' and its business 'so secretly managed by old fashioned Russians who have a crafty illiberal system of management that it is difficult to do any thing with them'. The uncharitable Simpson also found, incidentally, that most of the directors were 'Stupid to a Degree'; the company's chief director, Andrei Severin, was 'a Stupid old thief who professes to know every thing about the country & Trade but really knows nothing'.[17]

Second, the more that the Russian government controlled the company, the more decisions were made on political rather than economic grounds. For instance, in 1818, following the dismissal of Russian America's first and last merchant governor, the Head Office prohibited the sale of colonial furs to foreign ships, and in 1821 the tsar issued a decree banning foreign vessels from the coast of Russian America and setting 51° North as the colony's southern boundary. New Archangel, or Sitka, as it was increasingly called, was thereby deprived of its usual source of supply – Yankee fur-trading vessels, which had been bringing provisions and manufactures in exchange for fur-seal skins, but also selling guns and spirits to the Tlingit Indians in colonial waters and allegedly inciting them against the Russians. Now Sitka had to rely on Mexican California, where crop failures were periodic and export charges sizeable, and on European Russia, whose shipments via Kronstadt were twice as costly as American deliveries.[18] As a result, the dividend that the company paid its stockholders in 1820 and 1821 was only half that of 1818 and 1819, and from 1822 to 1826 no dividend at all was paid, with the company facing bankruptcy.[19] So the company reopened its colonial waters and ports to American ships in 1824 and to British ships in 1825 under the terms of ten-year conventions. The ultimate non-economic decision affecting the company was the sale of its territory to the United States in 1867. When the Russian government raised the prospect in the last half of the 1850s, the Russian-American Company was still very much in the black. It was still serving its economic purpose (to make money) but it was no longer meeting its political purpose (to promote Russian imperialist expansion). By then there were no longer any imperialist opportunities left in North America; they had been conceded to Great Britain and the United States, and Russian America was outflanked. But there *were* attractive opportunities in Asia, and they were much closer to home. Just as the decline of the Sublime Porte had raised the Eastern Question and eased Russian expansion into the Caucasus, so now the waning of the Manchu dynasty weakened its indirect control over the steppe pasturelands, irrigated croplands, and mercantile cities of western Turkestan and its direct control over the supposed bread basket, fur reserve, and commercial waterway of the Amur basin. In addition, the decline of the Tokugawa Shogunate invited Russian encroachment on Japan's northern marchlands of Sakhalin and the Kurils. And this realignment of imperialist policy was facilitated by the mood of reform in Russia following its disastrous defeat in the Crimean War, the same conflict that underlined the indefensibility of Russian America by the overtaxed imperial navy, headed by the tsar's brother, Grand Duke Constantine, who favoured a sale. So the empire's sole overseas colony was relinquished in favour of plumper prospects abutting the motherland.[20]

Third, the Russian-American Company was increasingly militarized as well as politicized and bureaucratized. The military element surged from the late 1810s, when Russian America was inspected by a naval officer, Vasilii Golovnin, who was sharply critical of the concern.[21] This ascendancy did not quell the class conflict that had erupted between Russian shipmasters and the first governor, Aleksandr Baranov, an old-style trader who was described by Washington Irving as 'a rough, rugged, hospitable, hard-drinking old Russian; somewhat of a soldier; somewhat of a trader; above all, a boon companion of the old roystering school, with a strong cross of the bear'.[22] The worst incident occurred in 1816, when Lieutenant Mikhail Lazarev, commander of the *Suvorov*, left New Archangel against Baranov's orders and under fire.[23] The naval officers, who belonged to the nobility and gentry, disdained the untitled and untutored merchants as socially inferior and administratively unfit, while the merchants considered the officers commercially inept.[24] The latter, although they might be able administrators, were neither trained nor experienced in business. The Bay man, James Douglas, noted this failing:

> A decidedly vicious and ill advised feature in the management of this business is the appointment of Naval officers, a class of men ignorant of and by their previous habits of life the most unqualified to manage commercial undertakings, to the principal direction [of the company] and these after holding their stations five years and acquiring some knowledge of business are withdrawn and replaced by others who have also every thing to learn & who are in like manner removed at the moment they are qualified to render efficient service.[25]

Furthermore, as a mercantile monopoly, the Russian-American Company was bound not to be in the best long-term interests of its colony in a couple of other respects. The company had been chartered to administer and develop its territory exclusively. And in the best mercantilist tradition, just as the Russian government exerted economic control through the mechanism of a trading company, so, too, did the company exercise its mandate to the benefit of the motherland first and the colony second. These priorities, of course, favoured the permanence of the former over the latter. Also, as a monopoly, the company was deprived of the need to maintain a competitive edge, and it became complacent and inefficient. Hence, in part, its overstaffing. Hence, too, the high price of goods in the colony. As a government inspector found in 1860–61,

> the Company assumed responsibility for provisioning the colonies through its own means with all necessities. There was no competition from anyone. This has led to the situation that all items supplied to the colonies are to a large degree either cheaply made or of a very mediocre quality, and they are sold at very high prices.[26]

The company imposed a mark-up of 42 per cent on such imports to cover hauling and handling. This surcharge covered costs and even left a profit; in addition, however, another mark-up of 35 per cent was put on their retail prices, and the resultant profit was so great as to constitute one of the company's chief sources of revenue.[27] Competition from either British or American goods would have lowered prices and improved quality.

The company had to import provisions because of the lack of agricultural settlers. And this lack was indicative of a larger constraint: the shortage of manpower, despite the firm's topheaviness. The colony's total white population seldom exceeded 700 (it peaked at 823 in 1839).[28] Again, the immobility of serfdom was partly responsible, but even non-serfs were reluctant to go to Russian America. The other corners of the empire – Siberian, Far Eastern, Transcaucasian, Central Asian – were less remote and less brutish. And Russian America was rendered even more unattractive by its rainy climate, heavy work, meagre pay, and spare diet.[29] Hence a churchman's remark that 'it is better to go into the army than to go to [Russian] America'[30] (and at that time military service normally lasted twenty-five years). Even the colonial capital, where goods and services were better than elsewhere in the colony, was referred to as 'barbarous, desolate Sitka' by Governor Semen Yanovskii (1818–21), and in 1842, when with some 1,000 residents it vied with San Francisco (Yerba Buena) as the largest town on the entire Pacific Coast of North America, it was ranked by a well-travelled British visitor as the 'most wretched and most dirty' place that he had ever seen.[31] In 1838 Governor Ivan Kupreyanov bemoaned the 'utter shortage of workers in the colony at present', and in 1846 Governor Mikhail Tebenkov complained that 'there is much work but no men.'[32] Those who died or left often outnumbered new recruits. From 1838 to 1842, for example, there was a loss of 181 workers and a gain of only 67 for a deficit of 114.[33] Furthermore, the few men who did opt for Russian America were mostly of the worst sort: drunkards and hooligans. Only they were foolish enough or desperate enough to countenance the punitive working conditions. The commandant of Okhotsk reported in 1815 that most of the company's workers were boozers and ruffians.[34] In 1852 ex-governor Tebenkov acknowledged that 'not only will a *good* worker not go to the colony but a good man can get there only accidentally'.[35] By contrast, the company enjoyed several very able colonial governors, such as Ferdinand von Wrangell, Adolph Etholen, and Tebenkov himself, but their efforts were frustrated by the riff-raff of workers. Moreover, employees were debilitated further by corporate neglect of their welfare. There was no doctor or infirmary at New Archangel before 1820. In 1860 Pavel Golovin, a government inspector, was sailing from San Francisco to Sitka aboard the company's ship *Tsaritsa* when a Finnish crewman died of pneumonia, and the inspector commented:

> *The Company does not provide either a doctor or a feldsher on its ships*, and since neither the captain nor the navigator had any knowledge of how to treat this illness, although they are good naval specialists, the poor sailor, lacking adequate treatment, departed from this world to the next, *where he will probably be better off than in the service of the Russian American Company*.[36]

Increasingly the company relied upon Alaska's natives and creoles (mixed bloods) for manpower.[37] Their life-style and value system, however, did not always satisfy Russian requirements. Also, their numbers were decimated by epidemics of smallpox in the last half of the 1830s[38] and the early 1860s, and measles in the late 1840s, just as the Russian workers were debilitated by scurvy and respiratory and rheumatic ailments associated with malnutrition, drunkenness, and dankness. Russian America remained chronically undermanned.

The colony also remained undersupplied, especially with respect to food.[39] The Russian colonists were neither numerous enough nor competent enough to support local manufacturing. And Alaska's physical environment – even if sufficient peasants had been available – severely limited agricultural output. The growing season was short and cool and the soil cover was limited and mediocre, even in coastal, insular, and southern Alaska, where the Russians were overwhelmingly concentrated. And the natives – Aleuts, Eskimos, and Indians – were fishers and hunters, not farmers. So the Russian-American Company was left with three logistical options: shipment from European Russia either overseas around the Horn or the Cape on company and navy ships or overland across Siberia to Okhotsk, Russia's foremost Pacific port, and thence across the far North Pacific; extra-territorial colonization of promising places not far from Alaska; and international trade with visiting vessels (mostly American Nor'west coasters), foreign colonies (chiefly Alta California), and rival companies (mainly the Hudson's Bay Company). The first option took too long and cost too much, largely because it was crippled by three factors that in themselves helped to both define and defeat Russian America: remoteness, maritimity, and backwardness. New Archangel, the colonial capital, and St Petersburg, the imperial capital and company headquarters, were almost exactly halfway around the world from each other, or nearly 10,000 kilometres apart as the crow flies (but considerably more, of course, as the Russian rode, and much, much more as he sailed). This 'space friction', or 'tyranny of distance' to an Anglocentric Australian, prolonged transportation and communication. If Tsar Nicholas I really did say that 'Russia suffers from its distances', then Russian America must have been in a good deal of pain. To extend a Siberian saying, God was too high above and the tsar was too far away. During his tour of inspection of the colony in 1860–61 Captain Golovin remarked:

> Here it is just as if we were in some desert where the voice of educated persons is rarely heard . . . if it were not for the isolation from the rest of the world, and the severe climate, then it would be possible to live here. All the same, thank God I do not have to.[40]

Moreover, as Russia's only overseas colony (and therefore, by some definitions, Russia's only true colony) Russian America had to be reached in part by sea, and the disposition of the colony itself, of course, was maritime, since its *raison d'être* was the hunting of two marine mammals, the sea otter and the fur seal. Russians did have plenty of experience in riverine and coastal boating but not in oceanic shipping.[41] They did not circumnavigate the globe until 1806, nearly 300 years after Magellan did so for Spain and 225 years after Drake for England (and even fifteen years after Gray for the United States). Foreigners had to be enlisted as shipwrights and navigators (the Dane, Vitus Bering, comes immediately to mind), and young Russian midshipmen were sent abroad for training in the British and French navies (such as Adam von Krusenstern and Yurii Lisianskii themselves, who commanded the first Russian circumnavigation, and on two ships, moreover, that had been bought in England). The Russian-American Company, too, had to buy foreign ships and hire foreign mariners (and it employed not a few Finnish seamen after Finland became a duchy of the empire in 1809). During the twenty years of its first charter the company built fifteen vessels in the colony and bought thirteen from foreigners, mainly Americans.[42] The situation improved considerably when naval officers were appointed governors of the colony and commanders of company ships from 1818.

Nevertheless, distance and other problems remained. On the Siberian overland route winter cold, spring *rasputitsa* (breakup), summer *gnusy* (literally, 'vile ones', that is, winged, blood-sucking insects), and autumn *bezdorozhe* (literally, 'roadlessness') were formidable barriers. Particularly problematical was the 1,100-kilometre-long obstacle course between Yakutsk and Okhotsk. During the first half of the nineteenth century from 10,000 to 15,000 Yakut pack-horses annually hauled freight on this trail, and up to half of them died every year.[43] The well-travelled George Simpson, who in his passion for expedition and endurance had himself gained a well-deserved reputation as a hard driver of man and beast, was appalled by the toll of horses when he took the route in the summer of 1842:

When compared with this corner of the world, England, which is sometimes said to be the hell of horses, must be contented with the secondary honour of being their purgatory. The unfortunate brutes here lie down to die, in great numbers, through famine and fatigue; and this road is more thickly strewed with their bones than any part of the plains on the Saskatchewan with those of the buffalo.[44]

Around 1820 a shocked Mikhail Speranskii, who was serving as Governor-General of Siberia on his way back into official favour after his sudden fall from grace in 1812 as one of Tsar Alexander I's most influential ministers, urged that the Russian Far East and Russian America be supplied overseas in order to avoid the equine carnage.[45] (Incidentally, Speranskii, one-time liberal reformer, became more conservative upon his return to favour, and in 1826 he was the most active member of the tribunal that tried the Decembrist plotters. One of the five who were sentenced to death, the brilliant Pavel Pestel, was the leader of the Southern Society, the most radical of the conspiratorial groups, and the son of a notorious Governor of Siberia. One of the 116 who were sentenced to Siberian exile, Vladimir Shteingel, was the son of a former commandant of Kamchatka.)

Speranskii's advice notwithstanding, the oceanic route was little better, what with enemy warships, storms, calms, reefs, fog, and scurvy. During its first twenty-year charter the Russian-American Company owned thirty-two ships, and exactly half of them were wrecked.[46] Spoilage of foodstuffs one way and furs the other by heat and damp was not uncommon. Also, the building of ships and the training of sailors was costly. Oceanic supply in the first half of the 1820s (with the loss of three ships and one-third of the crew of another) nearly broke the company, even though the expense of transport on naval vessels should have been mitigated by the fact that they served other purposes as well, namely, to show the flag in the international arena of the North Pacific, to protect Russian America from native enemies and foreign rivals, to train Russian seamen, and to discover and explore.[47] Still, the overseas route was much cheaper than the overland channel. It cost the company from two to three and a half times as much to send supplies across Siberia as far as Okhotsk only, as around the world all the way to Sitka.[48]

Backwardness was a proverbial Russian condition, exemplified by the retention of serfdom until 1861, the lateness of industrialization (the last third of the nineteenth century), the prolongation of autocracy until 1917 (even, some might argue, until 1953), and the rural dominance of the population until 1961 (when, for the first time in Russian history, at least half of all citizens were urban). The country was, to borrow the phrase of the compilers of some Elizabethan accounts of Muscovy, a 'rude and barbarous kingdom'. Or, as one of the condemned Decembrist leaders is supposed to have said on the gallows when his executioners botched the first attempt, 'Poor Russia, they don't even know how to hang properly!' (and Ryleev, another of the condemned whose hanging was bungled, is alleged to have exclaimed: 'I have failed at everything, even at dying!').[49] In Russian America managerial and technological backwardness were more critical than elsewhere because here there was simply less room for error, conditions being so marginal. Indeed, the colony, given its distant location, small population, and technological atavism, was a classic example of peripheralization. Backwardness marked two of the Russian-American Company's principal activities: hunting and shipping. The promyshlenniki never even bothered to learn how to bag sea otters from a kayak,[50] being content instead to enserf the expert Aleuts and Kodiaks. Pelts were poorly cured, and their resultant mediocre quality reduced their competitiveness on the international market. From 1800 to 1802 one-third of the take of 900,000 fur-seal skins on the Pribilof Islands spoiled, and in the last half of the decade another 1,000,000 skins were lost.[51] In 1827 a Russian naval officer found that the company's best ships at New Archangel were those that had been bought from American traders, and in 1832 another officer decried the shortage of healthy, skilled sailors in the colony.[52] Richard Henry Dana, Jr, was certainly not impressed with the company's brig *Polifem* or its crew at San Francisco in 1835, writing as follows in his *Two Years Before the Mast*, a classic account of the California hide and tallow trade:

Though no longer than the Pilgrim [Dana's ship], she had five or six officers, and a crew of between twenty and thirty; and such a stupid and greasy-looking set, I never saw before. Although it was quite comfortable weather and we had nothing on but straw hats, shirts, and duck trousers, and were bare-footed, they had, every man of them, double-soled boots, coming up to the knees, and well greased; thick woollen trousers, frocks, waistcoats, pea-jackets, woollen caps, and everything in true Nova Zembla rig; and in the warmest days they made no change. The clothing of one of these men would weigh nearly as much as that of half our crew. They had brutish faces, looked like the antipodes of sailors, and apparently dealt in nothing but grease. They lived upon grease; ate it, drank it, slept in the midst of it, and their clothes were covered with it. To a Russian, grease is the greatest luxury. They looked with greedy eyes upon the tallow-bags as they were taken into the vessel, and, no doubt, would have eaten one up whole, had not the officer kept watch over it. The grease appeared to fill their pores, and to come out in their hair and on their faces. It seems as if it were this saturation which makes them stand cold and rain so well. If they were to go into a warm climate, they would melt and die of the scurvy.

The vessel was no better than the crew. Everything was in the oldest and most inconvenient fashion possible: running trusses and lifts on the yards, and large hawser cables, coiled all over the decks, and served and parcelled in all directions. The topmasts, top-gallant-masts, and studding-sail booms were nearly black for want of scraping, and the decks would have turned the stomach of a man-of-war's-man. The galley was down in the forecastle; and there the crew lived, in the midst of the steam and grease of the cooking, in a place as hot as an oven, and apparently never cleaned out. Five minutes in the forecastle was enough for us, and we were glad to get into the open air.[53]

Not surprisingly, at the beginning of the 1800s it took Russian American sea-otter skins a year to reach the China market at Kyakhta on the Mongolian frontier south of Lake Baikal (thus the company tried long and hard but in vain to be allowed to barter instead at Canton, which a sailing ship could make from Sitka in two months). Consequently, as North China's merchants found, the price of sea-otter skins at Canton was 'much below' that at Kyakhta (they also found, incidentally, that the British woollens available at Canton were superior to the Russian woollens brought to Kyakhta).[54] In the middle of the 1840s an exchange of correspondence between New Archangel and St Petersburg took a year and a half.[55] In 1860 Captain Golovin complained that the company's Head Office in St Petersburg did not maintain regular contact with Sitka.[56] At that time communication by ship between the imperial and colonial capitals took from seven to eight months; by contrast, mail went from San Francisco by pony express to St Louis, railroad to New York, steamship to France, and railroad to St Petersburg in one and a half months.[57] Cyrus Field's transatlantic cable would have improved communication greatly, of course, but it was laid too late (1866) to benefit Russian America (it also killed Western Union's much longer overland telegraph line, which would have linked motherland and colony via the Bering Strait).

Thus, the logistical approach of shipment from what Russians commonly called Russia, that is, the country west of the Volga and north of the Caucasus, was unsatisfactory. So, too, was the development of colonial exclaves in balmier locales. The short-lived venture of 1815–17 in the Hawaiian Islands was really a farce staged by an egotistical employee.[58] Russian California, however, was a serious long-term effort by the company to cure some of its colonial ills. It began in 1812 with the building of Fort Ross on the narrow coastland 150 kilometres north of the Golden Gate (it had been intended, incidentally, to found the establishment on the lowermost Columbia but the Astorians got there first). Ross Counter also included a port, Port Rumyantsev (Bodega Bay), and several farms. The exclave was planned as a farming base for feeding Alaska, a hunting base for tapping the Californian sea-otter rookery, and a southern foothold for winning the international competition for the North-west Coast.

Shipbuilding, brick-making, and tanning were also undertaken, but the Californian oak proved unsuitable for vessels, and the sea otters and fur seals were soon depleted (although a few continued to be bagged by means of hunting on halves with Mexican citizens and American settlers). From the middle 1820s the Counter concentrated on producing grain, vegetables, fruits, beef, mutton, pork, butter, wool, and hides for Alaska, but the farms did not thrive, thanks mainly to the want of skilled farm hands and the lack of suitable farm lands. In the middle of the 1830s the company tried to overcome both of these shortcomings by negotiating an enlargement of the exclave with the Mexican authorities and by recruiting a professional agronomist. But Tsar Nicholas I, the so-called 'gendarme of Europe', disdained dealings with Mexico's revolutionary government, and the company agronomist was left to apply his skills to the limited ploughing and grazing land between the coast and the northernmost Hispanic missions and ranchos. In 1841 Russian California was sold to New Helvetia's John Sutter, who eventually paid – in grain.

The remaining logistical option of international trade was likewise flawed. American shipmasters began to visit New Archangel as soon as it was founded in 1799, and from 1803 they began to trade more or less regularly with the Russians, exchanging provisions (mostly flour, millet, sugar, salt, molasses, vinegar, tea, coffee, rum, gin, wine, and tobacco) and manufactures (chiefly soap, blankets, cloth, guns, and gunpowder) and even ships for fur-seal skins and piasters (Spanish silver dollars).[59] The Yankee skippers brought the same goods to barter with the North-west Coast Indians anyway, so it was not difficult to bring more of the same for Sitka, and the company's purchases increased their profit margin. The 'Boston men', as they were termed in the Chinook trading jargon of the coast, were a mixed blessing, however. Although they supplied goods that were respectable in quality and reasonable in price, they also competed with the company in the coast trade, not hesitating to poach in what the Russians considered their territorial waters (even while at anchor in Sitka Sound under the very guns of the fort) and to engage in gunrunning and rumrunning to the Tlingits and turning them against the tsar's men. These subversive activities prompted the imperial edict of 1821 closing Russian America's ports and waters to foreign vessels. American ships were readmitted in 1824 after the Russian government realized that the colony simply could not afford to do without American supplies. By then, however, the heyday of the maritime fur trade was over, and fewer and fewer Yankee coasters visited Sitka. In 1837 the company's Head Office acknowledged that the Bostonian suppliers were unreliable.[60]

Fortunately for Russian America, when it was closed to American and other ships in 1821, Mexico declared its independence and opened Alta California's ports to foreign trade in the very same year. Heretofore provisions had been obtained from the bountiful missions only sporadically through either the liberality or venality of the Californian authorities. Henceforth, however, up to three Russian-American Company ships put into San Francisco or Monterey every year to take on wheat, beef, beans and peas, and tallow and lard in exchange for manufactures and silver dollars. But even this channel was doomed to disappointment. Transaction costs (custom duties and anchorage and tonnage fees) rose steadily, and American and British traders offered stiffening competition for the California market. Also, supply was periodically reduced by crop failures resulting from drought, wheat rust, and Indian burning; half of the 1820s, for example, experienced harvest failures. The final blow came in the middle 1830s with the secularization of the missions. The *peninsular* padres were ousted and the enserfed Indians freed; rancheros looted mission property, and fields reverted.

The Russian-American Company then turned to its British rival, the Hudson's Bay Company.[61] The latter had productive farms on the lower Columbia (Fort Vancouver) and lower Fraser (Fort Langley), as well as ready access to the agricultural surplus of the Willamette settlers.[62] The Honourable Company also had access to high-quality British manufactures via the 'London ship', which annually rounded Cape Horn and entered the Columbia river. Moreover, Governor George Simpson, the company's unlikeable but masterful field general in North America, saw the supply of New Archangel as a way of capturing the coast trade from what he called the 'American adventurers'. This tactic would not only halt the long-standing diversion of beaver pelts from the king's posts in the cordillera to Yankee ships on the coast but also offset the company's declining returns from the lower Columbia basin, which was being 'trapped clean' in the event of United States sovereignty. The Russian-American Company, for its part, would be rid of the troublesome Bostonians and able to shed the disappointing exclave of Russian California. So in 1839 the two firms signed a ten-year pact whereby the British agreed to supply Sitka with provisions and manufactures and to rent the Alaska panhandle in return for 5,000 land-otter skins.

This seemingly secure mode of supply, however, was – like the others – shortlived. The Russians soon discovered that they could obtain manufactures more cheaply from Europe on chartered vessels than on those of the Hudson's Bay Company, which charged high freight rates. In addition, in 1846 the joint occupation of the Oregon Country was ended when the 49th parallel was extended from the Rockies to the Pacific as the international boundary, thereby vitiating the Hudson's Bay Company's most productive farmlands (even Fort Langley missed being lost by only a few miles of latitude). More importantly, in 1848 gold was discovered at Sutter's Mill, and many of the Oregon Country's farmers abandoned their fields and joined the rush to California. Chief Factor Douglas told Governor Tebenkov in 1849 that two-thirds of the region's white inhabitants had gone to California's goldfields.[63] So when the 'Russian contract' was renewed in 1849 for another ten years, the supply clauses were dropped.

Thus, the supply of Russian America was generally unstable, so much so that in 1834, for instance, when supplies from California's missions and American coasters were still forthcoming, the colony's governor bemoaned the 'wretched state of the customary scarcity of the most necessary articles.'[64] And as late as 1855 and 1856 'provisionment was unusually meagre', in the words of another governor.[65] Sitka even became heavily dependent upon the local (and not always friendly) Tlingits for large amounts of fish (138,096 pounds in 1851), venison (2,774 carcasses in 1861), and potatoes (1,060 barrels in 1845) (the latter, incidentally, had been adopted from the Euroamericans by the coastal Indians).[66] That the Russian-American Company's colony was able – barely – to manage logistically was due in large part to the acquiescence of its very rivals for the Pacific Slope of North America. That position was hardly one of strength.

Indeed, this point raises the last constraint on Russian tenure that needs to be discussed. Russia had advanced rapidly across Siberia towards Alaska, partly because of the powerful lure of precious sable fur and the facility of the dense river network, but also because of the feebleness of native resistance and the absence of foreign opposition. Siberia's indigenes were not at all numerous, they did not unite against the Russian interlopers, and they were at a low technological level (few farmed or smelted, for example, and most had no written language). Other powers were not interested in Siberia, perhaps because it was too remote or too cold or too wild. China and Japan were close enough and strong enough to intervene but chose not to do so, for both came under isolationist regimes just as Russia was advancing eastwards: the Manchu or Ching dynasty in 1644 and the Tokugawa Shogunate in 1603 (only when the Russians encroached upon the Amurian homeland of the Manchus did China ract vigorously). So Russia had a free hand in Siberia.

Such was not the case in Alaska, however. Here Russia entered a New World which Britain, France, and Spain had already long contested and which they and the fledgling United States were now foreclosing in the very north-western quarter where Russia had just arrived. In this competition for the territory, resources, and peoples of the Pacific Slope the Russians stood to lose. In terms of the maritime fur trade they did enjoy the advantage of an earlier start, their rivals not entering the business until the middle 1780s, more than forty years after the Russians. The tsar's men also monopolized the habitats of the most valuable sorts of sea otters (and fur seals, too, for that matter) – the Kurilian-Kamchatkan and the Aleutian, whose coats were larger, thicker, and darker than those of their North-west Coast and California cousins. The Russians likewise controlled the best hunters of sea otters, the Aleuts and Kodiaks, whose prowess with kayak and harpoon prompted their enserfment and allowed the Russians partially to forego the additional (and costlier) step of trading. Furthermore, the Russians had the support of permanent bases amid the sea-otter and fur-seal grounds, beginning probably with Captain's Harbour on Unalaska Island in 1774 or certainly with Three Saints' harbour on Kodiak Island in 1784.

But all this was not enough. The Americans – as befits New Englanders, perhaps – were keener and sharper traders, and they had more seaworthy ships and more seasoned sailors. Captain Otto von Kotzebue, son of the very popular and influential German dramatist (and paid tsarist agent) August von Kotzebue, visited New Archangel in 1824–5 during the second of his three round-the-world voyages, and was impressed by American maritime enterprise. ' . . . no people in the world', he asserted, 'surpass the citizens of the United States in the boldness, activity, and perseverance of their mercantile speculations'.[67] During his stopover the American brig *Lapwing* came safely to anchor in Sitka's harbour despite the intoxication of captain and crew: ' . . . the North Americans are such clever sailors', he exclaimed, 'that even when drunk they are capable of managing a ship.' He added:

> On my visit to the ship, I could not help remarking the great economy of all its arrangements: no such thing, for instance, as a looking-glass was to be seen, except the one kept for measuring the angle of the sextant, and that, small as it was, assisted the whole crew in the operation of shaving.[68]

The brig and its cargo, incidentally, were bought by the Russian-American Company for 21,000 fur-seal skins, and the vessel was renamed the *Okhotsk*.[69] The Yankee traders also enjoyed faster and easier, and therefore cheaper, access to the China market via the port of Canton, which was reached much more readily than Kyakhta, of course. Moreover, the Americans were quick to spread their commercial risk through diversification: smuggling and poaching along the western coast of Spanish America from the 1790s, sandalwooding on the Hawaiian Islands from the 1810s, whaling in the North Pacific, and hiding and tallowing in California from the 1820s. The Russians did not follow suit with coal, timber, fish, whales, ice, and tea until the 1850s.

The Russians were outcompeted by the British, too. The latter's trade goods were higher in quality and lower in price, and their managers were more knowledgeable and more efficient (George Simpson, John McLoughlin, and James Douglas are prime examples, but there were others, like Peter Skene Ogden and John Work). The 'King George's men', as they were known in Chinook, also benefited from less strained logistics, including food production in the adjoining Oregon Country. And their financial resources were greater, thanks to their profitable prosecution of the beaver-based continental fur trade since 1670 (and the Hudson's Bay Company's absorption of the rival North-West Company in 1821). Just as the Americans were able to offer the North-west Coast Indians from two to three times as much for furs as the Russians in the middle 1810s, so, too, could the British pay the natives just as much again as the Russians in the early 1830s.[70]

In fact, Russia's competitive position was more akin to that of Spain.[71] Both struggled on the margins of the North-west Coast theatre, and both were hampered by the secrecy of their activities and the neglect of conservative motherland rulers (the Bourbons and Tsars Alexander I and Nicholas I). Although stuck with the less prized Californian subspecies of sea otter, the Spanish were nevertheless more experienced mariners than the Russians, and they had readier access to the China market via the yearly Manila galleon. And New Spain was a proximate and plentiful supply base. Even so, Spain's role gradually atrophied with the Nootka Sound Convention of 1790 with Great Britain, the Transcontinental Treaty of 1819 with the United States, and Mexico's declaration of independence in 1821.

Even the coastal natives thwarted the Russians. The Aleuts and Kodiaks were easily overcome, but the stalwart and numerous Tlingits were, as the tsar's men might have said, *iz drugoi opery*, that is, quite another matter. Thanks to their temperate environment's bounty of fish and timber, the Koloshes, as the Russians called them, were, like the other groups of North-west Coast Indians, able to develop an elaborate and vigorous culture without the benefits of farming or smelting. Each Tlingit village comprised several independent clans whose intervillage ties took precedence over their intravillage ties, resulting in tribal solidarity. And they quickly acquired and mastered firearms, thanks to American military aid. So the Tlingits presented a strong and united front to the Russians, particularly after the latter were so rash as to invade and occupy Tlingit territory, notably at New Archangel. The Tlingits even seized and razed the colonial capital itself in 1802 (it had to be refounded two years later), and as late as 1855 they besieged New Archangel and destroyed nearby Ozersk Redoubt. Captain Golovin found in the early 1860s that Sitka was 'constantly in a state of siege,' with no Russian daring – 'until recently' – to venture fifty paces from the fort unarmed.[72] Little wonder that the Russian-American Company always classified the Tlingits as 'completely independent'. For their part, the Indians said that they 'tolerate the Russians.'[73] In Siberia only the Chukchis were similarly able to keep the Russians at bay, apart from the nomadic Kirgiz of the Turanian steppe.

Finally, Russian America suffered from St Petersburg's indifference. Russia was preoccupied with European affairs, and justifiably so, since its principal warring and trading partners, and enemies, were European. Asian affairs were of little consequence because there was nothing or nobody there of much import. No serious threat had come from the east since the thirteenth century, and now China and Japan stood aloof. Russia seems not to have devised a definite and forceful policy towards its eastern frontier until the 1850s, when the growing United States appeared poised to envelop North America, and China and Japan were succumbing to British and American inroads. The *perestroika* prompted by Russia's ignominious defeat in the Crimean War called for the abandonment of the chequered overseas colony and the exploitation of Chinese weakness in Central Asia and the Far East. So Russian America became the Territory of Alaska, and western Turkestan became Russian Turkestan and the river basin of the Black Dragon that of the Amur.[74] The tsar's new Asian lands were largely incorporated and assimilated into the empire. That had not happened to Russian America, so it was more expendable. And unlike Russia's other colonies, it was not contiguous to the motherland, so what happened there was of less moment, and for that reason, too, it was more expendable. Thus, Russian America was sold to the United States in 1867 for two cents an acre. The same year saw the birth of the Canadian dominion and the finalization of the political map of North America.

NOTES AND REFERENCES

1   See Janet Martin, *Treasure of the Land of Darkness: The Fur Trade and its Significance for Medieval Russia* (London and New York: Cambridge University Press, 1986).

2   See Raymond H. Fisher, *The Russian Fur Trade, 1550–1700* (Berkeley and Los Angeles: University of California Press, 1943); Robert J. Kerner, *The Urge to the Sea: The Course of Russian History. The Role of Rivers, Portages, Ostrogs, Monasteries, and Furs* (Berkeley and Los Angeles: University of California Press, 1946); and George V. Lantzeff and Richard A. Pierce, *Eastward to Empire: Exploration and Conquest on the Russian Open Frontier to 1750* (Montreal and London: McGill-Queen's University Press, 1973).

3   Basil Dmytryshyn and E.A.P. Crownhart-Vaughan (trans.), *The End of Russian America: Captain P.N. Golovin's Last Report 1862* (Portland, Oregon: Oregon Historical Society, 1979), p. 111.

4   See James R. Gibson, 'Diversification on the Frontier: Russian America in the Middle of the Nineteenth Century', in J.H. Bater and R.A. French (eds), *Studies in Russian Historical Geography* (London: Academic Press, 1983) 1: 199–242.

5   See François-Xavier Coquin, *La Sibérie: peuplement et immigration paysanne au XIX siècle*, (Paris: Institut d'études Slaves, 1969), and Donald W. Treadgold, *The Great Siberian Migration: Government and Peasant in Resettlement from Emancipation to the First World War* (Princeton: Princeton University Press, 1957).

6   S.B. Okun, *The Russian-American Company*, trans. Carl Ginsburg (Cambridge, Mass.: Harvard University Press, 1951), pp. 97–8.

7   N.N. Bolkhovitinov, *Russko-Amerikanskie Otnosheniya 1815–1832* (Moscow: Nauka, 1976), p. 509.

8   Okun, *The Russian-American Company*, op. cit., p. 108; Patrick O'Meara, *K.F. Ryleev: A Political Biography of the Decembrist Poet* (Princeton: Princeton University Press, 1984), pp. 62–3, 143–4.

9   D.I. Zavalishin, *Zapiski dekabrista*, 2nd edn (St Petersburg, n.d.), p. 131.

10 See Okun, *The Russian-American Company*, op. cit., pp. 106–15 and O'Meara, *K.F. Ryleev*, op. cit., pp. 61–7, 142–5; see also N.N. Bolkhovitinov, 'Dekabristy i Amerika', *Voprosy istorii* 4 (1974): 91–104.

11 Okun, *The Russian-American Company*, op. cit., p. 113.

12 Ibid., p. 116.

13 See James R. Gibson (trans.), 'Russia in California, 1833: Report of

Governor Wrangel', *Pacific Northwest Quarterly* 60 (1969): 305-15.

14　James Douglas, 'Diary of a Trip to the Northwest Coast, April 22-October 2, 1840', British Columbia Provincial Archives, Ms AB40 D75.2A, 21 May 1840.

15　Glyndwr Williams (ed.), *London Correspondence Inward from Sir George Simpson 1841-42* (London: Hudson's Bay Company Record Society, 1973), p. 70.

16　Sir George Simpson, *Narrative of a Journey Round the World, During the Years 1841 and 1842*, 2: 188 (London: Henry Colburn 1847).

17　Alice M. Johnson (ed.), 'Simpson in Russia', *The Beaver* 291 (1960): 7, 10-11.

18　See James R. Gibson, 'Bostonians and Muscovites on the Northwest Coast, 1788-1841', in Thomas Vaughan (ed.), *The Western Shore: Oregon Country Essays Honoring the American Revolution* (Portland, Oregon: Oregon Historical Society, 1975), pp. 81-119.

19　Dmytryshyn and Crownhart-Vaughan, *The End of Russian America*, op. cit., p. 92; Okun, *The Russian-American Company*, op. cit., pp. 67-9.

20　See James R. Gibson, 'The Sale of Russian America to the United States', *Acta Slavica Iaponica* 1 (1983): 15-37.

21　See V.M. Golovnin, *Around the World on the Kamchatka, 1817-1819*, trans. Ella Lury Wiswell, (Honolulu: Hawaiian Historical Society and University Press of Hawaii, 1979).

22　Washington Irving, *Astoria: or, Anecdotes of an Enterprise beyond the Rocky Mountains*, clatsop edn (Portland, Oregon: Binfords and Mort, n.d.), p. 420.

23　P.A. Tikhmenev, *A History of the Russian-American Company*, trans. Richard A. Pierce and Alton S. Donnelly (Seattle and London: University of Washington Press, 1978), p. 120.

24　P. Tikhmenev, *Supplement of some Historical Documents to the Historical Review of the Formation of the Russian-American Company . . . ,* trans. Dimitri Krenov (Seattle: Works Progress Administration, 1938), pp. 309-16.

25　Douglas, 'Diary of a Trip', op. cit., 21 May, 1840.

26　Dmytryshyn and Crownhart-Vaughan, *The End of Russian America*, op. cit., p. 111.

27　Ibid., pp. 97, 111.

28　See Svetlana G. Fedorova, *The Russian Population in Alaska and California Late 18th Century-1867*, trans. Richard A. Pierce and Alton S. Donnelly (Kingston, Ontario: Limestone Press, 1973), appendix, pp. 275-81.

29　See Winston Lee Sarafian, 'Russian-American Company Employee Policies and Practices, 1799-1867', unpublished PhD dissertation, University of California at Los Angeles, 1970.

30　Ivan Barsukov, *Innokenti Mitropolit Moskovskii i Kolomenskii po yego sochineniyam, pismam i razskazam sovremennikov* (Moscow: Sinodalnaya tipografiya, 1883), p. 10.

31　Simpson, *Narrative of a Journey*, op. cit., 2: 190.

32　United States, National Archives and Records Service, 'Records of the Russian-American Company 1802-1867: Correspondence of Governors General', File Microcopies of Records in the National Archives No. 11, roll 40, fo. 246; roll 51, fo. 426.

33   Russian-American Company, Head Office, *Otchet Rossiisko-Amerikanskoi Kompanii Glavnago Praveleniya za odin god* . . . , (divers, 1843–65) (St Petersburg, 1843), p. 25.

34   Russia, Ministry of the Navy, *Materialy dlya istorii russkikh zaselenii po beregam vostochnago okeana* 1: 8 (St Petersburg: Tipografiya Morskago Ministerstva 1861).

35   United States, 'Records of the Russian-American Company', op. cit., roll 20, fo. 21; roll 34, fo. 141v.

36   Pavel N. Golovin, *Civil and Savage Encounters: The Worldly Travel Letters of an Imperial Russian Navy Officer 1860–1861*, trans. Basil Dmytryshyn and E.A.P. Crownhart-Vaughan (Portland, Oregon: Western Imprints, 1983), p. 79.

37   See James R. Gibson, 'European Dependence Upon American Natives: The Case of Russian America', *Ethnohistory* 25 (1978): 359–85.

38   See James R. Gibson, 'Smallpox on the Northwest Coast, 1835–1838', *BC Studies*, winter 1982–3: 61–81.

39   See James R. Gibson, *Imperial Russia in Frontier America: The Changing Geography of Supply of Russian America, 1784–1867* (New York: Oxford University Press, 1976).

40   Dmytryshyn and Crownhart-Vaughan, *The End of Russian America*, op. cit., p. 130.

41   See Samuel H. Baron, 'Shipbuilding and Seafaring in Sixteenth-Century Russia', in Daniel Clarke Waugh (ed.), *Essays in Honor of A.A. Zimin* (Columbus: Slavica Publishers, 1985), pp. 102–29.

42   Gibson, *Imperial Russia in Frontier America*, op. cit., p. 64.

43   James R. Gibson, *Feeding the Russian Fur Trade: Provisionment of the Okhotsk Seaboard and the Kamchatka Peninsula 1639–1856* (Madison: University of Wisconsin Press, 1969), pp. 97, 120–1.

44   Simpson, *Narrative of a Journey*, op. cit., 264–5.

45   Gibson, *Feeding the Russian Fur Trade*, op. cit., p. 122.

46   Okun, *The Russian-American Company*, op. cit., p. 99.

47   See N.A. Ivashintsov, *Russian Round-the-World Voyages, 1803–1849 With a Summary of Later Voyages to 1867*, trans. Glynn R. Barratt (Kingston, Ontario: Limestone Press, 1980); N. Nozikov, *Russian Voyages Round the World*, trans. Ernst and Mira Lesser (London: Hutchinson & Co. Ltd, n.d); and E.F. McCartan, 'The Long Voyages – Early Russian Circumnavigation', *Russian Review* 22 (1963): 30–7.

48   Tikhmenev, *History of the Russian-American Company* op. cit., p. 236.

49   Mikhail Zetlin, *The Decembrists* (New York: International Universities Press, Inc., 1958), p. 278.

50   Dmytryshyn and Crownhart-Vaughan, *The End of Russian America*, op. cit., p. 76; A.P. Lazarev, *Zapiski o plavanii voyennogo shlyupa Blagonamerennogo v Beringov proliv i vokrug sveta* . . . , (Moscow: Gosudarstvennoe izdatelstvo geograficheskoi literatury, 1950), pp. 186, 235, 282.

51   Gibson, *Imperial Russia in Frontier America*, op. cit., pp. 14, 37.

52   Frédéric Lutké, *Voyage autour du monde* . . . , trans. F. Boye (Paris: Didot Frères, 1835) 1: 106–7; United States, 'Records of the Russian-American Company', op. cit., roll 20, p. 21.

53   Richard Henry Dana, Jr, *Two Years Before the Mast: A Personal Narrative*, large-paper edn, (Boston and New York: Houghton Mifflin Company,

1949) 2: 282–3.

54 John Meares, *Voyages Made in the Years 1788 and 1789, from China to the North West Coast of America* (London: Logographic Press, 1790), p. xxxvi.

55 Russian American Company, *Otchet*, op. cit., 1846, p. 21.

56 Golovin, *Civil and Savage Encounters*, op. cit., p. 75.

57 Ibid., pp. 144–5; *Doklad komiteta ob ustroistve russkikh amerkanskikh kolonii* (St Petersburg: Tipografiya Departamenta Vneshnei Torgovli, 1863–4) 1: 186.

58 See Richard A. Pierce, *Russia's Hawaiian Adventure, 1815–1817* (Berkeley and Los Angeles: University of California Press, 1965).

59 See Gibson, 'Bostonians and Muscovites', op. cit., and Mary E. Wheeler, 'Empires in Conflict and Cooperation: The "Bostonians" and the Russian-American Company', *Pacific Historical Review* 40 (1971): 419–41. See also Howard I. Kushner, *Conflict on the Northwest Coast: American-Russian Rivalry in the Pacific Northwest, 1790–1867* (Westport: Greenwood Press, 1975) which, however, largely ignores the Russian sources.

60 United States, 'Records of the Russian-American Company', op. cit., roll 13, fo. 104v.

61 See James R. Gibson, 'The "Russian Contract": The Agreement of 1839 Between the Hudson's Bay and Russian-American Companies', paper presented to the Second International Conference on Russian America (Sitka, 1987).

62 See James R. Gibson, *Farming the Frontier: The Agricultural Opening of the Oregon Country, 1786–1846* (Vancouver: University of British Columbia Press, 1985).

63 United States, 'Records of the Russian-American Company', op. cit., roll 55, fo. 150v.

64 Ibid., roll 36, fo. 43v.

65 Ibid., roll 61, pt. 1, fo. 85v.

66 See Gibson, 'European Dependence Upon American Natives', op. cit.

67 Otto von Kotzebue, *A New Voyage Round the World in the Years 1823, 24, 25 and 26* (London: Henry Colburn and Richard Bentley, 1830) 2: 63–4.

68 Ibid., p. 65.

69 Ibid., p. 64. In fact, the Russians paid 24,235 fur-seal skins for the *Lapwing* (K.T. Khlebnikov, *Colonial Russian America: Kyrill T. Khlebnikov's Reports, 1817–1832*, trans. Basil Dmytryshyn and E.A.P. Crownhart-Vaughan (Portland, Oregon: Oregon Historical Society, 1976), p. 60).

70 Semen Yakovlevich Unkovskii 'Zapiski russkogo moryaka nachala XIXv.', Lenin Library, Manuscript Division, fond. 261, carton 20, fo. 74; United States, 'Records of the Russian-American Company', op. cit., roll 8, fo. 330v.

71 See Warren L. Cook, *Flood Tide of Empire: Spain and the Pacific Northwest, 1543–1819*, (New Haven and London: Yale University Press, 1973). See also Christon I. Archer's forthcoming book on this subject.

72 Dmytryshyn and Crownhart-Vaughan, *The End of Russian America*, op. cit., p. 27; Golovin, *Civil and Savage Encounters*, op. cit., p. 85.

73 Dmytryshyn and Crownhart-Vaughan, *The End of Russian America*, op. cit., p. 27.

74 See James R.Gibson, 'Russia on the Pacific: The Role of the Amur', *Canadian Geographer* 12 (1968) 15-27, and Mark Bassin, 'A Russian Mississippi? A political-Geographical Inquiry into the Vision of Russia on the Pacific 1840-1865', unpublished PhD dissertation, University of California at Berkeley, 1983.

7 Russia's 'Wild East': exile, vagrancy and crime in nineteenth-century Siberia[1]

Alan Wood

According to Alexander Solzhenitsyn, 'Man invented exile first and prison later'.[2] Old Testament fundamentalists may believe that God pre-empted Man's ingenuity in this respect by first expelling Adam and Eve from the Garden of Eden and condemning them to a lifetime of hard agricultural labour. This, together with the fate of their son, the fratricide Cain, as 'a fugitive and a vagabond in the earth',[3] curiously prefigures one of the most vexatious problems facing the Siberian exile administration in tsarist Russia – the related phenomena of vagrancy (*brodyazhestvo*) and violent crime. Since this earliest recorded sentence of administrative banishment, various forms of ostracism, deportation and exile have been used by political and administrative authorities throughout the ages as a means of ridding society of criminal, antisocial or otherwise undesirable members. And in modern history, Siberia has earned itself a peculiar notoriety in the grim gazetteer of remote and inhospitable locations for compulsory settlement or confinement.

Despite the universal ill repute of Siberia as a place of exile and punishment, and despite the considerable amount of scholarly material recently published in the Soviet Union about the workings of the exile system, particularly with regard to *political* exile, a comprehensive history of the origins, development and decline of Siberian exile in tsarist Russia still remains to be written.[4] No one has yet done for Siberia what Robert Hughes has done for Botany Bay.[5] Although there are certain similarities between the British transportation system to Australia and the Russian government's penal policies in Siberia, there are also obvious differences of both a qualitative and a quantitive nature. Of these, perhaps the most significant is that whereas almost the entire non-aboriginal population of settlers in the Antipodes were there in the first place only by virtue of the establishment of the convict colonies – either as prisoners, guards, officials or their dependents – in Siberia exiles accounted for only a very small percentage of the total population. In 1662, eighty years after Yermak's original expedition across the Urals, the Russian and other immigrant population of Siberia stood at 70,000 males, of which 7,400 were exiles, that is, 10.5 per cent.[6] In the late nineteenth century, according to the 1897 census, the total population of Siberia was 5,760,000; at 1 January 1898, government figures put the exile population at 309,25, that is, only 5.2 per cent – a proportional drop of about 50 per cent.[7] Of these, only about 1 per cent were political exiles, that is, state criminals or those administratively isolated by the police for security reasons. The major factor in the population growth of Siberia was, therefore, not compulsory settlement, but a combination of voluntary migration, state service (military, commercial, administrative), and natural procreation.[8]

This obviously dents the vulgar image of Siberia as little more than a vast penal settlement populated by criminals, dissidents and zeks.[9] However, what is indisputable is that, despite the comparatively low proportion of exiles, they nevertheless made a disproportionate impact on civil society in Siberia in terms of their responsibility for the territory's alarming rate of brigandage and violent crime. To shift the geographical and historical analogy, in the nineteenth century Siberia bore as many similarities to the American 'Wild West' as to the Australian outback. Both the historical reality and the Hollywood legend of the West as a rough, tough frontierland roamed by outlaws, gunslingers, gold-diggers, bounty hunters and pesky Indians is to some extent replicated in the practically lawless expanses of the Siberian taiga where thousands of escaped criminals, dangerous vagabonds and desperadoes terrorized the province's free citizenry, native peoples and honest settlers. It is in this sense that the image of Siberia as Russia's 'Wild East' is used in the present chapter.

Of course, the lawlessness which the American pioneers faced as they blazed their way across the continent towards the Pacific was not deliberately encouraged by Washington. Nor, presumably, was it the considered purpose of St Petersburg to turn Siberia into the Russian Empire's principality of crime. However, it is the object of this essay to demonstrate that the government's policy of purging metropolitan Russia of her miscreants and malcontents by annually deporting them in their thousands beyond the Urals was directly responsible for generating and exacerbating the very problems of vagrancy and violent crime which the exile system was partly designed to combat, eliminate and punish.

During the first century of its operation, Siberian exile was regarded as a positive institution, replacing, as it increasingly did, the gruesome forms of capital punishment practised in Muscovite Russia, and simultaneously adding to the manpower which the central government and local authorities needed to stock, administer and defend the newly-conquered territories.

Exile soon in fact became established as the tsarist government's most common form of punishment for a wide variety of criminal offences and acts of political, civil and religious disobedience.[10] There was, moreover, a conscious attempt to direct the exiles to the locations and kinds of occupation for which they were most fitted or trained, and many of the more serious social problems with which the exiles infected the region in later centuries had not yet become endemic.[11]

However, despite the system's positive side, it was not without its serious drawbacks and disadvantages. Indeed, to talk of an exile *system* is to employ a euphemism, as the whole rather chaotic operation was from the start beset by a wide range of difficulties and marked by a hopeless inadequacy of proper regulations, surveillance, transport and provisioning, and by a high incidence of disease, desertion and mortality. Underpinning the inefficiency and confusion of the Siberian exile administration was the basic incompatibility between the aims of punishment and the aims of colonization. Notwithstanding the example of the Australian penal colonies' eventual transformation into a flourishing civil society, the physical, legal and material constraints placed upon the Siberian exile population were not, on the whole, conducive to their successful settlement and exploitation of the territory's agricultural and other natural resources.

The practical and technical impediments posed by climate, distance, terrain and maladministration were further complicated by the rather obvious factor of the 'quality' of the human material involved. In addition to the increasingly wider variety of serious crimes and petty offences punished by exile to Siberia, legislation enacted by the Empresses Elizabeth and Catherine II in the late eighteenth century allowing serf-owners to hand over uncooperative and insubordinate peasants for transportation to Siberia unwittingly augmented the flow of totally unsuitable personnel into the region. The wording of the relevant decrees determined that only young, virile and healthy peasants – accompanied by their womenfolk and not flogged or mutilated so badly as to render them unfit for work – be so disposed of.[12] However, unscrupulous landlords regularly took advantage of the law to get rid of the old, the infirm and otherwise unprofitable in return for the promised military recruit quittance. The *de facto* abolition of the death penalty for criminal offences in 1753 also helped to ensure that many a dangerous and violent offender who would otherwise have ended his days on the scaffold or the block was now added to the motley collection of thieves, bandits, forgers, rapists, poisoners, prisoners-of-war, schismatics and insurgents, as well as fornicators, drunkards, layabouts and hooligans who were banished beyond the Urals in ever-increasing droves.

Another major obstacle to the success of enforced colonization was the chronic shortage of women. The problems caused by sexual imbalance in

Siberia have been dealt with elsewhere by the present author and need not be repeated here.[13] Suffice it to say that ever since the time of Ivan the Terrible, repeated government efforts, either by threat or inducement, to boost the female population of Siberia, had conspicuously failed to meet the insatiable demand for more women or to prevent the development of a situation in which rape, abduction, prostitution, incest, buggery, bestality and venereal disease were rife. None of this, of course, was especially conducive to domestic tranquility, efficient husbandry, or a harmonious and settled community life.

Given, therefore, the inauspicious combination of a hostile natural environment, a brutal and corrupt administration, inadequate supervision. a collective background of criminal or antisocial behaviour and an absence of any personal motivation or material incentive to settle down, it is hardly surprising that so many exiles responded to their miserable plight by absconding from their appointed places of settlement or imprisonment, taking to the forests and reverting, or turning, to a life of vagrancy and crime, joining the huge, shifting underworld of beggars, bandits and *brodyagi* (vagrants), popularly known as 'General Cuckoo's Army'.

The quaint cuculine image pertains to the local belief that it was the call of the first cuckoo each spring which acted as a signal for the start of the vernal exodus of vagabonds and villains from their places of settlement or confinement to a short-lived freedom in the wilderness of the taiga. Less romantic was the description of a one-time Governor-General of Western Siberia, Prince Gorchakov, who referred to the intractable problem of mass vagrancy in his province as the 'ulcer' or the 'running sore' (*nastoyashchaya yazva*) of Siberia. What were the origins of this phenomenon, and what were its immediate and long-term effects on Siberian society?

Despite a centuries-long pattern of compulsory service to the state, military conscription and serfdom, with all the attendant oppressive paraphernalia of collective responsibility, internal passports and man-made barriers to social and geographical mobility, Russia was in fact a country with a rich variety of nomadic and migratory traditions. A huge internal diaspora of runaway peasants, cossacks, pilgrims and peripatetic sectarians, caravans of merchants, peddlars, gypsies, schools of *skoromokhi* (wandering players), bands of migrant hunters, craftsmen and *promyshlenniki*, as well as the nomadic tribes of steppe, forest and tundra – all for countless generations had been the collective personification of Russia on the move. Indeed, many of these 'travelling folk' (*gulyashchie lyudi*) had played a prominent role in Russia's expansion across Siberia in the first place. Yermak himself, the pioneering cossack *ataman*, is often portrayed as a mercenary, roving pirate chief.[14]

None of these popular manifestations of circumforaneous activity is of course peculiar to Russia: internal migration, nomadism and vagrancy are a universal feature of pre-industrial societies, as is the combination of envy and suspicion, admiration and fear, with which its practitioners, whether tramps, outlaws and gypsies, have traditionally been regarded by the more sedentary communities through which they roam. There are also countless examples in history and legend of outlaw heroes, vagabond kings, highwaymen and popular brigand chiefs whom Eric Hobsbawm has designated as 'social bandits' and of which Robin Hood is the archetypal figure, plundering the rich to feed the poor and by his illegal activities championing the people's inarticulate struggle against political oppression and social injustice.[15] In this category may or may not be included such often idealized characters as the buccaneer Henry Morgan, Rob Roy, Stenka Razin, Dick Turpin, Jesse James, Ned Kelly, Pancho Villa and even the twentieth-century *Mafioso*, Salvatore Giuliano. While it is true that many of these characters in fact and fable protected the poor, fought oppression and lived by a code of honour which allegedly forbade molesting defenceless maidens and allowed attacks only on corrupt officials, wicked landowners and fat abbots, it is nevertheless 'a mistake', as Hobsbawm acknowledges, 'to think of bandits as mere children of nature roasting stags in the greenwood'.[16]

As far as Siberia's escaped convicts, brigands and brodyagi are concerned, the case for any kind of romanticization is very tenuous indeed, and for generations they continued to plague Siberian society, providing a living, but deadly, proof that the exile system could be neither an effective penological measure nor make a positive contribution to the social and economic development of the territory. As society in European Russia became more structured, central institutions of government more formalized, and rudimentary notions of citizenship established, vagrancy as a mass phenomenon, including large-scale banditry, began gradually to disappear. This, according to some authorities, was beginning to occur in the mid-eighteenth century.[17] But it was precisely at this time that brodyazhestvo in Siberia was artificially boosted to become a numerically and territorially significant phenomenon as a *direct* result of the increased use of judicial and administrative exile. The combination of unfortunate and debilitating circumstances noted above brought about a situation in which for many the hazards and uncertainties of a life on the run were preferable to the unaccustomed hardships of compulsory settlement and the certain torments of forced labour (*katorga*). Escape, flight and recidivism were therefore everyday facts of Siberian exile life.

The act of flight itself (*pobeg*) took on a variety of forms. Sudden, individual dashes for freedom (known as *pobeg na 'uru!'*) from the marching exile convoys were comparatively rare and actively discouraged, not only by the obvious risk of being shot down in the attempt, but by the collective authority of the prisoners' commune (*artel*).[18] This was done in order that privileges – such as the removal of the heavy iron ankle fetters which all prisoners were compelled to wear on the journey – could be obtained from the convoy officer in return for the artel's collective promise that no one would escape, thereby ensuring that a full complement of prisoners would be handed over to the next relay of guards. When such bolts did occur, the would-be escaper faced not only official punishment by the authorities on recapture, but the even grimmer retribution of a savage flogging at the hands of the merciless artel whose word had been broken. Often the convicts would make up their own search party to hunt down the fugitive, and, if unable to find the right person, would either bribe or bludgeon some other unfortunate soul they chanced upon into joining the convoy in order to keep the artel's side of the bargain for the communal good.[19]

Escape from prison, fortresses and forced labour compounds were difficult but not infrequent and were often marked by astonishing ingenuity and bravado. All the familiar stock-in-trade of the famous great escapes was there: tunnels, lock-picks, forged papers, filed bars, bribed warders, dummies in the bed and ropes of knotted sheets. The nineteenth-century ethnographer, S.V. Maksimov, tells a tale of one veteran brodyaga and amateur conjuror named Tumanov who brought off an audacious vanishing act in the fortress at Tobolsk by leaping over the prison's wooden pallisade from the top of a human pyramid formed by fellow prisoners during a display of acrobatics and prestidigitation which was being performed before an audience of the governor and his invited guests in the gaol courtyard. Maksimov goes on to relate how a search party failed to find Tumanov, but discovered, nailed to the prison wall where he had landed, a large false beard made of flax which he had used as one of his theatrical props. As a rather burlesque finishing touch to the story, it was later said that the provincial governor was so outraged by the whole affair that he ordered the prison commander to wear the beard 'to his dying day' as a mark of his gullibility and shame! What happened to Tumanov, escapologist *extraordinaire*, is not recorded.[20]

By comparison, flight from non-custodial centres of settlement, whether the established villages of 'old' Siberian peasants (*starozhily*), or purpose-built exile communities, was a simple exercise which was often tacitly or actively connived at by the local village authorities. The starozhily regarded the compulsory settlers (*poselentsy*) in their midst with an understandable mixture of resentment, enmity and fear which contrasted with the deep compassion with which the exiles were generally treated by the Siberian illagers while actually on their dreadful journey. Once they were forcibly registered or billeted at their appointed destination, the exiles represented a conspicuous social and economic threat to the local community, and any erstwhile charitable feelings towards them gave way to suspicion and open displays of hostility which bordered on the xenophobic. The new arrivals, far from making a positive contribution to the successful agricultural development of their new localities, only proved to be a heavy collective incubus on the community, straining its economic resources, raising levels of local crime and, as the exiles were mostly young, single men, aggravating the already serious imbalance between the sexes. It was therefore in both the exiles' and the villagers' mutual interest that they should move elsewhere. This circumstance, together with the chronic shortage of police personnel to enforce restriction of movement (as required by the Exile Regulations) facilitated the departure of the exiles in their tens of thousands.

If anything, the rate of desertion from the specially-built exile settlements was even higher, and in some areas the proportion of exiles who managed to put down roots and establish a settled existence was as low as 10 per cent. For example, in 1898 the chief of the Main Prison Administration, on a tour of inspection in Western Siberia, discovered that in seven settlements especially constructed ten years earlier in the Tara district, out of a grand total of 1,210 persons registered as dwelling there, only 136 were still there in person.[21] The other 90 per cent had drifted away and taken to the road, either finding casual employment in the farms, river-ports or gold-fields, or else enlisting in 'General Cuckoo's army'.

Of course, the precise numbers of Siberia's 'bolters and bushrangers',[22] those officially listed as 'whereabouts unknown' (*v bezvestnoi otluchke*), cannot by the very nature of the problem be accurately calculated. Many obvious factors such as inadequate or inaccessible statistical materials, fluctuating rates of detection, the brodyagi's use of multiple pseudonyms (of which the most widely used was the ubiquitous *Ivan Nepomnyashchii* – literally, 'Ivan Forgot-my-name'), variations in local practice, and the inherent fluidity of the phenomenon, militate against the establishment of exact figures. However, sufficient data can be gleaned from the sources to allow the formation of a reasonably accurate impression of the size and scope of the problem. George Kennan reckoned that the annual number of desertions in Siberia as a whole 'exceeds 30,000', while the Siberian regionalist writer, N.M. Yadrintsev, put the figure in the 1880s at between 30,000 and 40,000 out of a rough total figure of 330,000, that is, about 12 per cent.[23] There are grounds, however, for supposing that these may be underestimations. For example, figures provided by the Inspector of Prisons for Irkutsk guberniya in 1897 suggest that within his jurisdiction alone no less than 62 per cent of the entire exile population were listed as 'v bezvestnoi otluchke'.[24] The Soviet historian, A.D. Margolis, who also quotes this figure, gives a breakdown of the numerical and regional distribution of absentees among the exile population of Eastern Siberia at 1 January 1898, as shown in Table 7.1.

Table 7.1 Numerical and regional distribution of absentees among the exile population of Eastern Siberia at 1 January 1898

Yeniseisk guberniya	11,556 (22.65%)
Irkutsk guberniya	29,403 (40.95%)
Zabaikal oblast	3,374 (23.44%)
Yakutsk oblast	1,277 (24.66%)
Amur oblast	484 (71.27%)
Primore oblast	1,817 (85.82%)[25]

The Far Eastern districts therefore had the highest percentage of runaways, while the largest concentration in absolute numbers was in Irkutsk guberniya, straddling, as it did, the direct 'vagabond road' (*varnatskaya doroga*) from the prison camps and mines of Transbaikal. Particularly high concentrations of brodyagi were also to be found around the west Siberian towns of Mariinsk and Kainsk. 'In this way,' to quote Yadrintsev once more, 'from Eastern Siberia to the Urals there exists an endless *perpetuum mobile* of brodyagi'.[26] Taking all the evidence as a whole, it would probably not be unsafe to suggest that, in the last quarter of the nineteenth century, as many as one-third (about 100,000 souls) of the exile population of Siberia were constantly 'on the run'.

Such an intolerable situation obviously called for drastic measures to deal with it and the exile authorities and local police forces had a formidable battery of corporal and custodial punishments at their disposal which they did not spare to inflict on recaptured offenders. However, brutal floggings, increased terms of katorga, starvation diets, permanent chaining to a wheelbarrow and other fearsome sanctions failed to staunch the flow. Harbouring escaped criminals was also a serious offence, technically known as *pristanoderzhatelstvo*, which could itself be punished by a term of exile. This posed a problem for the Siberian villagers who, if they refused to give shelter, might very well find their house burned down around their ears. However, the main target of the legislation were the owners of illegal dens and doss-houses, often run by Jews, where for a small sum, commonly fixed at 10 per cent of any gambling gains, wandering ruffians might find a night's refuge and indulge their passion for playing at cards and dice and hard drinking. Despite the heavy penalties, such thieves' kitchens were commonplace throughout Siberia.

In addition to the legal penalties for escape, other dubious methods were also employed to try and combat the problem. On the island of Sakhalin, and in some other parts of Siberia, an unofficial bounty of three roubles a head was offered for the return of an escaped prisoner or exile. The Karym people of mixed Russian and Buryat blood in Eastern Siberia were particularly feared as relentless bounty-hunters, and there was a popular saying that a fugitive's hide was worth more than the pelt of a squirrel (*gorbach* [that is, a brodyaga] *vse zhe dorozhe belki stoit*). Though not officially encouraged, it was widely acknowledged that the Siberian peasants and natives had little compunction in hunting down such human quarry. According to the exiled Decembrist, D.I. Zavalishin, had the peasants not culled so many exiles in this way, Siberia would never have been able to cope with them all.[27] Naturally, the brodyagi bands exacted cruel reprisals on the bounty-hunting villagers, and the literature is full of horrific stories of acts of bloodcurdling vengeance, turning Siberia into what Yadrintsev describes as 'a constant field of battle'.[28] It was not unknown for a prison commandant to bribe his prisoners not to escape; while on the other hand some gaolers and turnkeys actually connived at successful escapes and deliberately failed to report them in order to carry on drawing the absconded prisoners' subsistence allowance and clothes, using them for personal profit.[29] Finally, one of the most excruciating methods of preventing flight, according to Maksimov, was the practice of slitting a habitual runaway's heels and stuffing the wound with finely chopped horse's hair! (On this painful subject, the same writer maintains that sometimes would-be absconders used this irritant material to insert inside self-inflicted incisions on the penis; the consequent lesions, inflammation and suppuration resembled the symptoms of syphilis, which might gain the desperate malingerer admission to the prison hospital-wing (*lazaret*), whence escape was considerbly easier.)[30]

Faced with this seemingly intractable problem, in 1895 the government began to punish those found guilty of brodyazhestvo by deporting them all to the dreaded penal colonies on the island of Sakhalin. Such was the terror inspired by the prospect of being confined in this final circle of the exile hell that there was immediately a steep and massive drop in the number of convictions and, as a government report in 1900 drily commented, an equally remarkable rise in the number of those masquerading as 'Ivan Nepomnyashchii' who suddenly remembered their real name.[31] But despite the falling conviction rates, flight, vagrancy and brigandage continued to poison the body of Siberian society for as long as the system of judicial and administrative exile remained in operation.

It was not, however, the case that all of those who took to the road were necessarily professional brodyagi or dangerous recidivists. Many drifted away from their places of official registration, not with any criminal intent, but simply because they were physically or temperamentally incapable of settling on the land and preferred to wander in search of casual employment, especially in the gold-fields and, at the turn of the century, on the construction of the Trans-Siberian Railway. These itinerant odd-job men and hobos did not, by and large, present any particular danger to the community. On the contrary, they were regarded as fair game by the starozhily, who not only paid them a pittance for their seasonal labour when required, but also, particularly in the violent, anarchical world of the Siberian gold-fields, swiftly relieved them of the earnings by selling illicit liquor, tendering their wives and daughters for prostitution, or simple robbery – or a combination of all three. These relatively harmless drifters and vagrants were popularly referred to as *zhigany*.

The really serious problem of banditry in Siberia was caused by the thousands of veteran brodyagi who had served their time at katorga and spent many seasons on the run, who knew the ways of the forest, whose lives alternated between the fortress and the taiga, and who survived through a mixture of devious cunning, brigandage and violent crime. The word most commonly used to describe these most dangerous denizens of the Siberian underworld was *varnak*, which George Kennan suggests was originally formed by the insertion of two letter 'a's among the initials V.R.N.K., signifying a flogged criminal (*vor, razboinik, nakazannyi knutom*), with which highwaymen were branded 'in the old times'.[32] During the short Siberian spring and summer they would roam in small groups or larger gangs through the villages and forests, begging or plundering as they went. In order to ward off possible attack, it was a common custom for the Siberian peasants to leave portions of food and drink outside their cottages to which the passing brodyagi could help themselves without physically threatening or molesting the inhabitants.

Even the larger Siberian towns were not immune from their depredations and during the summer hundreds would congregate on the city outskirts creating a huge suburban bivouac of tramps and robbers from which they would launch lightning raids and razzias (known as *strelki* or *letuchki*) into the downtown areas, terrorizing the population. Tyumen, in Tobolsk guberniya, was particularly notorious for its large summertime concentration of brodyagi, many of whom were attracted there by the prospect of casual employment on the river docks, but who also no doubt engaged in criminal activities. In Tomsk guberniya Tomsk itself, and also the towns of Kainsk and Mariinsk, both with large populations of exiles, had a reputation for attracting large numbers of vagrants and varnaki. The latter two centres were also remarkable for the fact that they each contained an officially tolerated refuge or asylum, run by charity and popularly known as the *zhiganskii dom*. In 1898 the shelter at Kainsk was visited by the Tomsk Provincial Prison Inspector who found so many wretched human beings packed into two smallish rooms in unutterably squalid and pathogenic conditions that it was impossible to conduct a proper count. Most were half naked and barefoot, there was a constant cacaphony of consumptive coughing, proper sanitation was non-existent, the atmosphere was mephitic, and the combination of insufficient clothing and the freezing temperatures outside made begging for food an impossibility. The overall picture, said the Inspector's report, was one of 'material and moral destitution that beggars the imagination'.[33] Quite how the maintenance of these institutions squared with laws against pristanoderzhatelstvo is unclear. It may be that they were tolerated in order to relieve the local prison authorities of responsibility for incarcerating the dossers in their own overcrowded cells.

It was in fact regular practice for the brodyagi, having survived the summer and autumn months on the run, to surrender themselves to the police authorities, declare themselves to be without identity papers (*bezpismennye*), offer an alias (for example, Ivan Nepomnyashchii) and hope to obtain shelter from the Siberian winter in the relative warmth and camaraderie of the fortress cells. Here, as an automatically affiliated member of the local chapter of the powerful brodyaga's commune (*brodyazheskaya artel*) the newly incarcerated fugitive would enjoy all the collective benefits of comradeship, personal security, ready cash from the communal chest (*artelnaya kassa*), illicit liquor, tobacco and gambling opportunities in the prisoners' own sutlery-cum-casino (the so-called *maidan*), and the knowledge that he was part of the 'exile prisons' aristocracy'.[34]

These 'aristocrats' of the exile underworld, these robber barons and pirate chiefs, were of course primarily responsible for Siberia's reputation as a vicious and violent continent, a land where brutal multiple murders, gang rapes and fiendish atrocities were routinely recorded in the regional press under 'current events'. Crimes which would have caused a journalistic sensation in European Russia hardly raised the collective eyebrow of the Siberian reading public.[35] And, of course, there was not a lot that the local police authorities could do in order to maintain civilized standards of law and order. The huge expanses covered by the Siberian police precincts, the scattered nature of the population and of population points – often hundreds of miles apart – the undeveloped or non-existent transport and communications system, and the chronic shortage of professional manpower, which had been a perennial complaint of Siberian governors since the seventeenth century, meant that even routine police duties were neglected, let alone the extra burden of maintaining special surveillance over the exile population of a given area. The vast majority of reported crime therefore went undetected, and one must naturally assume that an even greater proportion simply went unreported in the first place.

Of those crimes that *were* recorded, it is clear from the admittedly unsatisfactory and incomplete statistical material available that a disproportionately large percentage of them were committed by the exile, as opposed to the free, population of Siberia, and that of those crimes the greater percentage were of a serious and violent nature against both person and property. To give just one example: a government report published in 1900 reproduced a set of figures provided by the authorities in Yeniseisk guberniya itemizing the number and nature of recorded crimes committed by the exile population within its jurisdiction over a five-year period (unspecified, but almost certainly during the 1890s). Thirty-seven categories of serious and minor offences are listed – from homicide and robbery to brawling and blasphemy. Out of a total of 3,055 crimes recorded, the figures for the 'top ten' categories are as shown in Table 7.2.

Table 7.2 Serious crimes committed by exiles in Yeniseisk guberniya over a five-year period (1890s)

Theft	1,630
Murder and attempted murder	250
Insulting behaviour	182
Wounding and grievous bodily harm	180
Horse-stealing	134
Armed robbery	97
Fraud (*moshennichestvo*)	91
Arson	90
Embezzlement	63
Escape from custody	47

(Intriguingly, further down the list are eleven cases of bestiality, and just one of abduction of a married woman.) If one ignores insulting behaviour and gaolbreaks, then crimes against person and property (theft, murder, 'GBH', and so on) account for 83 per cent of the total. Moreover, the report adds a gloss on the fact that the incidence of murder and attempted murder (which averages out at one per week over the quinquennium) is one and a half times greater than that of wounding and grievous bodily harm, by noting that this was exactly the reverse of the situation in European Russia at the time.[36]

However, these statistics, chilling though they are, are not really surprising when one considers the records of those responsible. There is, of course, no documentary material directly relating the crimes listed above to their individual perpetrators, but if one looks at the criminal profiles and background of those exiled to Siberia by the courts for criminal offences, a clear correlation emerges between the types of crime for which the exiles were originally convicted and the pattern of crimes actually committed in Siberia. The first serious attempt at compiling proper criminal statistics in Russia was made by E.N. Anuchin in 1866. By subjecting the records of the Exile Bureau at Tobolsk to a meticulous analysis, Anuchin clearly demonstrated that, apart from brodyazhestvo itself, the vast bulk of the exile population was made up of convicted murderers, robbers and thieves. According to his painstaking researches (for which, incidentally, he was awarded the Constantine medal of the Imperial Russian Geographical Society in 1869), during the two decades between 1827 and 1846 the numbers of those dealt with by the Exile Bureau for selected offences were as shown in Table 7.3.

Table 7.3 Number of crimes punished by exile to Siberia, 1827–1846

Theft	40,660
Murder	14,531
Robbery with violence	5,068
Forging documents	3,545
Insurrection	2,411
Arson	1,918
Forging money	1,301
Grievous bodily harm	853
Sexual offences	853
Other miscellaneous offences	8,706
Total	79,846[37]

By comparing these two sets of figures (allowing for the chronological difference between them) it may be seen that the proportion (78 per cent) of those exiled to Siberia for serious crimes involving violence against person or property was roughly equal to the percentage of similar crimes committed by the exiles when in their place of banishment. Less reliable, though similar figures given by Maksimov for the number of serious offenders exiled to hard labour in the mines at Nerchinsk tell the same story. During the decade 1847 to 1857, out of a total of 6,230 prisoners received by the Nerchinsk mining administration, 2,179 were convicted murderers, 1,136 were sentenced for armed robbery or burglary, and 2,256 were being punished for crimes committed while on the run from imprisonment for previous offences, many of which were undoubtedly of an equally grave nature.[38]

It is therefore perfectly obvious, and indeed a matter of common sense, that it was the exile system itself which contributed more than anything else to the lawlesslness from which Siberia suffered and which helped to create the territory's 'Wild East' image. There was a quite literally vicious circle of crime, punishment, exile, escape, further crime and punishment which was, as the authorities themselves admitted, 'the fruit of the deeply imbued poison of the Siberian exile system'.[39]

Despite the constant dangers to which the villagers and citizens of Siberia were exposed, and despite the horrific nature of the crimes committed against them by the exile bandits and brodyagi, the literature nevertheless reveals that the hostility and fear of the starozhily towards the roving criminals was curiously mixed with a kind of admiration and respect which sometimes bordered on hero-worship. The Siberian folk memory retains the names of many famous bandit chiefs whose exploits made them a legend even in their own lifetime. Of these some of the most notorious were Gorkin, Korenev, Bykov, Chaikin, Sokhatyi and Kapustin – the Robin Hoods, Ned Kellys and Billy the Kids of the Siberian taiga, whose audacious deeds are now little remembered beyond the scene of their former crimes.[40] But in the nineteenth century tales and legends were still told about their boldness, their fortitude, physical prowess, animal cunning and even supernatural powers. Siberian children played not at cops and robbers or cowboys and Indians but at 'brodyagi and soldiers', and, according to Yadrintsev, peasant girls were often seduced into leaving their villages by fantasies of a life of excitement and glamour in the taiga as a Siberian ganster's moll.[41] The same writer, however, relates a gruesome anecdote which gives a more realistic and grimmer picture of the distress likely to be suffered by those unfortunate damsels who did fall into the brodyagi's clutches. This concerns a peasant woman who was abducted from her village and forced to accompany her brodyaga capturer on his travels. On the road they were joined by another brodyaga who wished to share the woman with the first. An argument ensued, but rather than falling out over who should have her, and thereby allowing a squabble over a woman to break the brodyagi's mutual bond, they decide to abandon her, but not without first gratuitously tormenting her for being the unwitting object of their dispute. Accordingly, they stripped her naked and left her hanging by her hair from a tree, where she was later discovered, almost dead, her bloated body eaten alive by gadflies and mosquitoes.[42]

Notwithstanding such barbarities, Siberian folklore nevertheless continued to perpetuate a mythology of outstanding robber-heroes, accrediting them not only with such physical attributes as enormous strength, great beauty and various bodily skills, but also with such admirable virtues as compassion for the poor and needy and a constant readiness to protect the downtrodden from oppression and exploitation: in other words, the classical Robin Hood syndrome of robbing the rich to feed the poor, which, while it may contain an element of truth, should not obscure the fact that in the absence of richer pickings from merchant caravans, state mail-coaches and grasping bureaucrats, the bandits of the taiga did not scruple to rape and pillage among the poorest peasants, townsfolk and native tribes of Siberia. It was not unknown for whole villages to be burned to the ground in acts of collective reprisal against a community suspected of collaborating with the police or military authorities in their search for criminals in the vicinity.[43]

As well as the legends, stories and myths, there were, too, other more tangible and observable memorials to the exploits of famous Siberian bandits. In some parts of Siberia, as elsewhere in Russia, geographical features such as streams, rivers, ravines, woods and swamps or even settlements often bore the name of a particularly memorable felon who operated in the locality. The region beyond Lake Baikal, for instance, which was infested with large robber gangs from the compulsory settlements established there by Emperor Paul I, contained hamlets known as Gorkin, Grigoriev and so on, named after well-known brigand chiefs.[44] But one famous bandit ataman, Mitka Bykov, who terrorized Kazan guberniya in the 1840s, left even more than his name to curious posterity. After his death, caused by the effects of being sentenced to run the gauntlet of a thousand men, Bykov's huge skeleton was preserved and placed on display in the museum of Kazan University, where, according to Maksimov, it made a striking impression by 'the fine proportions (*proportsialnostyu*) of the bones, indicating a handsome figure even in the anatomical meaning of the word'.[45]

One recurrent theme in both the oral and written literature about popular bandit heroes everywhere is that they were driven to commit their initial crime by some grave social injustice or personal insult or injury inflicted by officialdom. In the case of Siberia's exiles and criminals there is no doubt that many were driven to their original acts of insubordination, felony or worse by the overall oppression, inequality and rampant injustice of the tsarist social and political system. However, even if there is some truth in the maxim that every criminal is in a sense a martyr of the social order, and even though murderers, robbers and cut-throats are sometimes transmogrified in the popular imagination into enviable daredevils, rebels against tyranny, champions of the poor or well-meaning redistributors of the social wealth, it is not simply to the folklore and legends, but also to the criminal statistics, court reports and police records that one should turn in order to place their activities into proper perspective. As mentioned above, Siberian newspapers in the nineteenth century were replete with stories of such sickening crimes that it may be indelicate to repeat them here.

However, just a few examples will serve to convey something of the 'rude and barbarous' nature of life and death in Russia's 'Wild East', though it is, of course, possible that the mass barbarisms committed throughout the world in the twentieth century and the lurid reportage of crimes involving sex and violence in the contemporary western media may have inured us to their impact.

On 28 February 1875, it was reported in the Ishim newspaper, *Birzha*, that during one evening the previous week three young thugs had careered into the middle of the town, snatched a thirteen-year-old girl off the street, driven off with her in their sleigh and taken her out of town. There, each of them raped her in turn, and then drove back into town and threw her onto the street. An 'energetic' but fruitless search was made for her assailants and the girl died of her injuries on the following day.[46] Similarly, an article in *Otechestvennye zapiski* in July 1875 tells how a Siberian town was terrorized throughout one winter by a gang of youths who regularly galloped round the town in their troika, carousing and capturing unwary passers-by with lassos and boat-hooks.[47] This must have been a common sport, for George Kennan was later to report similar disturbances in the major town of Tomsk:

> Even the city of Tomsk itself was terrorized in February 1886, while we were there, by a band of criminals who made a practice of riding through the city in sleighs at night and catching belated wayfarers with sharp grappling hooks.[48]

In neither case are we told whether the kidnappers and gang-rapists were escaped exiles, brodyagi or varnaki, but both Yadrintsev and Maksimov provide accounts of other ghastly incidents in which the perpetrators were invariably discovered to have been exiled criminals. One concerned the disappearance of a young chambermaid from the Krasnoyarsk girls' high school. Soon after her disappearance was reported, a number of grisly human remains were discovered: first a mutilated head, then a severed arm being dragged along by a dog, from which *disjecta membra* the victim's identity was established, and eventually the poor girl's torso, horribly disfigured with the breasts hacked off and the genitals savagely mutilated. Suspicion fell on the school caretaker and on a clerk from a local office, both of whom had disappeared at about the same time. When they were finally arrested and their guilt established, the investigation revealed that both were escaped exile convicts living under false identities.[49] (The assumption of a false persona was, of course, a standard ploy for avoiding recognition as a wanted fugitive, and Maksimov tells of one rogue who for a long time passed himself off as a *yurodivyi* – a 'holy fool' – growing his hair and beard long to conceal the tell-tale criminal brand marks on his face, and another escaped exile who managed to get himself taken, in grand Gogolian fashion, for a Government Inspector or *revizor!*[50])

Multiple murders were also distressingly common. On 5 October 1873, the widow of an Irkutsk merchant, her daughter, their janitor and a Buryat servant were all killed and their bodies thrown in the river Angara. The killers also assaulted their young cook, raped her, tortured her and finally strangled her, leaving her for dead. Amazingly, however, she survived her ordeal and was able to identify her assailants who turned out to be three exiled settlers (*poselentsy*) and three brodyagi. At their trial they apparently showed complete indifference to the enormity of their crime. Three were later hanged. During 1897 and 1898, according to a government source, the whole major city of Krasnoyarsk was in a virtual state of siege as a result of the criminal depradations of large gangs of exiles who had gathered there ostensibly to labour on the construction of the Trans-Siberian Railway, but who in fact simply plundered the town with apparent impunity, often slaughtering whole families at a time. The report continues:

The whole town was terrorized by the exiles. No-one dared venture onto the streets alone after nine in the evening. Citizens would only go about in groups of several people, with revolvers at the ready.

But even fully-armed military patrols were attacked by gangs of criminals, and only the imposition of martial law (which included the death penalty) finally brought some measure of order to the town.[51] Elsewhere, not only whole families, but entire communities were wiped out. For instance, in his fascinating report of his investigations on the island of Sakhalin, Anton Chekhov tells of a massacre in which a gang of sixteen fugitive criminal exiles raided a native Ainu village, tortured and killed the menfolk, raped all the women and hanged all the children.[52]

Partly in response to the increasingly frequent reports of such harrowing incidents, and partly under the pressure of protests from the Siberian public and also international opinion, a serious attempt was finally made by the appropriate ministries to subject the whole exile operation to a thorough-going official investigation in the last years of the nineteenth century. Unable any longer to ignore the mounting campaign to end the system which, far from enhancing the successful colonization and development of Siberia, only damaged its chances of orderly, peaceful and prosperous progress, the government finally promulgated the Exile Reform Law of June 1900, a measure which Lenin considered to be as important to Siberia's future as the building of the Trans-Siberian Railway.[53] While the new legislation did have a certain limited success in ameliorating some of the system's more obvious and distressful abuses, it could do little in the short term to alter the formidable reputation of Siberia's far-flung wastes as the Russian

Empire's principal realm of crime and punishment. And the breakdown
of tsarist authority during the revolutions of 1917, the chaotic complexity
of the years of civil war, political fragmentation and foreign military
intervention, meant that the entire territory from the Urals to the Pacific
continued to be the scene of mass violence, lawlessness and social anarchy
which had been one of the singular hallmarks of the exile system.

It is interesting to note in conclusion that even now, in the last decade
of the twentieth century, not only has the region not lost its notoriety as
a hard, tough frontierland, but also – in addition to the perennial problems
of manpower shortage, communications difficulties, sexual imbalance,
vagrancy, inadequate social and cultural infrastructure, interethnic hostilities
and increasing resentment at the continuing centralization of political and
economic decision-making in Moscow – the disturbing fact remains that
Siberia and the Soviet Far East still suffer from a higher concentration of
crime and criminals in comparison with other regions of the USSR. This
situation has, too, been blamed on the continuing use of Siberia as a major
location for corrective labour camps and prisons to which are despatched
those convicted of participation in the Soviet Union's recently rocketing
crime rate.[54] Less recently, the Soviet film, *Cold Summer of 'fifty-three*,
tells the story of a gang of criminals, released from prison camp following
the amnesty after Stalin's death in 1953, who brought violence and terror
to a remote Siberian village; all the 'bad guys' were finally killed in a
dramatic shoot-out with the hero, a resident political exile.[55] When it was
shown on British television in January 1990, the presenter described it as
a 'film with all the elements of a classic "western" '. The incident depicted
was itself no doubt fictional, but it was explicitly based on real-life conditions
in post-Stalin Siberia. While it would, of course, be fanciful to apply the
'Wild East' analogy used in this chapter to the Siberia of today, the echoes
and vestiges of her unruly history evidently still persist.

NOTES AND REFERENCES

1   A slightly different version of this chapter was originally presented as a paper
    at the international colloquium on 'La Sibérie: Colonisation, Développement et
    Perspectives (1582–1982)' in Paris, May 1983.
2   Aleksandr Solzhenitsyn, *Arkhipelag GULag* (Paris: YMCA, 1975), p. 351.
3   Genesis 4. 12.
4   Among the most useful recent Soviet works are the five collections of essays
    edited by L.M. Goryushkin: *Ssylka i katorga v Sibiri (XVIII – nachalo XX v.)*
    (Novosibirsk: Nauka, 1975); *Ssylka i obshchestvenno-politicheskaya zhizn v Sibiri
    (XVIII – nachalo XX v.)* (Novosibirsk Nauka, 1978); *Politicheskie ssylnye v Sibiri
    (XVIII – nachalo XX v.)* (Novosibirsk Nauka, 1983); *Politicheskaya ssylka v
    Sibiri, XIX – nachalo XX v. Istoriografiya i istochniki* (Novosibirsk Nauka, 1987);
    Politicheskaya ssylka i revolyutsionnoe dvizhenie y Rossii, Konets XIX – nachalo

XX v. (Novosibirsk Nauka, 1988). See also L.A. Ushakova, *Sovetskaya istoriografiya sibirskoi narodnicheskoi ssylki* (Novosibirsk Nauka, 1985). In English, the best-known study is that by the American journalist, George Kennan, *Siberia and the Exile System*, 2 vols (New York: The Century Co., 1891); for an 'inside' view see Leo Deutsch, *Sixteen Years in Siberia: Some Experiences of a Russian Revolutionist* (London: John Murray, 1903). See also the following articles by the present author: Alan Wood, 'Siberian Exile in Tsarist Russia', *History Today* 30 (1980): 19–24; 'Sex and Violence in Siberia: Aspects of the Tsarist Exile System', in John Massey Stewart and Alan Wood, *Siberia: Two Historical Perspectives* (London: GB-USSR Association and School of Slavonic and East European Studies, 1984), pp. 35–61; 'Chernyshevskii, Siberian Exile and *oblastnichestvo*', in Roger Bartlett (ed.), *Russian Thought and Society 1800–1917: Essays in Honour of Eugene Lampert* (Keele, 1984), pp. 42–66; 'The Use and Abuse of Administrative Exile to Siberia', *Irish Slavonic Studies* 6 (1985): 65–82; 'Crime and Punishment in the House of the Dead', in Olga Crisp and Linda Edmondson (eds), *Civil Rights in Imperial Russia* (Oxford: Oxford University Press, 1989), pp. 216–33; 'Avvakum's Siberian Exile', in Alan Wood and R.A. French (eds), *The Development of Siberia: People and Resources* (London: Macmillan, 1989), pp. 11–34; 'Administrative Exile and the Criminals' Commune in Siberia', in Roger Bartlett (ed.), *Land Commune and Peasant Community in Russia: Communal Forms in Imperial and Early Soviet Society* (Macmillan, London: 1990), pp. 395–414.

5 Robert Hughes, *The Fatal Shore: A History of the Transportation of Convicts to Australia 1787–1868* (London: Pan Books, 1988).

6 N.V. Turchaninov, 'Naselenie Aziatskoi Rossii', in *Aziatskaya Rossiya* I (St Petersburg, 1914), p. 81; N.M. Yadrintsev, *Sibir kak koloniya. Sovremennoe polozhenie Sibiri. Yeya nuzhdy i potrebnosti. Yeya proshloe i budushchee* (St Petersburg, 1882), p. 127.

7 Turchaninov, op. cit., p. 81; A.D. Margolis, 'O chislennosti i razmeshchenii ssylnykh v Sibiri v kontse XIX v.', in Goryushkin (ed.), 1975, op. cit., p. 235.

8 There is a large statistical and analytical literature on the population dynamics of Siberia: see, for example, Turchaninov, op. cit.; V.M. Kabuzan and S.M. Troitskii, 'Dvizhenie naseleniya Sibiri v XVIII v.', in *Sibir XVII–XVIII vv. Materialy po istorii Sibiri: Sibir perioda feodalizma* 1, Novosibirsk, Izd. Sibirskogo otdeleniya AN SSR: 1962), pp. 139–57, and 'Chislennost i sostav naseleniya Sibiri v pervoi polovine XIX v.' in *Russkoe naselenie pomorya i Sibiri (Perioda feodalizma)* (Moscow: Nauka, 1973), pp. 261–77; V.M. Kabuzan, 'Zaselenie Sibiri i Dalnego Vostoka v kontse XVIII – nachale XX veka (1795–1917 gg.)', *Istoriya SSSR* 3 (1979): 22–38; N.I. Nikitin, *Sluzhilie lyudi v Zapadnoi Sibiri XVII veka* (Novosibirsk: Nauka, 1988); Donald Treadgold, *The Great Siberian Migration* (Princeton, 1957); Terence Armstrong, *Russian Settlement in the North* (Cambridge University Press, 1965); F.-X. Coquin, *La Sibérie: peuplement et migration paysanne au XIX siècle* (Paris, 1969). See also the chapter by Leonid Goryushkin in the present volume, pp. 140–57.

9 *zek*: Russian prison slang for 'convict' or 'prisoner'. In the nineteenth century, Yadrintsev was particularly contemptuous of the notion that 'criminal blood' (*varnatskaya krov*) flowed in the veins of most of the Siberian population: N.M. Yadrintsev, 'Kolonizatsionnoe znachenie russkoi ssylki', *Delo* 2 (1872): 1–34.

10 I. Ya. Foinitskii, *Uchenie o nakazanii v svyazi s tyurmovedeniem* (St Petersburg, 1889), pp. 260–6.

11   *Ssylka v Sibir. Ocherk yeya istorii i sovremennago polozheniya* (St Petersburg, 1900), pp. 6–9; see also the comments on the sound sense of the exile system by a contemporary exile, in J.M. Letiche and B. Dmytryshyn, *Russian Statecraft: The Politika of Iurii Krizhanich* (Oxford: Blackwell, 1985), p. 127.

12   For a discussion of the wording and implication of these decrees, see A.D. Kolesnikov, 'Ssylka i zaselenie Sibiri', in Goryushkin (ed.), 1975, op. cit., p. 42.

13   Wood, 'Sex and Violence', op. cit., pp. 39–43.

14   Terence Armstrong (ed.), *Yermak's Campaign in Siberia*, (London: Hakluyt Society, 1975), pp. 9–18. Armstrong's reiteration of the traditional view that 'he [Yermak] undoubtedly was a pirate' (ibid., p. 12) is indirectly challenged by R.G. Skrynnikov, who adduces archive evidence which 'is noteworthy for disposing of myths about Ermak's supposed brigandage. . . . ' and ' . . . shows that Moscow knew Ermak well and valued his services'. See his article, 'Ermak's Siberian Expedition', *Russian History/Histoire Russe* 13 (1) (1986): 1–39 (quotation, p. 7).

15   E.J. Hobsbawm, *Bandits* (London: Pelican Books, 1972).

16   Ibid., p. 85.

17   N.M. Yadrintsev, *Russkaya obshchina v tyurme i ssylke* (St Petersburg, 1872), pp. 351–9.

18   On the function, powers and organization of the Siberian exiles' artel, see Wood, 'Administrative Exile and the Criminals' Commune in Siberia', op. cit., pp. 402–12.

19   Kennan, op. cit., I: 393; S.V. Maksimov, *Sibir i katorga*, 3rd edn (St Petersburg, 1900), pp. 17–18.

20   Maksimov, op. cit., pp. 47–8.

21   *Ssylka v Sibir*, op. cit., pp. 161–8.

22   The phrase is borrowed from Hughes's chapter on escaped convicts in Australia, *Fatal Shore*, op.cit., pp. 203–43.

23   Kennan, op. cit., II: 153; Yadrintsev, *Sibir kak koloniya*, op. cit., p. 189.

24   *Tyuremnyi vestnik* 9 (1898): 447.

25   Margolis, 'O chislennosti. . . ', op. cit., p. 231.

26   Yadrintsev, *Russkaya obshchina*, op. cit., p. 363.

27   *Ssylka v Sibir*, op. cit., p. 263, note 2.

28   On 'lynch law' in Siberia, see Yadrintsev, *Russkaya obshchina*, op. cit., pp. 488–500; Maksimov, op. cit., pp. 74–78; Kennan, op. cit., II: 463–4.

29   Kennan, op. cit., II: 156.

30   Maksimov, op. cit., p. 49.

31   *Ssylka v Sibir*, op. cit., p. 277. During the four years, 1891–4, the average number of brodyagi punished by 'exile for resettlement' (*ssylka va vodvorenie*) was 1,205; for the four years *after* Sakhalin became the main destination (1895–8), this dropped to an average of 426 and in 1898 was as low as 263; *Ssylka v Sibir* (Prilozhenie 2: 9–12).

32   Kennan, op. cit., II: 463, note 5.

33   *Ssylka v Sibir*, op. cit., p. 266.

34   Yadrintsev, *Russkaya obshchina*, op. cit., p. 415.

35   *Ssylka v Sibir*, op. cit., pp. 304–5; Yadrintsev, *Sibir kak koloniya*, op. cit., p. 205.

36   Ibid., p. 302.

37   E.N. Anuchin, *Issledovaniya o protsente soslannykh v Sibir v period 1827–1846*

godov. *Materialy dlya ugolovnoi statistiki Rossii* (St Petersburg, 1873), pp. 17–22.
38 Maksimov, op. cit., p. 194.
39 *Ssylka v Sibir*, op. cit., p. 305.
40 Maksimov, op. cit., pp. 171–95, 237–47; Yadrintsev, *Russkaya obshchina*, op. cit., pp. 400–3.; V. Ptitsyn, 'Iz proshlago. Zabaikalskie razboiniki', *Istoricheskii vestnik* 40 (1890): 237–9.
41 A.P. Chekhov, *Ostrov Sakhalin*, in *Polnoe sobranie sochinenii i pisem v tridtsati tomakh* 14–15: 272 (Moscow: Nauka, 1978); Yadrintsev, *Russkaya obshchina*, op. cit., pp. 403–12, 424–5.
42 Ibid., p. 411.
43 *Ssylka v Sibir*, op. cit. p. 264.
44 Maksimov, op. cit., p. 239.
45 Ibid., p. 245.
46 Yadrintsev, *Sibir kak koloniya*, op. cit., p. 202.
47 Ibid., p. 205.
48 Kennan, op. cit., II: 462, note 3.
49 Yadrintsev, *Sibir kak koloniya*, op. cit., pp. 202–3.
50 Maksimov, op. cit., p. 86.
51 *Ssylka v Sibir*, op. cit., pp. 207–8.
52 Chekhov, *Ostrov Sakhalin*, op. cit., pp. 328–9.
53 A.D. Margolis, 'Sistema sibirskoi ssylki i zakon ot 12 iyunya 1900 goda', in Goryushkin (ed.), 1978, op. cit., p 126.
54 *Izvestiya*, 4, 5 and 7 August, 1988. The startling information contained in the *Izvestiya* articles is analysed by Leslie Dienes, 'Crime and Punishment in the USSR: New Information on Distribution', *Soviet Geography*, 29(9) (Nov. 1988): 793–808.
55 'Kholodnoe leto pyatdesyat tretego . . .', directed by Konstantin Stenkin, Tvorcheskoe obedinenie 'ZHANR', Mosfilm Studios, Moscow.

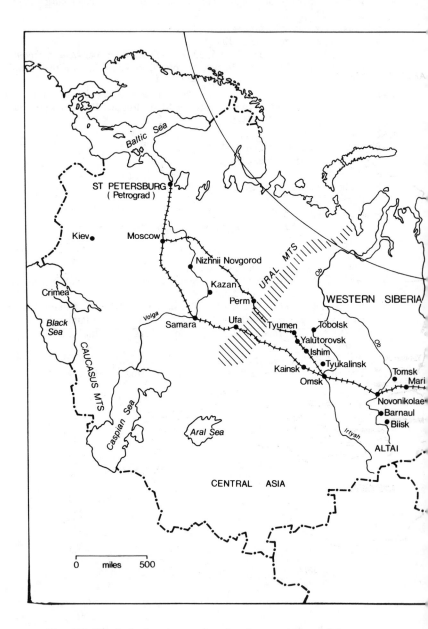

Map 7.1 Siberia in the nineteenth and early twentieth centuries
Courtesy of John Haywood.

8 Migration, settlement and the rural economy of Siberia, 1861–1914

Leonid M. Goryushkin
(translated from the Russian by Alan Wood)

The great Russian historian, V.O. Klyuchevskii (1841–1911), once remarked: 'The history of Russia is the history of a country undergoing colonization'.[1] After the abolition of serfdom in 1861, many peasants, driven by land-hunger and the oppression of the landlords (*pomeshchiki*), migrated to the southern Ukraine, the Caucasus, Central Asia and Siberia. By the end of the nineteenth and the beginning of the twentieth centuries, Siberia had become the country's principal region for colonization. Between 1896 and 1914 Siberia received approximately 80 per cent of all emigrants from European Russia. In settling this harsh and distant territory, the migrants laid new roads, built new villages, cleared the forests for agriculture and cultivated crops. The major role in the economic development of Siberia from the mid nineteenth to the early twentieth century was thus played by peasants, workers and artisans. The object of this chapter is to examine the process of this migration and its influence on the numbers and composition of the population, the opening up of new territories, and the development of agriculture, animal husbandry and cottage industries.

From 1861 to 1914, around 3,800,000 people migrated and settled in Siberia and the Far East, including Akmolinsk oblast. The rate and size of the movement, which was unevenly spread over the period, depended on a combination of social, economic and political factors. In rough figures, between 1861 and 1885 around 300,000 settlers crossed the Urals, that is, about 12,000 per year. At this time the tsarist government was attempting to curtail the movement of migration to the borderlands in order not to deprive the private landlords of an adequate labour force. However, the development of capitalist relationships, and the intensification of the land problem in European Russia, forced the government, without departing from its basic policy of restricting migration, to make certain concessions. In 1881 the 'Provisional Regulations for Peasant Migration' came into effect, which permitted the departure of peasants only with the agreement of the Ministries of Internal Affairs and State Lands, but in 1889 a new law was passed according to which those who had received permission to migrate were entitled to travel grants and loans to help them establish farmsteads. During the ten-year period from 1886 to 1895 there were 611,000 immigrants to Siberia, that is, an average of more than 61,000 per year.

With the building of the Trans-Siberian Railway, which greatly facilitated both the export of agricultural goods out of, and the movement of settlers into, Siberia, the inflow of migrants increased significantly. Between 1896 and 1900, 670,000 settlers (134,000 per year) moved into Siberia and the Far East, but the next five years (1901–5) saw a marked decline to 226,000 (45,000 per year), as a result of increasing agrarian unrest in European Russia and the peasants' mounting hopes of acquiring more land from the pomeshchiki in their own homeland. After the revolutionary upheavals of 1905–7, the government began to force the pace of migration once more in an attempt to diffuse the revolutionary mood of the peasantry by encouraging them to move to far-off Siberia, thereby blunting the acuteness of the land question in central Russia. As a result, from 1906 to 1914 around two million people (220,000 per year) migrated to Siberia and the Far East.[2]

Among the new settlers were peasants of various social levels, but until around the 1880s the majority of them consisted of 'middle peasants' or *serednyaki*. Later on, and especially after the opening of the Trans-Siberian Railway, the proportion of 'poor peasants' (*bednyaki*) began to increase, so that by the beginning of the new century they comprised the majority of new immigrants. In terms of nationality, most were Russians. In the 1880s and 1890s more than 80 per cent of all emigrants were from the black earth regions, particularly Kursk, Tambov, Poltava, Kharkov and Voronezh gubernii. However, at the turn of the century there was an increase in the number of migrants from the south-west regions (for example, Kiev and Podolsk gubernii), the western provinces (Minsk, Mogilev, Vitebsk) and the southern steppes (Kherson, Yekaterinoslav (now Dnepropetrovsk), and so on).

In Siberia the immigrants naturally tried to settle in those places which were most conducive to agricultural development, and which were the easiest and least expensive to reach. From the mid-1890s the main body (up to 40 per cent) of settlers headed for Tomsk guberniya, and also for Akmolinsk (now Tselinograd) oblast and Yeniseisk guberniya. They selected their areas of settlement in accordance with the recommendations of scouts (*khodoki*), that is, peasant representatives who had been sent ahead to reconnoitre suitable plots of land, or according to the letters and accounts of their compatriots who had migrated earlier. In this way particular areas of Siberia were often settled overwhelmingly by peasants who had originated from the same region of European Russia. Consequently, peasants from the steppes or forest belt of European Russia would settle in similar locations in Siberia. They made careful calculations about the ecological characteristics of various soil and climatic zones, and naturally preferred to establish their new settlements on land near rivers and lakes, with fertile soil and close to a forest.

In the process of migration and settlement, various channels were created which allowed mutual economic influences to develop between the new settlers and the old inhabitants (*starozhily*) of Siberia. One such channel of influence resulted from the pattern of peasant settlement. From the 1860s to the 1880s the majority of immigrants acquired land in the villages of the starozhily, paying a certain sum of money for it to the village commune (*selskoe obshchestvo*). It was easier for the new settlers to find accommodation, work for wages, and buy essential goods in the starozhily villages until they had built their own home and established their own farm. They could also count on the help of the community (*obshchina*) in the preparation and ploughing of their plots of land. In this process of mutual assistance, the newcomers benefited from the agricultural skills of the starozhily, and, in turn, passed on to the old Siberians their own experience derived from European Russia.

In the first decades after the 1861 reform, most of the immigrants settled in the villages of the Siberian starozhily. However, the number of those who preferred to live in newly-established settler communities gradually increased, and by the beginning of the twentieth century they began to form a majority. While living in these settlements, they continued to mix with the starozhily and work for them as hired labour. During the first years of their arrival in Siberia many of the migrants worked for wealthy starozhily and other settlers in order to accumulate sufficient capital to buy their own farm. Mingling with the Siberian peasants they soon familiarized themselves with local agricultural practices, both of crop production and livestock rearing.

The historical literature has often regarded the phenomenon of repeated resettlement within Siberia as a 'sorrowful symptom' of the immigrants' dissatisfaction with the poor quality of the land they acquired on their first arrival,[3] and the unsatisfactory nature of the help received from the immigration and settlement administration.[4] There is some justification for this view, but the process of continuous resettlement has another side to it which investigators have failed to take fully into account. The movement of internal 'remigration' within Siberia helped to open up new territories, provided a means for the wider distribution of agricultural experience, and extended the influence of the settlers on the development of Siberia's agrarian economy. According to official figures, in 1910 the proportion of new inhabitants acquiring land in Tobolsk and Tomsk gubernii who wished to resettle in other regions was between 5 and 6 per cent, and in Yeniseisk guberniya, 12.6 per cent.[5] In 1913 around 7,000 migrants from Akmolinsk oblast – almost 15 per cent of recent arrivals – chose to resettle, mainly in the Far East.[6] In this way, the process of internal migration within Siberia furthered the process of colonization and many remote areas were settled by emigrants from, as it were, transitional, intermediate regions.

The movement of migration and settlement had a powerful influence on the dynamics and composition of the population of Siberia, the region's greatest productive force. In 1858 the total population of Siberia (excluding the Far Eastern provinces) stood at 2.7 million; by 1897 this had risen to 5.8 million, and in 1913 to 10.3 million. At the turn of the century, the rate of population increase in Siberia was twice that of European Russia. This was due both to the influx of new settlers and to the higher rate of natural increase in population in Siberia. Between 1861 and 1896 immigration accounted for approximately one-third of the total population increase, and for two-thirds in the period 1897 to 1913. The highest population growth rates were in Akmolinsk oblast and Tomsk and Yeniseisk gubernii, which were, of course, the most popular regions for immigration and settlement. The rate of natural increase of population in Siberia (1.8 per cent), was higher than the national average of 1.4 per cent, and is explained by the greater prosperity of the Siberian peasantry in comparison with the peasantry in the traditional serf-owning regions of the country, and also by the natural conditions of the newly-settled borderlands which demanded an increase in the number of inhabitants and working hands.

Another artificial source of population increase was the Siberian exile system. According to approximate figures of the Main Prison Administration, between 1861 and 1898 around 535,000 people were banished to Siberia, including family members who voluntarily accompanied their exiled relatives.[7] However, the exile system did not on the whole play an especially significant role in the colonization and settlement of Siberia. The vast majority of exiles were single men, often of advanced years, many of them only temporarily resident in Siberia. Only a very small proportion of them actually produced families and settled down to permanent residence (see Chapter 7).

The circumstances in which Siberia was colonized also had an effect on the age and sex structure of the population. The majority of the population was male: in European Russia for every 100 men there were 103 women; in Siberia there were 95 (with the exception of Tobolsk guberniya, which was geographically closest to Europe and where the ratio between the sexes was roughly equal). The reason for the imbalance is that during the colonization of Siberia, the proportion of males of working age and old men was higher, and that of children and young people under twenty years of age lower, than in European Russia. Moreover, the further one moved from west to east and from south to north, that is, from the more to the less inhabited and settled regions, the greater was the tendency for there to be a lower percentage of minors, and a higher percentage of working-age adults in the population. Migration was therefore the most important source in the population growth of Siberia – a territory which is richly endowed with everything else except human beings (in 1913 there was less than one inhabitant per square kilometre).

As the migratory movement across the Urals gained pace, so did the proportion of new settlers in the rural population of Siberia almost double from 27 per cent in 1897 to 49 per cent in 1914. The main direction of settlement was along the Moscow Tract, and then along the route of the Trans-Siberian Railway with deviations to the south (the Altai and the Minusinsk Depression) and along the course of the major rivers. The majority of immigrants stayed in the mixed forest-steppe zone, and in the process of settlement opened up 16.5 million desyatinas (one *desyatina* equals 1.09 hectares or 2.7 acres) of new lands, of which around 8 million were brought under the plough.[8] Thousands of new population centres were established. From 1898 to 1912 alone, more than 6,400 new rural communes were created, and by 1917 almost half of the population centres in Yeniseisk guberniya consisted of villages and settlements which had been founded predominantly between the mid-1880s and 1914.[9]

The migration process naturally encouraged the development of agriculture. In the last four decades of the nineteenth century the area of sown land in Siberia increased by 42 per cent, and the total yield by as much as 87 per cent. The most spectacular growth took place in those areas which were most populously settled by the incomers (Akmolinsk oblast, Tomsk and Yeniseisk gubernii) and during the period which saw the greatest wave of immigration after the opening of the Trans-Siberian Railway. With the increase in sown area and cereal crop yield, the agricultural productivity of Siberia per head of population outstripped that of European Russia. In keeping with the pattern of migration and settlement, agricultural production in Siberia moved gradually southwards to the forest-steppe and steppe zones. With Siberia's entry on to the all-Russian and the world market after the construction of the Trans-Siberian Railway and the massive flood of migration across the Urals, the rate of growth in the area of sown land increased not just fourfold (as happened from the 1860s to the 1890s), but by more than five times in comparison with corresponding indicators in

European Russia. According to statistics compiled by the migration authorities, in 1913 37,620 families of settlers arrived in Siberia, thereby increasing the total population by 226,000, the number of active workers by 113,000, the area of sown land by 150,000 desyatinas and the grain harvest by 6,000,000 puds (one *pud* equals 16.38 kilogrammes or 36 pounds).[10] By 1917 Siberian grain production had outstripped all the other colonial borderlands of the country – the northern Caucasus, Transcaucasia, and Central Asia including Kazakhstan.[11]

The development of commercial-capitalist relationships in the Siberian countryside in the late nineteenth and early twentieth centuries brought with it a change in the pattern of sown crops: for instance, there was a sharp rise in the proportion of spring wheat grown predominantly for the market, which accounted for almost half the total sown area. The settlers brought with them improved types of seed corn (Russian names – *beloturka, kitaika, krasnokoloska*), which became widely disseminated throughout Siberia, and in the northern regions they experimented with the sowing of winter wheat. Already at the end of the seventeenth century attempts had been made to cultivate flax in Siberia, and in 1847 flax seeds purchased in St Petersburg and Vologda guberniya were sown for the first time in Kamchatka. In the 1850s settlers from Vitebsk province disseminated flax seed in the Ishim district of Tobolsk guberniya which was of a much higher quality than any previously known in Siberia, the fibres being much thicker and twice as long as earlier strains. Consequently, considerable areas were given over to flax cultivation.[12]

After 1906–7, settlers from the flax-growing regions of European Russia – Smolensk, Pskov, Novgorod and other provinces – imported seeds of a long-fibred flax (*lën-dolgunets*) and began its large-scale industrial production. In the 1830s Himalayan barley began to be propagated in Siberia, and the 1850s saw the first attempts to introduce sugar-beet. A major role was played by the immigrants in the distribution of these and other crops, for example, millet, buckwheat and sunflowers, in Siberia. In Nizhneudinsk, Balagansk and other districts of Eastern Siberia the new settlers widely extended and improved sheep-farming, and also laid out melonfields with different types of melon and water-melon, infecting the starozhily with their example. In the steppe regions of Yeniseisk guberniya the settlers cultivated raspberries and gooseberries, the seddlings of which they imported with them, and in Kansk district immigrants from the Baltic region grew a special sort of strawberry called the 'Victoria' which produced an even heavier crop than in its native soil. Settlers also brought fruit-farming to the Altai, especially the cultivation of apple trees.

Changes in agricultural methods also accompanied the immigrants from European Russia. For instance, in the northern regions where the soil was not particularly fertile for grain production, the settlers began the practice of fertilizing the ground with animal dung – a practice which was soon adopted by the starozhily. Even before the building of the Trans-Siberian Railway and the mass importation of agricultural machinery, the settlers had already introduced new types of agricultural equipment and tools. Among other things they changed from the traditional Siberian wooden plough (*sokha-kolesukha*) to the Russian plough (*plug*), and also began to manufacture harrows, winnowing machines and both hand- and horse-powered threshers. The change-over to mechanized agriculture on a large scale began with the opening of the Trans-Siberian Railway and, in the early 1890s, with the creation by the Migration Administration of special funds to finance the purchase of farm machinery. This opened the floodgates for major Russian and foreign manufacturers. In 1897 Omsk became the base for representatives of American firms specializing in the production of agricultural machinery such as MacCormick, Osborn, Champion and others, which in 1902 united to form the 'International Harvester Company', part of the Morgan finance group.[13]

On the eve of the First World War there were eighteen domestic and foreign firms marketing agricultural machinery throughout Siberia and the Far East, with around 600 trading centres and eighty-three depots, with many branches belonging to the Migration Administration. Dominating the market was the International Harvester Company, which specialized in the sale of mowers and reapers. In the immediate pre-war years Siberia accounted for one-quarter of all the trade in agricultural machines in Russia, at an average annual value of twenty million roubles. They were used mainly by wealthy peasants, both settlers and starozhily, who not infrequently also employed hired workers. On 2 November 1913 the newspaper *Yeniseiskaya zhizn* commented that agricultural machinery was most widely used 'in regions of intensive settlement'. The faster the growth in the area of sown land, the more vigorous was the formation of a stratum of prosperous peasants.

The wider distribution of factory-produced machines did not eliminate the need for craftsmen and craft workshops. For instance, co-operatives of immigrant craftsmen in the Tara district of Tobolsk guberniya continued to manufacture threshers for the peasants, and in the town of Kurgan a settlers' depot entrusted the repair of its farm machinery to local craftsmen, providing them with the necessary materials and spare parts. In 1910 immigrant craftsmen in Barnaul set up the 'Siberian Labour Co-operative' (*Sibirskaya trudovaya artel*) which fulfilled orders from settlers' depots. The co-operative also had branches in Pavlograd, Ust-Kamenogorsk and other population centres.

At the same time as passing on the experience of the Russian peasantry to their Siberian cousins, the immigrants were also quick to adopt Siberian farming methods. Like the local peasants, they practised the 'seizure' (*zakhvat*) method of landownership and the fallow-field system of field-crop cultivation. Woodland was cleared and brought under cultivation by rooting out trees and ploughing up the virgin land. The immigrants were obliged to take account of new soil and climatic conditions, choosing appropriate methods of working the land in accordance with these and often abandoning their previous practices. In areas of taiga, for instance, they avoided deep ploughing and were forced to prepare the ground for sowing spring crops in the autumn. It was particularly important to select the correct location for different types of crop: for example, it was dangerous to sow winter crops on high ground which was unprotected by the forest, as they would be killed off by the heavy frosts; on low ground, however, they would rot beneath the deep cover of snow.

The newcomers paid dearly for their mistakes. Thus, by sowing seed-corn brought in with them from their native province which was not hardened to Siberian conditions, they produced crops which had extremely long stalks, but no actual grains. Settlers who tried to establish farms in the taiga region, concentrating purely on the cultivation of cereal crops, frequently experienced failure. Many of the taiga-dwellers combined crop raising with livestock farming and other economic activities (*promysly*) which allowed them to exploit the agricultural conditions of the forest zone to their full advantage. Moreover, keeping animals helped the peasants to transform the taiga into arable and meadow land. A few head of large cattle and a herd or flock of smaller stock would quickly trample down a wide area around the settler's cottage, effectively getting rid of the taiga undergrowth and weeds which it would be almost impossible to eliminate by any other means. For this reason a large area would be fenced off to graze the animals, thereby creating a kind of pasturage (*poskotina*).[14]

From the 1860s to the 1880s it was still possible to find the pasturing system of cattle raising, whereby only the milking and working cattle were fed with ready-made dry fodder during the three or four winter months. The rest of the animals were left out to graze, even in winter, searching for grass beneath the snow. There were very few heated byres, and cattle was raised primarily for beef. However, in Tobolsk, Tomsk and Yeniseisk gubernii the peasants produced boiled butter which was bought up by dealers and transported to the markets at Ishim and Irbit, and thence along the Kama and Volga rivers to Nizhnii Novgorod (now Gorkii) from where it was taken to the southern ports. In all, about 300 puds of boiled butter were exported from Siberia.[15]

The flood of migrants and the increasing number of peasant farms brought with them a significant rise in the number of head of cattle in Siberia – almost doubling from 5,671,000 in the 1860s to 11,167,000 in the second decade of the twentieth century. But even more important than quantity were the qualitative changes which took place in the development of the cattle and dairy industry. The first Siberian butter factory was established in 1886 in the village of Chernaya Rechka (Tyukalinsk uezd, Tobolsk guberniya), and within a year new creameries had appeared in many other villages. But the real breakthrough in the dairy industry came with the opening of the Trans-Siberian Railway. This greatly facilitated the export of dairy products from Siberia, which acted as a stimulus to further production. From the mid-1890s there began a steady though rapid increase in the number of dairy factories utilizing mechanical separators. In 1894 only 2 such factories were in operation; in 1895 there were 15, in 1900 – 277, in 1905 – 1,181, and in 1910 – 3,109. They sprang up like mushrooms after rain, not only in Tobolsk and Tomsk gubernii, but all over Siberia – in the Akmolinsk, Zabaikal and Amur districts and in the national regions of Gornyi Altai, Buryatia and Yakutia.[16] Butter factories and creameries were opened by merchants, wealthy peasants – both starozhily and new immigrants – and by members of the tsarist regional administration in Siberia.

An important role in the foundation and development of the Siberian butter industry was played by N.V. Vereshchagin (brother of the famous battle-painter) who had already successfully organized dairy production in Tver (now Kalinin) province and suggested a similar development in Siberia. Immigrants from the northern and western provinces of European Russia, where the industry was already widely established, also made a major contribution. Alongside privately-owned enterprises there also appeared co-operative creameries. The first of these was organized in January 1896 by six peasant households from the village of Morevo (Yalutorovsk uezd, Tobolsk guberniya). By 1913, out of 4,092 creameries operating in Siberia, around half were run on co-operative lines. In 1907 they joined together and established the 'Union of Siberian Butter-manufacturing Co-operatives' (*Soyuz sibirskikh maslodelcheskikh artelei*). The majority of the creameries were tiny enterprises with only two or three workers and a very small output.

According to the results of an enquiry conducted by the Tomsk Juridical Society in 1905, 60 per cent of all peasant households – both starozhily and immigrant – supplied milk for the butter manufacturers,[17] but the main bulk of marketed milk came from the major farms with large dairy herds. The excellent composition of the grass ensured that milk from Siberian cows was marked by a high fat content (on average, 4 or 5 per cent), and butter by its high quality and low cost. It is not surprising therefore that it effectively conquered the west European markets. On the eve of the First World War

Siberia accounted for 60 per cent of Russia's and 16 per cent of the world's exports of butter.

More than a dozen export organizations were occupied in the trade, of which the leading firm was the 'Siberian Company'. The Siberian Company bought from private manufacturers and exported over one million puds of butter, mainly to England, but also to Germany and Denmark. Butter produced by the co-operative creameries was exported by the Union of Siberian Butter-manufacturing Co-operatives, which in 1912 entered into a joint-stock company called 'Union', organized with the English entrepreneur, T. Lonsdale, to market their product. In 1900 a centner (a German measure of about one hundredweight) of Danish butter sold on the London market at 122–126 shillings; Dutch butter at 110–120 shillings, and Russian butter at 82–86 shillings.[18] Cheap butter from Siberia therefore found a wide market in England.

The old revolutionary, N.S. Korzhanskii, who visited Lenin's London apartment during the fifth congress of the Russian Social Democratic Workers' Party in April–May 1907 records the following:

> I was amazed at the wonderful, beautiful-smelling creamy butter, and was just about to burst out with some remark about the wealth of the British, when Vladimir Ilyich said, 'Yes. That must be ours. From Siberia'. He then turned to the landlady and asked her something in English. She answered him for two or three minutes, and when she had finished, he assured me:

> 'That's right. Siberian. She even told me which region it's from – the Barabinsk steppe . . . Her geography's not too good, though. She's convinced that that's somewhere beyond Lake Baikal. Actually it is in the west, between Omsk and Tomsk. I passed through it twice – on my way into exile and back again. A marvellous place. With a great future. The English-woman told me that they all know Barabinsk butter and Chulym cheese.'[19]

The development of the butter industry resulted in a shift from raising beef to dairy herding, and led to a large increase in the size of the herds. In 1917 there were seventeen to eighteen head of cattle to every hundred of the population in European Russia; in Siberia there were forty-two. Most of the cattle and the butter factories were located in the forest-steppe zone of Siberia, where the main body of immigrants were settled. Changes in the methods of animal husbandry also took place. The peasants began to prepare more hay and other feedstuffs for the winter, and there was also an improvement in the cattle's fodder ration. The new settlers also extended the practice of stalling the animals in heated buildings, which the starozhily, under the influence of the immigrants, also began to build. The settlers also introduced merino sheep into Siberia. In the nineteenth century the farming of fine-woolled sheep was widespread in the Crimea and the Tauride province. However, in 1884 the shortage and high cost of grazing land there compelled sheep-farmers to migrate with their flocks to the borders of Stavropol guberniya. But even here they encountered problems. Then, two sheep-farmers, M. Ya. Sosednov and S.P. Sizov, travelled to Siberia and concluded an agreement with the government administration in the Altai to rent 50,000 desyatinas of grazing land on the Korostelevsk steppe in Zmeinogorsk uezd. They decided to drive their sheep there on foot. In March 1904 the flocks left Stavropol and after a year and a half's exhausting journey and a winter rest near the town of Atbasar, 3,750 sheep finally arrived on the Korostelevsk steppe at the end of September 1905. After them, others chose to drive their flocks along the same route.

The local peasants also began to buy and rear merinos, and by 1909 there were 17,000 head of them. The sheep-farmers also began to sow grass and root crops for fodder and changed their methods of herding and feeding their flocks. The second region where merino sheep-farming was established in Siberia was at Marionovka station, situated between Omsk and Petropavlovsk, where twenty-seven farms were in operation with 50,000 head of sheep. The Department of Agriculture also arranged for 'Rambouillet' sheep to be sent from the State Agricultural College in Kharkov guberniya to Akmolinsk oblast to be reared there in local conditions. In Yeniseisk province there was an enormous and well-known sheep-farm run by two businessmen named Alekseev and Chetverikov, who kept 39,000 head of sheep on 60,000 desyatinas of land rented from the government.[20] They also owned separate farms in Tobolsk guberniya.

The historical literature on the migration movement to Siberia has tended to concentrate on the agrarian development of the territory, as reflected in such phrases as 'peasant settlement', 'agricultural colonization' and the like. Less well investigated is the role played in the migratory movements by workers, artisans and craftsmen who established industrial and transportation enterprises, and developed many different trades and crafts in Siberia. Of the 4,307 families who were settled on state lands in Tomsk guberniya before 1893, around 35 per cent of them comprised craftsmen who had followed various trades in European Russia.[21] Those who migrated from the central black-earth provinces mainly specialized in working with 'animal' raw materials (tanners, saddlemakers, furriers, and so on), while those from the non-black-earth, forest zone specialized overwhelmingly in 'vegetable' raw materials (for example, joiners, carpenters and coopers).

In their homeland some of these had worked by undertaking orders from individual consumers and therefore represented the primary stage of industry – that is, handicraft; others had supplied manufactured goods for the impersonal market and were thus representative of light industrial goods production. Among the immigrants who were involved in cottage industries (*kustarnye promysly*) were included some who were quite prosperous and owned their own workshops, and others who were ruined peasants and hired themselves out for labour; but the majority were producers of light manufactured goods. The proportion of craftsmen was higher among migrants from the non-black-earth provinces where cottage industries had reached a higher level of development than elsewhere. Consequently, when the inflow of migrants from these areas increased at the beginning of the twentieth century, there were far more craftsmen among them than in the preceding decades.

In Siberia the immigrants benefited from their experience of cottage industry and continued to ply their various trades. Apart from working for wages, they used the income from their craftsmanship to accumulate the necessary finances to set up an establishment of their own. Possessing all the necessary skills and experience, but no capital, many were employed as wage labourers in the workshops of wealthy starozhily and became producers of light industrial manufactured goods. During the late 1880s, in Biisk and the Biisk region of the Altai, the majority of cottage workshops engaged in the manufacture of felt footware, felt hats and sewn goods, and other similar commodities were founded by new settlers. On their initiative, too, shoemakers', joiners' and coopers' workshops were established in Ust-Ishimsk district (Tara uezd, Tobolsk guberniya), and metalsmiths', blacksmiths', carpenters' and other craft shops in the villages of Yeniseisk guberniya.

Immigrants from Minsk, Mogilev, Vitebsk and other western provinces were responsible for extending domestic industrial production of cloth and knitwear (scarves, belts, gloves, and so on) in the Yalutorovsk district of Tobolsk guberniya, while others from Vyatka province introduced the manufacture of winnowing fans and wicker-work furniture. In response to questionnaires asking when certain trades were started in their area, the starozhily would usually reply, 'When the immigrants moved in'. The peasants' responses indicated that the majority of craft workshops in settlements established in Tomsk guberniya between 1861 and 1893 were actually founded during the 1880s when the movement of migration got properly under way. In Yeniseisk guberniya, the majority of manufactories operating on the eve of the First World War were started during the great wave of migration after the opening of the Trans-Siberian Railway, especially after 1907.[22]

Whereas the proportion of settler families engaged in cottage industries and crafts in their native provinces was about 34 per cent, and the proportion of immigrants on state lands in Tomsk guberniya who accumulated capital by similar activities about 30 per cent – *after* they had successfully established their own household in a new location, the proportion went up to 36 per cent. In other words, quite a number of immigrants who had never followed a trade or craft in their own homeland turned their hand to it after they had arrived in Siberia: hence the increase in the number of households engaged in some kind of cottage industry. This is explained by the settlers' eagerness to establish their own economy in their new location as soon as possible, by the wider distribution of household industries, and the more favourable conditions for the development of trades and crafts in Siberia.

Carefully husbanding their resources, the peasant settlers would try to produce everything for personal consumption from within their own household economy: they made their own rudimentary tools, wove their own cloth and sewed their own clothes, tanned their own leather and made their own shoes. But most of them also produced handmade goods for sale, which reflected the commodity nature of their economic activity. The most successful families were those which possessed the necessary financial resources and were well supplied with male working hands. And the greatest expansion of cottage industry took place in the southern, most intensively populated areas of Siberia, where the largest numbers of immigrants from European Russia were settled.

The immigrants expanded already existing trades and crafts in Siberia, and also introduced new ones, prompting the old inhabitants to emulate them. For instance, migrants from Perm guberniya introduced the manufacture of wicker baskets in the Irkutsk region, and their example was soon followed by starozhily peasants from other districts. The production of wooden shaft arcs for horse-drawn wagons (*dugi*), brought in from European Russia in the mid-1860s to the villages around Tomsk, spread along the route of the major tracts as the transport and haulage industry developed. And in 1861 settlers from Vladimir province began producing sheepskin coats in the town of Barnaul. Obviously the severe climatic conditions in Siberia created a huge demand and a ready market for warm sheepskins, and both immigrants and starozhily became engaged in their manufacture.

Craftsmen from the central provinces quickly established themselves in Siberia and were readily accepted into the communities of the old inhabitants. They settled among the local peasants and soon passed on to them their skills and experience. Also, by creating their own settlements in previously unoccupied territories, the migrants helped to spread the development of cottage industry into new regions of Siberia. The economic base of most of these new settlements was unitary, with the inhabitants engaging in only one single trade. But as the flow of immigrants increased and production expanded, the village economies became more diversified. The expansion of cottage industrial production was especially vigorous in areas which were close to towns, tracts or the railway, that is, the major areas of settlement. In Tomsk guberniya the number of households engaged in light manufacturing rose from 6,700 in 1887 to 21,400 in 1914, more than a threefold increase.

In the inhabited areas of Tobolsk guberniya which did not attract a large number of immigrants, trades and crafts did not develop significantly, and indeed some of them even diminished.[23] The building of the Trans-Siberian Railway had an ambiguous influence on the development of Siberia's artisan economy. On the one hand the coming of the railroad boosted the movement of migration into Siberia, which in turn stimulated the creation of new manufacturing trades and expanded already existing ones. On the other hand, the railway opened up the way for the import of industrial goods from European Russia, thereby undermining certain local cottage industries. So, for instance, the import of factory-produced felt footwear into Siberia caused the decline of the local felt-shoemaking industry. Cheaper transport by rail also caused a decline in the local haulage industry and related trades such as harness-making, the manufacture of horse-drawn sledges and the like.

Evidence from the Yalutorovsk district of Tobolsk guberniya in the mid-1890s and seven districts of Yeniseisk and Irkutsk gubernii in the late 1880s shows that around two-thirds of all immigrant households were engaged in the manufacture of goods from vegetable raw materials, predominantly wood. Yalutorovsk district also had a relatively high proportion (about 20 per cent) of households working with animal raw materials (leather, fur, wool, and so on), and in the East Siberian districts a similar proportion dealing with mineral raw materials. These occupations played an important role in the immigrants' household budget. For example, around 12 per cent of expenditure on clothes was covered by the production of items of clothing within the household. Nine per cent of the income of settlers who had lived in Siberia for between five and ten years comprised revenues from household manufacturing.

In the taiga zone the equivalent factor reached 30 per cent, with income from manufacturing activities taking second place between agriculture and animal husbandry. In the forest-steppe and steppe regions, income from manufacturing took third place after agriculture and livestock rearing.[24] While the rich peasants engaged in manufacturing production in order to increase their personal prosperity, the poor peasantry did it simply in order to survive. The former were engaged in entrepreneurial activity (owning workshops, contracting for the supply of wood and building materials, and so on); the latter hired themselves out for wages, undertaking heavy labour such as hauling timber, making railway sleepers, bricks and so on.

Migration also stimulated the development of other, non-agricultural, seasonal trades. Immigrant craftsmen such as joiners, shoemakers and potters travelled to nearby villages where there were no cottage industries and no competition. Their activities thus helped to create and establish their trades in new regions. In winter, artisans from European Russia would make the journey to Tobolsk guberniya and the Altai looking for work, the opening of the new railway greatly increasing the numbers of these seasonal workers. Travelling from village to village, they undertook orders for the peasants or worked for the local market. Like the settlers, the seasonal workers lent their knowledge and experience to the development of cottage industry in Siberia and helped introduce it to the starozhily. The seasonal craftworkers did not just stay in Tobolsk guberniya, but also used it as a jumping-off point for other regions. In Tyukalinsk district, about one-eighth of all the immigrant households in 1910–11 sent out seasonal workers into other areas, who brought back with them higher earnings than were they were able to obtain in their own regions.

During the process of colonization and settlement, centres of light peasant industry were established throughout Siberia, creating a 'huge peasant factory' (*ogromnaya muzhichyaya fabrika*), as N.M. Yadrintsev called it. Many different factors influenced the pattern of this development – the occupation of the immigrants in their place of origin, the working traditions of the starozhily, the economic and environmental conditions obtaining in different regions of Siberia and the presence of raw materials, means of communication, markets, and so on. In the main agricultural areas of forest-steppe and steppe-land where the bulk of the immigrants settled, the predominant forms of light industrial production were in the manufacture of articles from animal and vegetable raw materials. In the much earlier inhabited and settled Tyumen district, the peasants produced leather, carpets, furniture, carriages and other items. Tyumen was popularly known at the time as the 'leathershop' or 'tannery' (*kozhevennyi tsekh*) of Siberia, and the inhabitants of the region as the Siberian 'Vladimirans' and 'Yaroslavans' – immigrants from Vladimir and Yaroslavl gubernii being especially famous for their skilled craftsmanship.

Among the most widely practised businesses in the southern regions of Siberia – Kurgan, Ishim, Barnaul, Minusinsk, and so on – were butter-making, flour-milling, soap-making and weaving. In Yalutorovsk district, in Barnaul, Biisk and their immediate vicinities, and in Petropavlovsk and Akmolinsk in Akmolinsk oblast, where sheep-farming was widespread, there was a flourishing industry in the manufacture of sheepskin coats. Further north in the newly-settled forest regions of Tobolsk, Turinsk, Tomsk, Krasnoyarsk and other districts, the opening of the Trans-Siberian Railway and the new wave of immigration encouraged the development of wood-working trades and crafts (carriage-making, cooperage, basket-making, and so on), as well as the manufacture of fur goods and fabric weaving.

In the mining communities of the Altai and the western regions of Tobolsk guberniya close to the Ural mountains, metalsmiths produced agricultural implements and spare parts, dishes, pans and other hardware. In the villages along the Moscow Tract in Irkutsk uezd the highly-developed haulage and horse-drawn transport industry provided work for ancillary tradesmen such as harness- and saddle-makers, blacksmiths, carriage-builders and so on. Settlements lying along the course of the major rivers produced boats, nets and fishing equipment. Moreover, by utilizing the advanced skills and experience of their various trades acquired in European Russia, the immigrants had a profound and positive influence on the development of manufacturing techniques and technology in Siberia. Among other improvements, they introduced the pedal-operated potter's wheel, oil of vitriol for use in the manufacture of felt footware and aniline dyes for decorated carpet-making.

In the process of colonization and settlement, Siberia became an integral part of Russia, inhabited overwhelmingly by Russians. The Siberian frontierland and the European heartland of Russia were intimately connected by the unity of their political and economic development, and by the community of the spiritual and material culture of the mass of the population. Their agricultural methods and techniques were basically the same, they employed similar equipment and cultivated similar crops. This created favourable conditions for the easy transmission of working traditions and skills from the centre to the periphery. At the same time the peculiarities of Siberia's own historical development (for example, virtual absence of serf-owning relationships and an abundance of unoccupied land), the specific character of the natural environment (harsh climate, vast forests, soils which are difficult to cultivate, and so on) forced the immigrants to modify their tried, tested and traditional working habits, adapt them to local conditions, and take full account of the agricultural methods which had been worked out by the old inhabitants.

What emerged was a two-way process: the settlers not only passed on their productive skills and experience, but also learned new methods and working practices from the starozhily. In Siberia the immigrants also continued to employ their traditional methods of cultivation, animal husbandry and craftsmanship, and their interaction with those of the starozhily took on many different forms. At first the newly-imported traditions coexisted, as it were, alongside local ones; then some of them gradually merged with those of the old Siberians and gained a wide distribution, others took root only in isolated instances and yet others were totally transformed or disappeared altogether.

The movement of migration across the Urals certainly had a positive influence on the population dynamics of Siberia and on the development of agriculture, animal husbandry and manufacturing skills. But the influence of the immigrants did not stop there.

The new Siberians also brought with them their own traditions of house construction, of food and clothing, their own empirical knowledge of the environment, and their traditional spiritual culture. Like the old Siberians, they came into close contact with the aboriginal, native peoples of Siberia and established good social, economic and cultural relations with them. The result was the creation of a new amalgam of peasant traditions and customs. In this process of mutual interaction, assimilation and exchange of productive experience between the immigrants and the starozhily, there developed a close unity in the material and spiritual culture of the peasantry of European Russia and Siberia.

NOTES AND REFERENCES

1 V.O. Klyuchesvskii, *Sochineniya v devyati tomakh* 1 *Kurs russkoi istorii* part 1 (Moscow, 1987), p. 50.

2 Figures calculated from: N.V. Turchaninov, *Itogi pereselencheskogo dvizheniya za vremya s 1896 po 1909 g.* (*Vklyuchitelno*) (St Petersburg, 1910), pp. 52–6; I. Yamzin, *Pereselencheskoye dvizhenie v Rossii s momenta osvobozhdeniya krestyan* (Kiev, 1912), p. 11; N. Turchaninov and A. Domrachev, *Itogi pereselencheskogo dvizheniya za vremya s 1910 po 1914 g.* (Petrograd, 1916), pp. 48–69.

3 A.A. Kaufman, *Pereselenie in kolonizatsiya* (St Petersburg, 1905), pp. 316–17.

4 L.F. Sklyarov, *Pereselenie i Zemleustroistvo v Sibiri v gody stolypinskoi agrarnoi reformy* (Leningrad, 1962), pp. 444–5.

5 *Pereselenie i zemleustroistvo za Uralom v 1906–1910 gg.* (St Petersburg, 1911), pp. 80–1.

6 Tsentralnyi gosudarstvennyi istoricheskii arkhiv (TsGIA), fond 1284, op. 1, delo 0, list 2.

7 *Ssylka v Sibir. Ocherk yeya istorii i sovremennago polozheniya*, (St Petersburg, 1900), Prilozhenie no. 1.

8 L.M. Goryushkin, *Agrarnye otnosheniya v Sibiri v period imperializma (1900–1917 gg.)* (Novosibirsk, 1976), pp. 134–6, 138, 142, 144.

9 TsGIA, fond 1291, op. 84 (1912), chast 11, list 334; Gosudarstvennyi arkhiv Krasnoyarskogo kraya, fond 262, op. 1, delo 30, list 11.

10 *Obzor selskokhozyaistvennoi zhizni zaselyaemykh raionov Aziatskoi Rossii za 1913 g. po dannym pereselencheskoi tekushchei statistiki* (St Petersburg, 1914), p. 99.

11 L.M. Goryushkin, *Sibirskoe krestyanstvo na rubezhe dvukh vekov. Konets XIX – nachalo XX v.* (Novosibirsk, 1967), pp. 138–41.

12 A.K. Kaufman, 'K voprosu o kulturnoi roli pereselentsev v Sibiri i ikh otnosheniyakh k sibiryakam-starozhilam', in *Put-doroga* (St Petersburg, 1893), pp. 521-2.

13 *Sibirskaya zhizn*, 27 October 1907.

14 *Trudy mestnykh komitetov o nuzhdakh selskokhozyaistvennoi promyshlennosti. LVII. Stepnoi krai* (St Petersburg, 1903), p. 90.

15 N. Makarov, *Khrestyanskoe khozyaistvo i ego evolutsiya* (Moscow, 1920); Gosudarstvennyi arkhiv Altaiskogo kraya, fond 4, op. 1, delo 653, listy 8-9.

16 *Vestnik melkogo kredita* 30 (1912): 936; TsGIA, fond 398, op. 69, delo 2164, list 67.

17 *Ekonomicheskoe issledovanie maslodeliya v Sibiri* (Kharkov, 1906), p. 78.

18 *Sibir pod vliyaniem relsovogo puti* (St Petersburg, 1902), p. 160.

19 *Vospominaniya o Vladimire Iliche Lenine* (Moscow, 1956), p. 160. (Chulym is the name of a river and a region in Western Siberia.)

20 *Sibirskii zemledelets i sadovod* 9 (1909): 390-1; *Istoriya krestyanstva Sibiri v epohku kapitalizma* (Novosibirsk, 1983), p. 262; TsGIA, fond 1284, op. 1, delo 0, list 6.

21 E.I. Soloveva, *Promysly sibirskogo krestyanstva v poreformennyi period* (Novosibirsk, 1981), p. 85.

22 M.N. Solovev (ed.), *Kustarnye promysly Tomskoi gubernii* (St Petersburg, 1909), pp. 27-30; A.G. Shlikhter, *Kustarnye promysly Yeniseiskoi gubernii* (Krasnoyarsk, 1915), pp. 41-2.

23 G.A. Bochanova, *Obratyvayushchaya promyshlennost Zapadnoi Sibiri, Konets XIX - nachalo XX v.* (Novosibirsk, 1978), pp. 35, 121.

24 V.G. Tyukavkin, *Sibirskaya derevnya nakanune Oktyabrya* (Irkutsk, 1966), pp. 180-1.

9 Siberia in revolution and civil war, 1917–1921[1]

John Channon

> When revolution did actually break out in 1917, Siberia became the broad stage for a long, bloody and complex struggle between many different contending military, political, regionalist and nationalist forces before Soviet power was finally established from the Urals to the Pacific in 1922 with the Red Army's occupation (liberation) of Vladivostok and the departure of the last Japanese interventionist troops.
>
> (Alan Wood)[2]

In the past, the attention of western scholars has focused principally on Petrograd and Moscow as the centres of political activity in 1917, and only recently has work appeared which concentrates on revolution in the periphery. Yet it was the activities that occurred here which were to assume such significance in the development of the revolution after October. The revolt by the Czech Legions, returning home via the Trans-Siberian Railway, not only marked the turn towards all-out civil war in Russia, but began a period in Siberian history notable for its chaos and confusion, which ended finally with the Bolshevik victories in eastern Siberia in 1922.

It is the intention of this chapter to provide a survey of the revolution as it unfolded in Siberia from February 1917, through the turmoil of civil war, to Bolshevik victory in the early 1920s. A number of questions inevitably arise. Why, for instance, in a region where the vast majority of the population was rural and better-off than the peasantry west of the Urals did the Whites not manage to harness popular support? Why did the Socialist Revolutionaries (SRs) whose best result in the elections to the Constituent Assembly was achieved in Siberia not do better there? Were the Kadet party and the various regionalist groupings, lacking solid foundations before 1917, always doomed to failure? Was the Kolchak coup really the great turning point in the anti-Bolshevik movement as traditionally claimed, or was there greater continuity with previous White administrations in Siberia? And, ultimately, why did Kolchak fail? Until recently, western writing on the subject has been curiously skewed. Much has been published on the role of foreign intervention in Siberia; but relatively little attention has been paid to domestic politics and even less to social and economic matters. After a brief excursus into pre-revolutionary Siberian history, the chapter will consider the revolutions of 1917, the early period of Bolshevik rule, the various short-lived Siberian governments, the Kolchak period and the final struggle for Bolshevik power.

BACKGROUND

At the time of the Emancipation Edict of 1861, Siberia was seen as a cold and unwelcome place, with its extremely harsh climate and isolation suitable only for the transportation of criminals and exiles. By the end of the nineteenth century, however, numbers had swelled dramatically with more than 80 per cent of the population comprising immigrants. The latter continued to grow until 1914, while the indigenous peoples became an even-smaller minority. A major spur to this influx from west of the Urals was tsarist migration policy, facilitated by the construction of the Trans-Siberian Railway, completed in 1904. For all these settlers Siberia held out a vision of a 'promised land', though by 1911 many had returned to European Russia when the reality of the extremely difficult conditions confronting them revealed the cloudiness of their original vision.[3]

The economic benefits of this migration were undoubted, principally as a stimulus to agricultural development.[4] In the two decades before the Revolution, Siberian sown area increased by 122 per cent (exceeding the growth of population), while approximately three-quarters of the annual harvest was marketed.[5] Much of this grain was exported while more advanced equipment was utilized than west of the Urals. Animal husbandry was intensively practised with dairy production being especially successful (see Chapter 8). Exports fast became the main reason for increases in peasant incomes. The commune (*obshchina* or *mir*) prevailed in much of Siberia – as in European Russia – though its more restrictive elements only came into play in the more densely populated and developed areas, especially in Western Siberia. The commune, in fact, facilitated the growth of butter enterprises and dairies, many of these in reality being commune-based and organized along co-operative lines.[6] Other products such as furs, wool and meat provided additional sources of trade. The First World War was a further boon from the economic point of view, enabling co-operatives to obtain lucrative contracts to supply the Russian army.[7]

Such developments meant that in general the Siberian peasant was better off than his counterpart in European Russia. To argue that the 'Siberian peasant was really a wealthy landowner' would seem to overstate the case, though living standards were clearly well above those in central Russia.[8] None the less, conflict was still present in the countryside as manifested in the disputes between the old settlers (*starozhily*) and the newer migrants (*novoseltsy*) – several of whom had settled there illegally – between peasants and cossacks and between peasants and government officials but, in comparison with central Russia, the land issue assumed less urgency.

Accompanying the growth in trade was a steady expansion of industry and urban development, much of it financed by foreign capital. In six of the largest towns (Tomsk, Irkutsk, Omsk, Vladivostok, Chita and Novonikolaevsk – now Novosibirsk) population growth ranged from a doubling to an eightfold increase. There was no large-scale manufacturing industry in Siberia, though metallurgical works were founded there in the eighteenth century and the mining industry (gold, copper, zinc, lead, salt and coal) contributed significantly to the region's economy. By 1914 metal-working comprised only 8 per cent of Siberia's industrial output and the vast majority of Siberian industrial expansion was in service and food-processing industries.[9] Siberia's working class was emerging, albeit slowly, with a total urban work-force in 1913 of about 250,000, the years between 1900 and 1912 showing a particular increase (22.9 per cent) in the number of workers (as well as a 22.2 per cent increase in the value of industrial production).[10] Ninety thousand of these workers were engaged in the export of raw materials to supply the manufacturing industries of the centre and many others on the railway.[11] On the eve of the Revolution, Siberia's population was still overwhelmingly rural (comprising, according to estimates, between 97.2 and 97.5 per cent of the total) while the region was the least industrialized part of the Russian Empire.[12]

What, then, were the political implications of this pattern of economic and social development? Some historians see Siberia as being characterized by a 'significant measure of political and social moderation', identifying co-operatives, in particular, with the forces of moderate reform (the liberal Kadets, the Right SRs and some regionalists). By far the largest section of Siberian society comprised the primarily conservative, middle echelons. This was one reason why in Siberia the division between the right wing of the SR party and the Kadets was 'virtually non-existent'.[13] Although it is debatable whether the splits within it were any less serious than those in European Russia, Social Democracy in Siberia was different from that west of the Urals in its reflection of a strong peasant sector, a small working class and an insignificant landed gentry.[14] All these conditions made for relative social stability and general calm in Siberia in 1917 in contrast to European Russia. As one Soviet writer (oft-quoted in the west) has declared: 'If the October revolution had not broken out in the heartland, there would have been no revolution in Siberia for decades'.[15]

Yet it would be wrong to portray Siberian society as harmonious. Both
the SRs and the Kadets, for instance, held views that were out of step with
popular aspirations, SR socialization conflicted with the landownership
notions of the Siberian peasantry, while the SRs seemed to oppose and the
Kadets minimize regional autonomy. In fact local government reforms via
the *zemstva* were only introduced into Siberia on 17 June 1917.[16] Neither
should it be forgotten that the seeds of disaffection towards the Russian
government were sown long in advance of Marxism. The Siberian
regionalists (*oblastniki*), for example, wished to free Siberia from its
exploitation as a central Russian colony. Not only would this provide
economic stimulus to the region (via disbandment of the internal customs
barrier operating to the advantage of European Russia and subsidies for
resettlement of migrants from the west of the Urals), but it would also lead
to the emergence of a regional self-consciousness, and a desire for regional
autonomy. Even if not all regionalists wanted complete separation, many
still shared common grievances: Russian-appointed and corrupt officials;
poor cultural and educational facilities; the condition of Sibera's non-Russian
native peoples; and the persistent use of the exile system.[17] Furthermore,
the exiling of many political activists to Siberia by the tsarist government
provided the region with revolutionaries intent on spreading propaganda
and organizing insurgency. Apart from railway workers and soldiers recently
returned from the front (*frontoviki*), it was the new settlers – most recent
peasant migrants – who have been seen as those most receptive to revolutionary agitation.[18] There was thus some basis of support for Social
Democracy. Working-class organization in the region might have been in
its infancy[19] but it was the massacre of striking workers in the Lena
goldfields of Eastern Siberia that ignited the industrial unrest in the Empire
in the years immediately preceding the war.

THE REVOLUTIONS OF 1917

With the February Revolution and the collapse of tsarism came competing
claims to power. Siberia during 1917 became a political arena for the Right
Socialist Revolutionaries, the party considered closest to the interests of
the Siberian peasantry (and sometimes referred to as the 'moderate left')
and the far right. The peasantry wanted neither tsar nor Bolsheviks but the
development of co-operatives and conditions to promote their development
as well as a resolution to the land disputes, while the minorities showed
little interest in politics or nationalism.[20] A peasant movement developed
in Siberia from March 1917, as throughout the entire country, although
factors specific to the region clearly conditioned this development. In March
and April seizure of land was still rare, though the illegal hewing of state and

Kabinet (that is, Crown) woodland and refusal to meet lease and tax payments was common. Peasant resolutions (*nakazy*) revealed changing political attitudes, and between May and July land seizures, executed principally by peasant communities and village and *volost* committees, became the main form of unrest. By the summer the role of forestry wardens had been considerably diminished (or altogether abolished), while revenue from forests was a mere fraction of the 1916 level. Between August and October mass seizure of land and the elimination of state control over its woodlands occurred almost everywhere in Siberia, involving the mass of the peasantry in two provinces in particular, Yeniseisk and Tobolsk. Although the forms of unrest in various provinces and districts differed in accordance with specific local factors (such as a high concentration of recent migrants or a prevalence of large cossack lessors), resistance to the Provisional Government's food policy was all-pervasive. Similar lack of faith in the government can be seen by the mass refusal of peasants to introduce zemstva into their villages, for both political and economic reasons, after zemstvo elections began in August. The elections lasted until the late autumn but only 35 per cent of those eligible to vote participated. Clearly the peasantry was concerned above all with its own local interests.[21]

Regionalism and autonomy also featured as political concerns in 1917 although, according to one recent western writer, even among the dominant Great Russian population there was no great sense of specificity. While the oblastniki were poorly organized in 1917, having no Constituent Assembly candidates, the Revolution brought to the fore the question of the realization of Siberian regionalism. Almost immediately a peasant congress in Tomsk voted for Siberian autonomy while the Provincial Assembly called for self-government through an All-Siberian Regional Duma (SRD). Yet a constituent conference of the latter in August was poorly attended, the most significant statistic perhaps being that only three of the sixty-seven delegates were peasants. More delegates were attracted to the All-Siberian Congress which met in October (in Tomsk) and drafted a constitution vesting supreme legislative power in the SRD. A further (Extraordinary) Congress in December came out in opposition to Bolshevik views, the leading roles being assumed by SRs, who evidently hoped to win support in the Siberian autonomous movement, having lost face in European Russia. The Congress created an executive organ, the Provisional Siberian Council, to call democratic elections for the SRD and to recruit an army from sympathetic Siberian frontoviki to provide the council with military support. In January 1918 the council decided to convoke an SRD which immediately called for Siberian autonomy within a federal Russian republic, and condemned the Soviet of Peoples' Commissars (*Sovnarkom*) for dispersing the Constituent Assembly and for negotiating a separate peace with Germany. Such a blatant counter-revolutionary stance led, perhaps predictably, to the dispersal of the SRD by Bolshevik forces on 28 January.[22] With a small working class, few really poor peasants, very few large landowners and a small intelligentsia, Siberian society contained little to suggest a potential base of support for the Bolsheviks. Although the SRs won their highest percentage of votes in Siberia in the Constituent Assembly elections of November 1917 – the Bolsheviks receiving only 10 per cent of votes – it was the Bolsheviks who captured urban votes. For the Siberian Bolsheviks the immediate tasks lay in consolidating their own ranks and gaining control of the soviets. With the repeal of tsarist laws on corporal punishment and exile, numerous leading Bolsheviks returned to European Russia, leaving only poorly-prepared local forces to carry on the revolutionary struggle in Siberia. Uniting and reinforcing the Siberian Bolsheviks was a slow process. In April 1917 a Bolshevik conference instructed the Krasnoyarsk District Bureau to establish communications with all Bolsheviks in Siberia, while in August a Central Siberian Regional Bolshevik Conference, also in Krasnoyarsk and attended by 5,000 members, established the Central Siberian Regional Bureau to direct party activity in Siberia. By mid-September the Social Democratic organizations of such major Siberian centres as Tomsk and Omsk had divided, coming into line with Bolshevik policy. Centred on Krasnoyarsk, extensive agitation amongst the soviets and party organizations was accompanied by encouragement to unify the soviets (especially those of workers and soldiers), vital for the creation of a Bolshevik power base. Gaining control of the soviets also involved temporary alliances with the Left and Internationalist SRs and Mensheviks, in the light of particularly fierce opposition from the Right SRs. Although such left forces opposed Bolshevik attempts to arm workers, small groups of these did gradually emerge, often led by soldiers who had recently returned from the front.

Carr has called the six months following the October Revolution an interregnum, when Bolshevik power was consolidated sporadically and spasmodically, and local soviet control had only occasional contact with Moscow.[23] 'Soviet' power in Siberia after the October Revolution was indeed shaky: Bolshevik party members in Siberia numbered only 12,000 in 1917, while even leaders who were from Siberia itself had often defected from the SRs.[24] Concentration in a few conservative urban areas amidst numerous scattered and isolated settlements, and remoteness from the key urban centres of European Russia, hampered Bolshevik progress further. Thus, only a combination of political manoeuvre with a limited military force could enable the Bolsheviks to gain control of Siberia.[25] Krasnoyarsk came under Bolshevik control on 29 October, Irkutsk and Vladivostok in

November and Tomsk and Khabarovsk in December, the only serious fighting being in Irkutsk. With the Buryats driven from Ulan-Ude (south of Lake Baikal) in February 1918, the Bolsheviks had now reached the eastern periphery of the former empire. But they were unable to consolidate these gains. Their advance had been facilitated initially by weak and disorganized resistance, yet it was Bolshevik control via soviets which, ironically, would in turn produce waves of anti-Bolshevism.

Less than six months of Bolshevik rule in Siberia did little to enhance the party's position, its unpopularity stemming principally from the policy of *prodrazverstka* – the forceful requisitioning of grain, other agricultural commodities and horses. Cut off from markets in European Russia and western Europe, large grain reserves had accumulated in Siberia, a situation of which Lenin had been aware since July 1917, and a factor influencing his consideration in early 1918 of moving the Bolshevik base to Siberia, fearing a German attack.[26] In the six months after the October Revolution 80 per cent of the grain collected at the centre came from Siberia. Between December 1917 and March 1918 grain was regularly transported from Omsk to Petrograd in exchange for manufactured goods, the best known of these expeditions being that of the Siberian Bolshevik, A.G. Shlikhter, in February.[27] Yet opposition to Shlikhter's campaign came hard and fast from Siberian Bolshevik leaders, viewing this as an infringement of their own spheres of competence. Other factors did little to boost Bolshevik support. Rural co-operatives were ruthlessly expropriated while the failure to resolve the general economic chaos, resulting from war and revolution, lost support in urban areas. As everywhere, effective political control was also lacking. The nominal centre was Irkutsk, where the Central Executive Committee of Siberian Soviets – *Tsentrosibir* – was based, though regional subcentres with *de facto* power existed in Omsk (Western Siberia) and Khabarovsk (Far East), the latter two often disagreeing with the policies of Tsentrosibir.[28]

Foreign military intervention was to bring an end to this period of Bolshevik rule. Seeing the advance of Bolshevism to the Russian Far East as a threat to its interests, especially in Manchuria, Japan (ostensibly to protect Japanese lives and property) landed its forces at Vladivostok on 5 April, subsequently advancing along the Trans-Siberian Railway to Lake Baikal, giving support en route to the Whites under General Semenov in Mongolia. But it was the revolt in May 1918 of the 15,000 strong legion of former Czech prisoners-of-war, whose evacuation through Vladivostok had been negotiated with the Bolshevik government, that finally sparked off all-out opposition to the Bolsheviks supported by allied intervention. Clashing with Bolsheviks in Western Siberia, the Czechs took armed action to safeguard their position, moving westward along the Volga (seemingly with allied encouragement), sealing off the whole of Siberia from Bolshevik power and temporarily annexing certain regions of eastern European Russia to Siberia. Tomsk, in fact, was the only major town where Bolsheviks were overthrown without active intervention from the Czechs. By mid-summer 1918 the Bolsheviks had lost the Urals and Siberia, the latter soon to provide the base for a general opposition to Bolshevism.[29] Having lost power, the Bolsheviks were then unable to organize effective underground resistance.

ANTI-BOLSHEVISM FROM MAY TO NOVEMBER 1918

Within weeks of the collapse of the Bolshevik regime in Siberia, no less than nineteen separate governments – according to at least one estimate[30] – sprang up between the Volga and the Pacific, including the institution of a Provisional Siberian government – the PSG – in Omsk in July.[31] Further east, the ataman of the Siberian cossacks, Semenov, having formed an army in Harbin during the winter of 1917–18 before moving into Siberia the following March (initially with French support), had come to terms with the newly-arrived Japanese forces, subsequently controlling much of the Transbaikal region. The first attempt to consolidate these separate governments through the creation of a single anti-Bolshevik authority came at the Ufa Conference of 8–23 September 1918, attended by representatives of the PSG at Omsk, of the Samara government, of the 'national' governments of the Kazakhs, Turko-Tatars and Bashkirs and of several cossack military governments plus other minorities. Semenov boycotted it. The Ufa Conference witnessed the last attempt to form an all-Russian anti-Bolshevik authority from below. On 23 September an act was signed constituting a 'Provisional All-Russia Government' (PARG), described by one recent writer as the 'last broadly-based government to exist on Russian soil'.[32] This compromise arrangement which resulted in an uneasy alliance between the Omsk and Samara groups, located in the former and to be run, pending convocation of a Constitutent Assembly, by a Directory (*Direktoriya*) of five (with the Right SR leader, N.D. Avksentev, as President) and with General V.G. Boldyrev as Supreme Commander in Chief, lasted only eight weeks.[33] Accounting for its brief existence tells us much about Siberian politics in the autumn of 1918.

First, how did those parties fare that gained votes in the Constituent Assembly? The SRs had held a predominant position at the end of 1917, possessing a large base in Siberia (for every twenty Constituent Assembly voters in Siberia, fifteen voted for SRs as against two for Bolsheviks and one for Kadets) and especially within the co-operative movement. Yet the SRs could do little to consolidate a position that initially held out such promise. Even if the Constituent Assembly vote had given them a 'right' to govern Siberia, the evidence from the Samara government did little to suggest that they would perform much better elsewhere.

Their main error was to allow the development of an anti-Bolshevik front in 1918, producing an army that had mushroomed from a small nucleus of officers and cossacks in the spring of 1918 to a force of well over 100,000 by the winter (mustered principally from refugee officers from the west and widespread conscription). SR attempts to open the SRD (created by the SR-dominated All-Siberian Regional Congress and closed by the Bolsheviks in January 1918) were blocked by the PSG (politically to the Right) in an attempt to reduce influence from the Left.[34]

The Kadets, on the other hand, never had much of a base in Siberia (obtaining less than their 8 per cent average nationally), since the Russian liberal professional classes and intelligentsia had drifted to the regionalist movement. They had been on the right-wing of the Party of Peoples' Freedom, fervent Kornilovites, claiming in August 1917 that the Provisional Government had been overthrown. Maintaining their Great Russian stance, local Kadets did not participate in either the Western Siberian Commissariat or the PSG, critical of their regionalist associations. Kadet notions of a Russian unity where national aspirations transcended class consciousness were soon revealed to be fantasy. Realising they would never obtain a popular mandate to govern in Siberia, the Kadets threw in their lot with the army, the institution best representing for them the true spirit of Russia. Three months prior to Kolchak's coup, at a Kadet conference, their preference for military dictatorship over Siberian autonomy was clearly revealed.[35] Their lack of administrative experience further aided Kolchak's concentration on military matters.

Second, what was the position of those groups not represented in the Constituent Assembly? Although they had suffered from poor organization in 1917 (holding their first general conference only in December) and lacked a Constituent Assembly slate, the regionalists, advocating Siberian self-government, comprised a further important civilian group. The extent of their popularity is debatable. Some believe them to have possessed considerable popular appeal, while others argue that (like the SRs) they never had genuine popular support and certainly not enough to bolster a war in aid of Siberian autonomy.[36]

All three groups (SRs, Kadets and regionalists), together with junior officials (many of whom were also Kadets or further to the right), who ran the day-to-day affairs of the government, and counter-revolutionaries who had fled from European Russia, comprised the key civilian element of the Siberian and Urals provisional governments. The PSG based in Omsk and formed on 23 June 1918 was the earlier and more important of the two, with P.V. Vologodskii, the veteran regionalist, being its most prominent figure. Though small in number and scattered, cossack hosts, based in Omsk, also played a part. Nearly 8,000 officers of various ranks (having fled to Siberia and a third of whom were in Omsk) comprised another element. It has not gone unremarked that civilian weakness in allowing the army to run the PSG was to have 'grave repercussions for the future'.[37] This new army, flying the green and white flag symbolizing the forests and snows of Siberia, seemed on fertile ground for raising support. In late June 1918 general mobilization was announced and by September the army comprised some 38,000 men.

What then were the problems that beset the PSG? The various administrations at Omsk (the Western Siberian Commissariat and the PSG) with SR or non-party majorities were constantly frustrated in their attempts to wield power, even though they could claim some political legitimacy, being descended from the short-lived Siberian government elected at Tomsk by the Siberian Regional Duma before its dispersal by Red Guards in January 1918. A further problem was the absence of reliable and experienced administrators to govern Siberia (the zemstva having only been introduced there in 1917), so that the more conservative oblastniki and ex-tsarist officials were recruited into the ministries at Omsk. Before the end of July 1918 the last vestiges of the Soviet regime were dismantled: soviets were banned, industry denationalized, the state trading monopoly was ended; and estates were to be returned to former owners.[38] In the urban areas unions and workers' organizations had been broken up while cossack atamans brutally suppressed peasant revolts. For Mawdsley, all of this revealed the 'continuing weakness of civilian politics in Russia', due partly to the small intelligentsia and to the lack of a tradition of participatory politics but also because of the impossibility of co-operation emerging between political parties (the Right considered the SRs as little better than the Bolsheviks while the SRs saw the Right as counter-revolutionary).[39]

If the PSG at Omsk had been moderate and regionalist in origin, it was soon to drift to the right under pressure from military groups and their reactionary sympathizers who had been gathering in Western Siberia, under cover of the Czechs' policing of the railway and the allies.[40] The PSG appeared to promise democracy and a Constituent Assembly but in reality proved incapable of preventing the dominance of the political Right and the army's recurrent outbursts of violence. In the judgement of one recent western writer, the PSG appeared as nothing more than a 'toothless coalition government', dispersing or eliminating those elements which supported the Constituent Assembly. The Right, it is claimed, hid behind the 'democratic' Directory while preparing international support and consolidating the power of the army.[41]

To what extent the Kolchak 'coup' marked a fundamental shift in the politics of the anti-Bolshevik movement and the collapse of the Directory signalled the end of the 'democratic counter-revolution', is debatable. Some would argue that the appellative 'democratic counter-revolution' is a misnomer for the previous governments, since Right SR members of the Directory accepted the continuation of former PSG measures (such as the transfer to it of the PSG's Council of Ministers), and assisted in the dispersal of local 'governments' in the Urals and the Far East as well as the Siberian Regional Duma, 'the sole remaining voice of socialist dissent against the central authorities in the region'.[42] The Omsk government had clearly failed to obtain popular support. Peasants had been antagonized by Bolshevik agrarian policies from the spring of 1918 but this did not mean that they automatically supported the Whites. The PSG's land and labour legislation did little to attract mass support, while it was gravely mistaken in assuming that the First World War had been popular and even more so in thinking that the population would readily accept the presence of foreign troops on Siberian soil. Hence the widespread resistance to the PSG's mobilization campaign of summer 1918.[43] Perhaps General Boldyrev's assessment of the Directory comes close to the truth: it was detached from the masses, created by the intelligentsia and 'absorbed too much in high-sounding principles . . . it had no contact with real life'.[44]

THE KOLCHAKOVSHCHINA

With the Bolshevik recapture of Kazan, Simbirsk (now Ulyanovsk) and Samara (now Kuibyshev), the authority of the PARG was restricted by early October to western Siberia, and less than two months after its inception, on the night of 17 November, it was overthrown by force. Two SR directors were arrested by a cossack detachment (with the approval of the Omsk garrison commander), claiming it was to prevent an SR plot, and Admiral A.V. Kolchak, the War Minister, was chosen as Supreme Ruler (*Verkhovnyi Pravitel*). He was to lead the White movement in Russia for the next fourteen months. A military dictatorship, which the army commanded, the political right and some influential allied representatives had been calling for throughout the summer, was now installed, organized by local right-wing civilians and by mid-ranking officers and cossacks from the garrison. There is 'no evidence of direct allied involvement' in the coup although it is believed that certain individuals from the allied nations, and Britain in particular, may have played a part.[45]

But Kolchak did not create a new government, simply taking over the Council of Ministers. In fact, Kolchak did not need to pass any radical new legislation since 'all the major pillars of the military dictatorship had been put in place long before his arrival on the Siberian scene, while the SRs were still theoretically in government'.[46] According to this view, there was no 'coup' since the events were not sudden and unexpected. After all, the 'coup' was bloodless while the SRs, Avksentev and Zenzinov, were exiled. This marked the end of the SR party as a serious political force in Russia.

Even then the White camp was not monolithic, since with the continuation of the Red advance during 1919 various groups vied to influence Kolchak, while large areas of Siberia and the Far East fell under the control of independent cossack atamans, the Japanese expeditionary force and peasant partisans.[47] The generals wanted less debate and politics and increased support for the army; civilian politicians desired the reverse.

By early 1919 increased mobilization had led to a White force numbering some 200,000 to 300,000, largely as a consequence of Bolshevik policies. Yet even this did not bring military success, and Kolchak's spring offensive of 1919 turned into a defeat that was to prove decisive to the White cause. Before the end of July the Red Army had broken through the Urals, depriving the Whites of their only industrial base, and spelling doom for Kolchak's forces which had been pushed back too far to threaten Central Russia. In early September the Whites, using a large cavalry force of Siberian cossacks, made a last serious counter-attack, eventually forcing the Reds to retreat some 150 kilometres to the river Tobol. By 4 November, however, the Reds had recovered and counter-attacked, taking Omsk without a fight a week and a half later.[48] The White regime had made no attempt to extend its popularity until it was too late, the reason lying in Kolchak's unswerving faith in victory and a naïve optimism stemming from the belief that Russia, God and the army provided the only requisites for success. It also led the Whites to shun anyone who was not an ardent supporter.

Military collapse was a major reason for Kolchak's downfall. His forces were both quantitatively and qualitatively weaker than those of the Reds, indiscipline being a particular problem frequently manifested in desertion, units changing sides and other difficulties. Encompassing an area with a larger population, the Reds could more easily find local reinforcements. Kolchak's population base has at most been estimated at one-third of the Bolsheviks', reduced with the loss of the Urals and a need for greater selectiveness in the light of troop unreliability. In addition, supply problems were acute. Officers and soldiers often had families accompanying them, the brunt of feeding them being borne by the local population. Little relief came from allied supplies, and even when these did get through at the end of spring 1919 they were ineffectively used. Chaos was rife.[49] With able officer commanders such as Tukhachevsky, Shorin and Eikhe, the Reds were clearly becoming more effective. By the summer the Whites now faced a regular and well-behaved army and no longer the 'motley rabble' of previous years. Although the path to Red success was far from smooth, summer and autumn 1919 witnessed eventual Bolshevik victories. Meanwhile White ineptitude continued, marked by tactical shortcomings. In an attempt to retake the Urals (the 'Ufa offensive'), a major battle in which both sides suffered heavy losses, the Whites still failed to achieve success. The inability of inexperienced troops to hold together was largely to blame. Even more capable White commanders could have done little in the face of such difficulties, a factor similarly revealed by the subsequent failure of the September offensive.

The allies had done little to help. Even during the winter of 1918–19, no front-line troops had been sent, while proposals for the setting up of an Anglo-Russian Brigade in 1919 came to nothing. The entire Japanese force was in eastern Siberia, the Czechs were still stationed in the rear protecting the railways, and in late summer of 1919 the European allies removed even the small garrisons in Kolchak's rear. Kolchak received support, though by no means wholehearted, as long as he was perceived to be advancing and this, in turn, led Kolchak into further blunders. In Paris on 26 May 1919, allied leaders announced their preparedness, with qualification, to assist the Kolchak government with munitions, supplies and food, in order to enable it to establish itself as the government of all Russia. Following a democratic policy and accepting the loss of some border areas was to be the cost. Although Kolchak consented to this, his troops ceased advancing from early May and so nothing materialized. Overall, allied policy in Siberia, particularly in relation to Kolchak, was 'both opportunistic and ill informed'.[50]

Personal and administrative weaknesses were also to blame. Kolchak himself has not been immune from criticism, in a personal, political and military capacity. His neurosis, incompetence, moodiness and indecision, not to speak of his drug addiction, clearly affected his judgement as a political and military leader. He was not a monarchist and did not call for a restoration of tsarism, but chose relatively young advisers of Kadet sympathies, conditioned possibly by his army role. Administrative problems prevented government from being effectively organized. Few experienced personnel existed from before the Revolution, a situation only worsened by the alienation of the pro-SR intelligentsia. The paucity of administrative personnel had even worse consequences at local level: if it was impossible to create an efficient administration in Omsk, doing so over the whole of Siberia was a chimera. The Kolchak government became, in effect, 'an organisation for supporting the army'. He was hated by the left and especially the SRs, as well as the Bashkir minority, and he had no control over the Orenburg and Ural cossacks. The local atamans (Semenov and Kalmykov)

– east of Lake Baikal – were a law unto themselves. In effect, the supply line for the Siberian army and economy was blocked.[51]

KOLCHAK'S ECONOMIC AND SOCIAL POLICIES

Kolchak's downfall lay as much in economic problems as in military, perhaps because he and his army commanders concerned themselves little with social reforms and economic management, the economy being deemed useful only for defeating the Bolsheviks. Little help was forthcoming from the few Siberian capitalists. The Urals was the Whites' only industrial region, but productive capacity there was much depleted, while the First World War isolated Siberia from its natural supplies and markets west of the Urals, with the result that consumer goods could now only be brought in along the rail link with the Pacific. Little aid came from the allies, and when it did it was not used efficiently.[52] The urban areas also suffered from poor food supplies and speculation, exacerbating the shortage of basic necessities. Yet Kolchak's administrative centre was far from Vladivostok whence war materials and manufactured goods would have to be supplied. Furthermore, the ports in European Russia through which were previously exported the produce from agricultural areas in Western Siberia (vital to pay for the imported goods) were now sealed off.

The urban working class and labour issues were identified in White minds with Bolshevism. The unions were virtually abolished by government decrees which gave little protection to the workers. Workers' rights were rapidly eroded: factory owners dispensed with collective bargaining, the eight-hour day, the six-day week and redundancy payments, while wages were cut and social security guarantees reduced. Under Kolchak, the government sided with factory owners who then turned to the military for backing. Much of this was due to the influence of Petrograd financiers and industrialists. Every strike that affected Siberia in 1919 had an economic cause, according to one Soviet historian of the 1920s. The chief grievance was low wages together with payment often several months in arrears, by which time money was worthless due to raging inflation.[53] Finances were in a dire state even before the military disasters of mid-1919, although some measures were taken in an attempt to improve the situation, such as the currency reform of April 1919 (intended to persuade peasants distrustful of the numerous worthless paper currencies available in Siberia, to part with their crops in exchange for new Kolchak roubles to feed the hungry towns). Yet the abolition of the *Kerenki* banknotes only aggravated the position concerning workers' wages. Kolchak refused to use the Imperial gold reserve to alleviate the situation, considering himself only the trustee. A further law followed in May threatening stiff penalties for speculation though, according to one recent writer, all these measures were 'applied too late and too unsystematically to be convincing or to have any beneficial effect'.[54]

Agriculture posed even greater problems. Although there was no 'land question' as in European Russia (namely, that between landlords and land-hungry peasants), there were conflicts between the state (as major landowner) and the peasantry, and between the new migrants and the earlier settlers. Peasants had redivided state and other non-peasant land during 1917–18 (see pp. 161–2), although the October land decree had never become effective. From mid-1918, White agrarian policy in Siberia was designed to appeal to certain sections of the peasantry (the better-off) but not at the expense of support from former landowners. This dilemma was ever present. The pronouncements, in a PSG resolution of 6 July 1918, returning estates to former owners, and in a circular of October, declaring that all redivisions of land should cease, challenged the very essence of local peasant decision-making. In attempting to take away land which peasants had seized from landowners, the PSG had revived the legislation of the Provisional Government and the use of the zemstva as a transmission mechanism for implementing their policies in the countryside.

The position seemed to change little after Kolchak's coup, with contradictions in the various statements on the land question:

> On the one hand, it was necessary to consolidate rights to land for the peasants in order to ensure the support of the upper strata of peasants in the struggle against Bolshevism; on the other hand, it was necessary to satisfy the demands of the refugees (*bezhentsy*) – pomeshchiki and generals – having been deprived of their estates but in the process of securing their return.[55]

In February 1919 support was openly given to small peasant proprietorship: ' . . . in the field of agrarian legislation the government prefers consolidation and the development of small landownership at the expense of large ownership and a "broad" land reform'.[56]

This line was continued two months later with the publication (on 8 April) of the 'Declaration of the Russian Government' which noted that 'the government is taking measures to supply the landless and land-short peasants', using privately-owned and state land. The transfer of non-workers' land to assist the development of 'small toiling households' (on the basis of individual consolidated holdings) was to be especially encouraged.

The land issue, it was declared, could be solved only by a Constituent Assembly, when the process of distribution would be conducted in an orderly manner: peasants were given firm warnings against redividing land on their own initiative, all 'illegal' (*samovolnye*) seizures and distribution of land being prohibited. Kolchak's fear of 'spontaneous' peasant behaviour appeared to match that of the Bolsheviks. One further point in the 'Declaration' permitted peasants to retain the harvest from the land they were currently using, a concession doubtless owing more to economic necessity than political astuteness.[57]

Only five days later (13 April) a decree was published which seemed to counter the spirit of earlier pronouncements supporting small, individual peasant landownership. This decree maintained that land which had been confiscated from pomeshchiki since the February Revolution should be returned (via the government) to its former owners (echoing the resolution of the PSG from the previous July).[58] Curiously few Soviet writers seem to discuss this *Polozhenie* which now appeared to resolve the dilemma regarding landownership, dismissing the right of all individuals to land.

Even such an ardent Kolchak supporter as Gins was critical of Kolchak's hesitant and indecisive stance on the land question in the Declaration. It seemed to have little relevance to peasants in Siberia who had never (or extremely rarely) experienced pomeshchik landownership. In fact, they might have experienced such for the first time under Kolchak. Clearly one of his purposes was to compensate pomeshchiki who had been deprived of their estates elsewhere in the country with new land from areas now under White control, though this in itself displayed a singular failure to understand the interests of the Siberian peasantry. It is also debatable, of course, whether the pronouncements of 8 and 13 April even amounted to much in reality.[59]

By the spring of 1919 the political and administrative weaknesses of Kolchak's regime made it difficult for him to muster popular support for the army. Requisitioning, taxation and mobilization, all frequently brutally enforced, served to alienate peasants most in Siberia and drove many towards the myriad partisan armies which opposed the regime in 1919. Yet it is doubtful whether the decisions and policies of the Omsk government actually penetrated the Siberian countryside, many of these merely emanating from the 'whim or caprice of local commanders'; in many instances peasants had never heard of Kolchak. The White propaganda organisation (*Osved*) did little to help either. It was organized too late, and was largely ineffective anyway.[60]

Peasant unrest eventually proved the main problem for Kolchak. With the emergence of the harsh measures of War Communism the pendulum of peasant support, in Pereira's words, 'swung back and forth'. Although few Siberian peasants supported Bolshevism, they believed there to be more justice on the Bolshevik side. This explains, for Pereira, why many peasants voluntarily left their land and families to join the Red Partisans when they reappeared.[61] In the Altai region peasant opposition to mobilization was first noted as early as 1914 while mass resistance was the response to the PSG's mobilization orders of August 1918.[62] Peasant uprisings mushroomed from November to December and by summer 1919 had taken hold of much of the region, the most serious occurring in central Siberia between Omsk and Lake Baikal. Peasants were suspicious of towns and desired local control and freedom to do as they wished, a consequence of their experiences during the war and having become used to governments lasting only a short period of time.[63] Furthermore, Siberian peasants before 1914 had had little experience of urban administration and control and several authors commented on peasant revolts against towns and the gulf which had emerged between the rural peripheries and the urban centres.[64] Peasants also resented forced requisitioning and attempts to suppress the distillation of *samogon* (home-made liquor), and frequently vented their hatred against the better-off cossack settlements which supported Kolchak. In some areas additional difficulties were present as, for example, in parts of the Altai and Yeniseisk area where peasants suffered particularly from the loss of exports markets.[65]

Peasant uprisings occurred all over Siberia; and wherever peasants found a vigorous leader there was also the beginning of a partisan band. These bands were to emerge gradually from the autumn of 1918, originally in response to conscription and often led by soldiers returning from the front. Partisans thrived in the thinly-settled taiga north and south of the railway line and even established 'partisan' republics, advocating local autonomy and resisting all central authority. White punitive expeditions served only to aggravate matters and by autumn 1919 the ranks of Red partisans in Siberia numbered well over 100,000.[66] Partisans were especially detrimental to the Kolchak cause, denying him resources, hampering the mobility of his forces and further undermining morale.[67]

WHITE COLLAPSE

Political and military failures were clearly closely connected. In the military sphere the army suffered from disorganization and poor supply, exhaustion after continuous fighting, a weakness of communication between officers and soldiers and from illiteracy and hare-brained schemes in the high command. Politically, White propaganda was never able to match that of the Bolsheviks, while government and society were ridden with moral turpitude (ambitious and self-centred individuals at the top with bribery and corruption rife), to say nothing of Kolchak's personal shortcomings.[68] The setting of a date for the convocation of the Constituent Assembly after the Bolsheviks had been defeated, promised to the allies in June 1919, hardly seemed likely with earlier rejection of the Assembly. The military hold on power at the centre and in the localities hardly augured any better for the institution of local self-government through the zemstva, also promised earlier. Promise of wider government, at the end of 1919 when the army had been defeated, came too late in the day to have any effect. Failure in internal politics was also linked to social and economic issues. The main problem came from partisan bands, not directly linked to the Bolsheviks. When the Whites encountered opposition in towns it was led by SRs. Bolshevik links with partisans in the taiga were weak and once Reds had captured towns, partisans often turned against them.[69] The Bolsheviks were undoubtedly unpopular (*vide* the 'Perm catastrophe' of December 1918, the 'extraordinary Tax' of 2 November 1918 on kulaks and middle peasants, the backbone of the partisan movement, while in many areas the local organs of the *Cheka* (counter-revolutionary police) were the only representatives of Bolshevik power), yet they were eventually successful. The Bolsheviks created a Siberian Bureau (*Sibbyuro*) to direct party work in the Urals and Siberia but the huge distances to be covered rendered it largely ineffective while its membership was appointed from Moscow. Initially the small Bolshevik underground which concentrated mainly on urban uprisings was soon destroyed by the Whites, the most spectacular defeat being the Omsk uprising of December 1918. Yet new Bolshevik policies came into practice between January and March 1919. While army and party-state administration was improved, stress was now placed on the middle peasant in an attempt to win as much support as possible in the countryside. Peasant antipathy towards the Kolchak regime increased the appeal of Bolshevism. The peasantry now looked towards practical alternatives, particularly the concretization of the peasant utopia most clearly manifested in the desire for independent communities under local control.[70]

THE DENOUÉMENT

After Omsk had fallen on 14 November 1919, the Red Army reached Irkutsk by the following March, having taken all of central Siberia to Lake Baikal. With the Red advance and partisans approaching from the south and north, the White armies, now crippled by typhus, were broken and dejected. Kolchak chose to cut himself off from both his government and his army.[71] A brief socialist opposition (dominated by Mensheviks and then SRs) was set up in January 1920 but soon replaced by the Bolsheviks through the Irkutsk Military Revolutionary Committee. Kolchak was subsequently handed over to Bolshevik forces on 6/7 February 1920 and he and his Prime Minister were both shot, a panic measure in the face of advancing White troops and in contravention of Lenin's orders.[72] Although it was over two and a half years after Kolchak's death before Bolshevism was completely victorious, a government in the form of the Far Eastern Republic (FER), nominally controlling all territory from Lake Baikal to the Pacific, was established in early 1920. Ataman Semenov (in Chita) controlled the bulk of Transbaikal but was unable to hold out for long, lacking support from the other east Siberian regions and from the Japanese who had withdrawn from Transbaikal. Chita fell on 22 October 1920, and in November Transbaikal (and most of east Siberia) passed under FER control. Baron Ungern-Sternberg (a former Semenov lieutenant) continued fighting from a base in Outer Mongolia, though Urga (now Ulan-Bator) was taken in February 1921 and Ungern-Sternberg overthrown (and executed) by the Red Army in the summer of 1921. This led to the establishment of the pro-Soviet Outer Mongolian Republic. There then followed eighteen months of confrontation between White survivors, the FER and the Japanese garrison. After one final White offensive (under Diterikhs) FER forces recaptured Khabarovsk in February 1922. Since their garrison had effec-tively kept the Whites in power, the withdrawal of the Japanese in October meant the end of a White foothold. The remaining Whites fled to Korea and Manchuria, and Red troops entered Vladivostok on 25 October. In November 1922 the Far Eastern Republic was absorbed by the Russian Soviet Federated Socialist Republic, and thereby became an integral part of the USSR. The Civil War was to all intents and purposes over; Soviet power was now established from the Urals to the Pacific, and the whole of Siberia once more reverted to the centralized control of Moscow.

NOTES AND REFERENCES

1   The author is particularly grateful to David Collins for advice on source materials and to Susanne for assistance in the preparation of this chapter. Thanks are also due to Bob Service and Alan Wood for their comments on an earlier draft.

2   Alan Wood, 'From Conquest to Revolution: The Historical Dimension' in Alan Wood (ed.), *Siberia: Problems and Prospects for Regional Development* (London: Croom Helm, 1987), p. 55. For general discussion of the Russian Civil War see D. Footman, *Civil War in Russia* (London, 1961); J. Bradley, *Civil War in Russia, 1917–1920* (London and Sydney, 1975); and Evan Mawdsley, *The Russian Civil War* (hereafter *RCW*) (London: Allen & Unwin, 1987).

3   Donald T. Treadgold, *The Great Siberian Migration* (Princeton, New Jersey, 1957); A.M. Anfimov, *Rossiiskaya derevnya v gody pervoi mirovoi voiny (1914 – fevral 1917 gg.)* (Moscow, 1962), p. 174.

4   See especially Treadgold, op. cit.; Daniel R. Kazmer, 'The Agricultural Development of Siberia, 1890–1917', unpublished PhD dissertation (MIT, 1973); N. Poppe, 'The Economic and Cultural Development of Siberia' in G. Katkov, *et al.* (eds), *Russia Enters the Twentieth Century* (New York, 1971).

This was not necessarily the case with industry, where the Trans-Siberian opened up Siberian manufacturing to outside competition (Jon Smele, 'Labour Conditions and the Collapse of the Siberian Economy under Kolchak', *Sbornik* (The Journal of the Study Group on the Russian Revolution) 13 (1987):32. See also Chapter 8 of the present volume.

5 Smele, 'Labour Conditions', ibid., p. 33.

6 For a recent discussion of the commune in Siberia see John Channon, 'Regional Variation in the Commune: The Case of Siberia', in Roger Bartlett (ed.), *Land Commune and Peasant Community in Russia. Communal Forms in Imperial and Early Soviet Society* (London: SSEES/Macmillan, 1990), pp. 66–85.

7 Smele, 'Labour Conditions', op. cit., p. 41.

8 This is partly accounted for by the fact that between 1907 and 1909 money invested in Siberian savings accounts accounted for almost one-third of all savings in the entire Empire, even though the population in Siberia accounted for only 11 per cent of the total (Poppe, 'The Economic and Cultural Development', op. cit., p. 148). Clearly living standards are judged in terms of early twentieth century rural Russia.

9 Smele, 'Labour Conditions', op. cit., p. 32.

10 N.G.O. Pereira (1987) 'White Power During the Civil War in Siberia (1918–1920): Dilemmas of Kolchak's "War Anti-Communism" ', *Canadian Slavonic Papers* 29 (1): 45–62; the total working class (including permanent rural proletarians) has been estimated by Soviet scholars as 500,000 (or even 650,000) (see *Krestyanstvo Sibiri v period stroitelstva sotsializma (1917–1937 gg.)* (Novosibirsk, 1983), p. 12; E. Kolosov, 'Krestyanskoe dvizhenie pri Kolchake', *Byloe* 20 (1922):224, gives a figure of 300,000–400,000 for the proletariat; Smele, 'Labour Conditions', ibid., p. 32.

11 Smele, ibid.

12 The total population is estimated at 9–10 million (Kolosov, 'Krestyanskoe dvizhenie', op. cit., p. 224) and the figure here is based on a total urban work-force of 250,000.

13 Pereira, 'White Power', op. cit., pp. 50–1.

14 Mawdsley, *RCW*, op. cit., p. 118; N.G.O. Pereira (1988) 'Regional Consciousness in Siberia before and after October 1917', *Canadian Slavonic Papers* 30 (1): 114. On Social Democracy west and east of the Urals see R.C. Elwood, *Russian Social Democracy in the Underground. A Study of the RSDRP in the Ukraine, 1907–1914* (Assen, 1974); and G. Swain, *Russian Social Democracy and the Legal Labour Movement, 1906–1914* (London, 1983).

15 Poppe, 'The Economic and Cultural Development', op. cit., p. 151.

16 Pereira, 'Regional Consciousness', op. cit., pp. 11, 14.

17 Alan Wood, 'Chernyshevskii, Siberian Exile and *Oblastnichestvo*', in Roger Bartlett (ed.), *Russian Thought and Society 1800–1917: Essays in Honour of Eugene Lampert* (Keele, 1983), pp. 42–66; Wood, 'From Conquest to Revolution', op. cit., pp. 35–61.

18 Pereira, 'White Power', op. cit., pp. 50–1; David Footman, 'Siberian Partisans in the Russian Civil War', *St. Antony's Papers*, Soviet Affairs, 1 (1956) challenges the idea that new settlers were more radical.

19 Wood, 'From Conquest', op. cit., p. 53; J.R. Adelman, 'The Development of the Soviet Party Apparat in the Civil War; Center, Localities and Nationality Areas', *Russian History* 9 (1) (1982): 86–110.

20 On this much neglected subject see Elena Varneck, 'Siberian Native Peoples

after the February Revolution', *Slavonic & East European Review*, 21 (1943): 70–88; and more recently, James Forsyth, 'The Indigenous Peoples of Siberia in the Twentieth Century', in Alan Wood and R.A. French (eds), *The Development of Siberia: People and Resources* (London: SSEES/Macmillan, 1989), pp. 72–94.

21   *Krestyanstvo Sibiri*, op. cit., pp. 13–22.
22   Mawdsley, *RCW*, op. cit., p. 23; Pereira, 'Regional Consciousness', op. cit., pp. 118–20.
23   E.H. Carr, *The Bolshevik Revolution* 1 (London: Macmillan, 1979).
24   Pereira, 'White Power', op. cit., p. 57.
25   Felix Patrikeeff, 'Siberia in Revolution', in H. Shukman (ed.), *The Blackwell Encyclopedia of the Russian Revolution* (Oxford: Blackwell, 1988), pp. 259–62.
26   Smele, 'Labour Conditions', op. cit., p. 42; Russell E. Snow, *The Bolsheviks in Siberia, 1917–1918* (New Jersey, 1977); Mawdsley, *RCW*, op. cit.
27   Of 500,000 tons of grain collected in the six months after November, 80 per cent came from Siberia (Mawdsley, *RCW*, ibid.); John Channon (1988) 'The Bolsheviks and the Peasantry: the Land Question During the First Eight Months of Soviet Rule', *Slavonic & East European Review* 66 (no. 4): 620–1.
28   Robert Service, *The Bolshevik Party in Revolution: A Study in Organisational Change 1917–23* (London, 1979), p. 78; Mawdsley, *RCW*, ibid., p. 102.
29   Mawdsley, *RCW*, ibid., p. 102; and for a discussion of possible allied encouragement, Carr, *The Bolshevik Revolution* 1: 351.
30   J. Smele, 'Introduction', in *Kolchak i Sibir*, (edited and introduced by D. Collins and J. Smele) (Study Group on the Russian Revolution/Kraus Thompson, White Plains, New York, 1988), p. ix.
31   G.K. Gins *Sibir, soyuzniki i Kolchak: Povorotnyi moment russkoi istorii 1918–1920 gg.* (Peking and Harbin, 1921) 1: 102–31.
32   Mawdsley, *RCW*, ibid., p. 106.
33   Smele, 'Introduction', op. cit.; Mawdsley, *RCW*, ibid., p. 104.
34   Mawdsley, *RCW*, ibid., pp. 107–11; Smele, 'Introduction', ibid., p. xv.
35   Smele, 'Introduction', ibid., p. xix; Pereira, 'Regional Consciousness', op. cit., p. 131.
36   Pereira, 'Regional Consciousness', op. cit., pp. 23; Pereira, 'White Power', op. cit. pp. 126–8; Mawdsley, *RCW*, op. cit. pp. 22, 103.
37   Mawdsley, *RCW*, ibid., p. 103.
38   Further study of the Siberian countryside during these years might reveal whether the return of estates to former owners was as meaningless as Smele claims ('Introduction', op. cit., p. xii).
39   Mawdsley, *RCW*, op. cit., p. 110
40   Patrikeeff, 'Siberia in Revolution', op. cit., p. 261
41   Smele, 'Introduction', op. cit.
42   Ibid., pp. xii, xiv.
43   Pereira, 'Regional Consciousness', op. cit., pp. 123–4; Pereira, 'White Power', op. cit., p. 60.
44   Smele, 'Introduction', op. cit., pp. xii, xiv.
45   Mawdsley, *RCW*, op. cit., pp. 108–9; Smele, 'Introduction', ibid., p. x.
46   Smele, 'Introduction', ibid., pp. xii, xiv.
47   Mawdsley, *RCW*, op. cit., pp. 109–10; Smele, 'Introduction', ibid., p. x.
48   Pereira, 'White Power', op. cit., p. 56; Mawdsley, *RCW*, ibid., pp. 134, 148–9.
49   Mawdsley, *RCW*, ibid., pp. 153–5.

50 For discussion of foreign intervention see Bradley, *Civil War*, op. cit., Chapter 3; G. Kennan, *The Decision To Intervene* (Princeton, New Jersey, 1958); R.H. Ullman, *Britain and the Russian Civil War* (Princeton, New Jersey, 1968); B.M. Unterberger, *American Intervention in the Siberian Civil War* (Boston, 1969); J.A. White, 'The American Role in the Siberian Intervention', *Russian Review* 10 (1951); M.J. Carley, *Revolution and Intervention: The French Government and the Russian Civil War 1917-1919* (Kingston and Montreal, 1983); J.W. Morley, *The Japanese Thrust Into Siberia, 1918* (New York, 1957).

51 Mawdsley, *RCW*, op. cit., pp. 135-7.

52 For details of one abortive effort see J.D. Smele, 'An Attempt to Utilize the Northern Sea Route to Siberia in 1919', *SIBIRICA* IV (1989): 28-39.

53 Smele, 'Introduction', op. cit., p. xxi, note 34.

54 Ibid., p. xxii. For further discussion of economic matters see Smele, 'Labour Conditions', op. cit.

55 *Sovetskaya sibirskaya entsiklopediya* (hereafter *SSE*), 2: 838.

56 I. Kaptsugovich, 'Krestyanskoe dvizhenie v 1917 godu i osushchestvlenie leninskogo dekreta o zemle v Permskoi gubernii, 1917-1919 gg.', unpublished *kandidat* dissertation (Perm, 1962), p. 301.

57 Gins, *Sibir, Soyuzniki i Kolchak* 2: 152-3; *SSE* 2: 838.

58 The full decree was entitled 'Polozhenie ob obrashchenii vo vremennoe zavedovanie pravitelstvennykh organov zemel vyshedshykh iz fakticheskogo obladaniya ikh vladeltsev i postupivshikh v faktichskoe polzovanie zemledelcheskogo naseleniya'.

59 *Istoriya VKP(b)* 4: 358-9; P. Parfenov, *Grazhdanskaya voina v Sibiri, 1918-20 gg.* (Mosccow, 1925), p. 95; G.V. Krusser, *Kolchakovshchina* (Novosibirsk, 1927), p. 28; Kolosov, 'Krestyanskoe', op. cit.; E. Kolosov, 'Sibir pri Kolchake. Vospominaniya, materialy, dokumenty' (Byloe, 1923); V. Averev (1929) 'Agrarnaya politika Kolchakovshchiny', *Na agrarnom fronte* 6 (1) and 8 (2); M.E. Plotnikova, *Sovetskava istoriografiya grazhdanskoi voiny v Sibiri (1918-pervaya polovina 1930-kh gg)* (Tomsk, 1974).

60 Smele, 'Introduction', op. cit. p. xx; *Osved* received little support from the army high command and too few resources.

61 Pereira, 'White Power', op. cit., p. 60. Such a statement requires more rigorous testing, but if confirmed adds much to our knowledge of peasant reactions to Bolshevism.

62 This was one reason why the Siberian peasantry preferred 'Russian' Bolsheviks to foreigners (Pereira, 'Regional Consciousness', op. cit., pp. 124, 127).

63 For the pattern of peasant revolts see Footman, 'Siberian Partisans', op. cit., pp. 25-6.

64 Pereira, 'Regional Consciousness', op. cit., p. 127; B. Yeltsin (1926) 'Krestyanskoe dvizhenie v Sibiri v period Kolchaka', *Proletarskaya Revolyutsiya* 2 (49): 25.

65 Footman, 'Siberian Partisans', op. cit., p. 31.

66 Pereira, 'White Power', op. cit., p. 57; 'Regional Consciousness', op. cit., p. 130; Footman, 'Siberian Partisans', op. cit., p. 31.

67 Partisans did not seriously threaten the railway or large towns until after the collapse of Kolchak's main front.

68 These were the observations of General Budberg, who was in charge or army supplies, and of Kolchak himself (Mawdsley, *RCW*, op. cit., p. 155).

69 For a recent discussion of the partisan issue see N.G.O. Pereira, 'The Partisan

Movement in Western Siberia, 1918–1920', paper given at a conference of the British Universities Siberian Studies Seminar, University of Glasgow, 4–8 September 1989. The present manuscript was already at an advanced stage by the time the paper appeared and so the views contained in it could not be examined here.

70 Footman, 'Siberian Partisans', op. cit., p. 28; Service, *The Bolshevik Party*, op. cit., p. 105; Mawdsley, *RCW*, op. cit., p. 150.

71 For Kolchak's reasons, see Mawdsley, *RCW*, ibid., p. 232.

72 For a time Lenin tried to hush up the matter, not wishing his opponents to acquire further ammunition for their cause.

Afterword: Siberia in the twentieth century

Alan Wood

The foregoing chapters have concentrated on important aspects of the history of Siberia from the time of the Russian conquest and colonization in the sixteenth and seventeenth centuries to the Revolution of 1917 and its aftermath. As pointed out in the Introduction, one of the objects of this book has been, within its limits, to demonstrate how the history of Siberia, while having its own intrinsic and specific importance, is an integral and fully contributing factor in the historical development of Russia as a whole. It has obviously been impossible to cover the whole ground, and many important issues – for example, the growth of towns; foreign relations with Siberia's neighbours, particularly in the Far East; more detail on the region's administrative structure; the role of the Orthodox Church and missionary activity in Siberia; the Siberian regionalist and separatist movement; industrial development and the building of the Trans-Siberian Railway; 1905 in Siberia; the rise of the Siberian working class; the Lena gold-field massacre; more specialized studies of the region's social and economic history, and so on – all these and much more must wait for a further volume.

And, of course, the story does not stop in 1917. Since the Revolution and Civil War, Siberia has played a vital part – for both good and ill – in the social and economic development of the Soviet Union, and will continue to do so into the twenty-first century. After the ambiguities and uncertainty of Lenin's New Economic Policy (NEP) during the 1920s, when Siberia was the scene of many exciting forms of social and economic experimentation – for example, in the well-meaning but not always successful efforts to advance the progress, education and opportunities of the Siberian native peoples – the territory was to acquire its greatest notoriety during Stalin's dictatorship as the principal location of forced labour, exile and the whole grim *univers concentrationnaire* of what Solzhenitsyn has described as the 'GULag archipelago'. Despite the often unacknowledged miseries of the Siberian exile system under the tsars, it is to the mass horrors and sufferings of Stalin's victims – admitted by contemporary Soviet sources to be numbered in tens of millions – that Siberia mainly owes its negative, indeed rebarbative, reputation in the modern era. The *GULag* (that is, the Main Prison-camp Administration) peopled the countless islands in its far-flung archipelago of punishment with multitudes of so-called 'enemies of the people', arbitrarily arrested, incarcerated and banished by the security forces to end up as slave-labourers in the process of fulfilling the unreal industrialization targets of the Five-year Plans, and in building Stalin's grotesque version of 'Socialism in One Country'. Old Bolsheviks and veterans of the revolutionary struggle against tsarism, enterprising peasants who had made an economic success of the NEP, writers, intellectuals and scientists, prominent government officials, hundreds of foreign communists fleeing from fascism in Europe, distinguished military officers and many other 'guilty' categories of ordinary Soviet citizens were transported in cattle-wagons to toil and die in the camps, factories, mines, construction sites and 'forbidden zones' of the frozen empire administered by the GULag and its sister organization, *Dalstroi*, the Far Eastern Construction Trust. Many of the new industrial complexes located in Siberia – in particular Magnitogorsk and the huge Urals-Kuznetsk iron and coal combine in West Siberia, and the mineral-extracting enterprises at Norilsk and Kolyma in the Far North – were right at the heart of the industrialization of the Soviet economy overall. In this sense, the phenomenal economic successes of the Soviet industrialization drive and the triumphant Five-year Plans were therefore achieved at the incalculable cost of millions of shattered human lives, and built on the bones of those who died in their enforced efforts to tear the mineral wealth of Siberia out of her permanently frozen earth.

Shortly before Napoleon's invasion of Russia in 1812, Alexander I is reported to have declared that he did not fear the attack, as the Russian tsar is always 'formidable in Moscow, terrible in Tobolsk, and invincible in Kamchatka'. In so saying, the emperor was acknowledging the tremendous strategic significance of Russia's enormous territories beyond the Urals and therefore, as it turned out, beyond the reach of hostile invaders from the west. During the Second World War – known in the Soviet Union as the 'Second Great Patriotic War' (after the defeat of Bonaparte in the first one) – Siberia contributed in a number of crucial ways to the ultimate allied victory over Germany and Japan. This is not the place to detail them (though Siberia's wartime role still awaits a western historian), but it is worth noting the following brief points.

After Soviet–Japanese clashes on the Far Eastern 'front' at Lake Khasan (1937) and Khalkhin Gol (Nomonhan) (1939), the Japanese decision to bomb Pearl Harbor in December 1941 (prior intelligence of which reached Stalin via his secret agent in Tokyo, Richard Sorge), rather than strike north into Siberia, meant that the immediate threat to the Soviet Union of a war on two fronts was lifted, and winter-toughened Siberian troops under Marshal Zhukov could be safely transferred west to join in the defence of Moscow. Siberia's reprieve as a theatre of hostilities meant that it was able to make a massive contribution to the nation's war effort in the production and supply of military *matériel*, and as a safe destination for the territorial diversification and relocation of industry from the western battlefronts and occupied zones. Whole enterprises and hundreds of factories with their attendant work-forces were uprooted from European Russia and replanted in Siberian soil, thereby guaranteeing continuing production of vital armaments, weapons, aircraft and ammunition. In the Soviet Far East, the port of Vladivostok became the major point-of-entry for the import of Allied war aid; indeed three-quarters of American Lend-Lease supplies entered the USSR via this route throughout the war, and more was ferried in by aircraft from Alaska to Yakutsk. Finally, Siberian military divisions and whole armies, many of them containing a disproportionate number of recruits from the native non-Russian peoples, made a distinctive contribution on almost every front, and suffered a consequently high number of war dead.

After the death of Stalin in 1953, Siberia's importance to the Soviet economy took a new turn and demanded new thinking. The GULag's empire was partially dismantled, and thousands of exhausted survivors returned home to piece together their shattered lives. A combination of economic imperatives and changed political circumstances now forced Soviet planners to make up for the shortage of labour supply in more acceptable ways. Power-intensive, rather than labour-intensive, industrial development was what was required, and Siberia was, of course, richly endowed with limitless energy resources, including the force of her mighty rivers. Accordingly, during the 1950s a massive programme of hydroelectric station (GES) construction was commenced which would not only feed electricity into the national grid, but also stimulate the growth of high energy-intensive industries. The 'cascade' of GESes established along the Angara and Yenisei river system, including the giant Bratsk station; Nikita Khrushchev's 'Virgin Lands' campaign for extensive agricultural development in the south and west of Siberia; and also the forward-thinking decision to found a major new scientific and academic research complex in the heart of the Siberian taiga near Novosibirsk, with the explicit purpose of further studying, exploring and harnessing the country's inestimable natural resources – all were outward and visible symbols of the Soviet government's new eastwards orientation, and of its determination and commitment to open up Siberia's still enormous potential.

The huge investment of financial, scientific and human capital in Siberia paid for itself beyond the wildest expectations with the discovery of giant oil and natural gas deposits in West Siberia during the 1960s. In the face of formidable natural obstacles, the swamplands, forests and tundra of western and north-western Siberia have since been transformed into the centre of the Soviet Union's most lucrative industrial development, with oil and natural gas exports accounting for over 50 per cent of the country's hard currency earnings.

New explorations and drillings in the Far North, the construction of extensive pipelines delivering their revenue-raising payload into the heart of Europe, the expansion of old and the building of new urban centres to accommodate the soaring population, the laying of an extended transport and communications infrastructure in the inhospitable terrain of the oil- and gas-fields are all continuing to guarantee Siberian development a high priority on the Soviet Union's economic agenda for the foreseeable future.

At the other end of the country, in Eastern Siberia and the Far East, the mammoth railway construction project popularly known as the BAM (Baikal–Amur Mainline), and at one time officially declared to be the 'construction project of the century', has unfortunately not so far come up to the ambitious prognostications as to its usefulness in opening up new areas of industrial development and in profiting from an increase in East–West trade via the new 'land-bridge' from the Pacific. Indeed, the BAM has been variously described in the late 1980s as a 'white elephant', as 'the most expensive monument to the Brezhnev era of stagnation', and the Director of the Siberian branch of the Academy of Sciences' prestigious Institute of Economics and Organization of Industrial Production in Novosibirsk recently remarked in public that, 'if they had asked me in the first place, the BAM would never have been started'.

However that may be, and it is obviously far too soon to make reliable predictions as to the new railroad's eventual cost-effectiveness and value to the economy as a whole, there is little doubt that even in the rapidly changing circumstances of Mikhail Gorbachev's *perestroika*, and a realignment of international relations in Europe, Asia and the Pacific, the human and natural resources of the lands beyond the Urals, their still untapped and even undiscovered abundance of minerals and raw materials, their gold, diamonds, timber, water, energy and latent productive forces will surely underwrite the continuing and exponential role of Siberia in the Soviet Union's future development, and indeed in the world's economy.

Overshadowed by more dramatic happenings elsewhere in the USSR and Eastern Europe in the early 1990s, Siberia is nevertheless pregnant with events of tremendous significance which only seldom catch the headlines of the western media. In 1989 Siberian and Arctic miners were at the forefront of nation-wide industrial unrest and dissatisfaction at the mismanagement of the economy, food shortages and lack of control over local affairs. Everywhere in Siberia there are social tensions caused by inadequate provision of basic amenities, poor housing and lack of job satisfaction, which are barely compensated for by higher regional wage differentials. There is an ominous renewal of regional self-awareness and a locally-oriented political consciousness arising, among other things, from mounting frustration at the continued centralization of economic decision-making affecting Siberia in the Moscow ministries. As elsewhere in the Soviet Union, though not so widely reported, there are bitter ethnic rivalries and racial hostilities which have expressed themselves in open clashes between the majority Russians and the indigenous peoples of, for instance, the Yakut and the Buryat Autonomous Republics. One important aspect of this problem is the destruction of native homelands and their natural environment by the encroachments of centrally-planned industrial development programmes. In this connection, the Siberian writer, Valentin Rasputin, is only the best known of the vociferous and persistent Siberian 'green' lobby, desperately concerned about what one author has called 'The Destruction of Nature in the Soviet Union'. Another social issue which has received fairly wide publicity inside the Soviet Union is the unacceptably high level of crime in Siberia and the Far East (in particular the Kemerovo and Irkutsk regions) resulting from the continued use of Siberia as a place of exile and imprisonment for criminals from all over the country, as discussed briefly at the end of Chapter 7.

More positively, prominent academics who have held senior positions at Siberia's high-powered research institutions, such as Abel Aganbegyan and Tatyana Zaslavskaya, have been at the forefront of the drive for economic modernization and reconstruction throughout the Soviet Union – indeed many of the ideas contained in Zaslavskaya's confidential memorandum of 1983, the so-called 'Novosibirsk Report', lie at the heart of Gorbachev's economic 'new thinking'. On the other hand, two of Gorbachev's most prominent critics, the 'conservative' former politburo member, Yegor Ligachev, and the radical 'populist' politician, Boris Yeltsin, are both natives of Siberia. In May 1990 Yeltsin was elected to the powerful political position of Chairman of the Supreme Soviet of the Russian Federated Republic which, of course, covers the whole of Siberia and the Far East, and has lent the weight of his name and his new authority to call for the greater independence of Russia from the Soviet Union. At the time of writing, the nature of the personal and political relations between Gorbachev and Yeltsin (described by one journalist as 'the big, blue-eyed Siberian') is a cause of intense speculation in the world's press. Finally, the USSR's interrelations with China, Japan and the United States are, of course, focused on Siberia's Eastern, Far Eastern and Pacific coastal regions as the country becomes more involved with the rapidly developing community of Pacific rim nations and their dynamic economies.

Obviously, the case of Siberia, a fully integrated part of the Russian Federated Republic and overwhelmingly Russian in its population and dominant cultural tradition for four centuries, is different from that of other, non-Russian, regions of the Soviet Union, some of which have made open and emotional bids for complete national independence and secession from the USSR which may well be achieved in time. As mentioned above, similar demands have also been made with regard to Russia itself. However, although resurgent Siberian regionalism has not yet taken on a full political colouration, and nothing as radical as calls for the total independence of Siberia seems imminent, events in all three major economic regions of West and East Siberia and the Far East will warrant future scholars' serious attention as an essential part of the unravelling history of the Soviet Union as it approaches the twenty-first century in a state of uncertain and troubled change.

Index

The method of alphabetization used is word by word. Maps, tables, illustrations and notes are not included in the index. Native peoples are listed alphabetically under the names of their groups.